# Ham's Sin
# and
# Noah's Curse
# and
# BLESSING UTTERANCES

## A Critique of Current Views

Nicholas Oyugi Odhiambo

authorHOUSE®

AuthorHouse™ LLC
1663 Liberty Drive
Bloomington, IN 47403
www.authorhouse.com
Phone: 1-800-839-8640

Published by AuthorHouse    08/21/2014

ISBN: 978-1-4969-3273-0 (sc)
ISBN: 978-1-4969-3274-7 (e)

TABLE OF CONTENTS

## DEDICATION

I dedicate this book to my immediate family (my wife of nineteen years and counting, Leonidah Kilonzo Odhiambo; my daughter, Khabaque Alimo; my son, Barakah Owinja), my departed siblings (Alfred Otieno, Christopher Ochieng, Bernard Argwings Kodhek) and dearly missed mother, the late Phelgonah Adoyo Odhiambo.

## ACKNOWLEDGMENTS

I express my heart-felt appreciation to the following. First, I am indebted to my wife, Leonidah, for making the hard decision to "leave her country, her kindred, and her father's household," and accompany me to a far-away land in pursuit of higher education and further ministerial training. For the duration of time that I have been in school, she has been my constant source of support and encouragement. Many thanks to you, Leonidah.

Second, my gratitude goes to NIST (Nairobi International School of Theology, Kenya), which equipped me well enough during my pursuit of the M.Div. degree there to cope with the rigors of higher education abroad. The non-exhaustive list of my teachers includes Dr. Michael Kyomya, Rev. Sam Owen, Rev. Gary Fredericks, and Rev. Pat Flynn.

Third, I am very appreciative of Dallas Seminary's Old Testament faculty for offering me excellent training and lots of encouragement along the way. Prof. Glenn served as my *de facto* mentor when he co-opted me into a group that he voluntarily brought together for weekly readings and discussions of the Hebrew text and when he challenged me to co-teach with him a number of classes. Dr. Taylor has been not just a model teacher but also a friend who invited my family to dine with his family. Dr. Merrill taught me well and agreed to serve as one of my readers. Dr. Johnston was a superb coach even before he accepted the role of dissertation advisor. Even though not a DTS faculty, Dr. Knut Holter agreed to serve as my third reader despite the fact that we did not know each other in person. His deep involvement in and contribution to Old Testament scholarship in Africa continues to make him an object of my admiration.

# ABBREVIATIONS

| | |
|---|---|
| *ABC* | *African Bible Commentary*. Edited by Tokunboh Adeyemo. Nairobi, Kenya: WordAlive Publishers, 2006 |
| *ABD* | *Anchor Bible Dictionary*. Edited by D. N. Freedman. 6 vols. New York, NY: Doubleday, 1992 |
| *Adam and Eve* | *Book of Adam and Eve* |
| *AHw* | *Akkadisches Handwörterbuch*. W. von Soden. 3 vols. Wiesbaden: Harrassowitz, 1965–1981 |
| *Ant.* | Josephus, *Jewish Antiquities* |
| *Arch* | *Archaeology* |
| ATLA | American Theological Library Association |
| *AUSS* | *Andrews University Seminary Studies* |
| *BASOR* | *Bulletin of the American Schools of Oriental Research* |
| BDB | Brown, F., S. R. Driver, and C. A. Briggs. *A Hebrew and English Lexicon of the Old Testament*. Boston: Houghton Mifflin, 1906. Reprint, Peabody: Hendrickson, 1996 |
| *BSac* | *Bibliotheca sacra* |
| *BN* | *Biblische Notizen* |
| *BZAW* | *Beihefte zür Zeitschrift für die altestamentliche Wissenschaft* |
| *Civ* | Augustine, *De civitate Dei* |
| *CTJ* | *Concordia Theological Journal* |
| *Doctr. Chr.* | Augustine, *De doctrina christiana* |
| *Dial.* | Justin Martyr, *Dialogus cum Tryphone* |

| | |
|---|---|
| *DCH* | *Dictionary of Classical Hebrew.* Edited by David J. A. Clines. 5 vols. Sheffield: Sheffield Academic Press, 1993–2001. |
| GBS | Guides to Biblical Scholarship |
| *Gen. Rab.* | *Genesis Rabbah* |
| GKC | *Gesenius' Hebrew Grammar.* Edited by E. Kautzsch. Translated by A. E. Cowley. 2d ed. Oxford: Clarendon Press, 1910 |
| *GTJ* | *Grace Theological Journal* |
| *HALOT* | Koehler, L., W. Baumgartner, and J. J. Stamm. *The Hebrew and Aramaic Lexicon of the Old Testament.* Translated and edited under the supervision of M. E. J. Richardson. 4 vols. Leiden: E. J. Brill, 1994–1999 |
| *Hist. Eccl.* | *Historia ecclesiastica* |
| *Hom. Matt.* | *Homiliae in Matthaeum* |
| *Hom. Gen.* | *Homiliae in Genesim* |
| *HUCA* | *Hebrew Union College Annual* |
| *IBHS* | *An Introduction to Biblical Hebrew Syntax.* B. K. Waltke and M. O'Connor. Winona Lake, Indiana: Eisenbrauns, 1990 |
| *IDB* | *The Interpreter's Dictionary of the Bible.* Edited by G. A. Buttrick. 4 vols. New York: Abingdon Press, 1962 |
| ICC | International Critical Commentary |
| *ISBE* | *International Standard Bible Encyclopedia.* Edited by G. W. Bromiley. 4 vols. Grand Rapids: Eerdmans, 1979–1988 |
| *JAAR* | *Journal of the American Academy of Religion* |
| *JASP* | *Journal of Applied Social Psychology* |
| *JBL* | *Journal of Biblical Literature* |
| *JBP* | *Journal of Black Psychology* |
| *JETS* | *Journal of the Evangelical Theological Society* |

| | |
|---|---|
| *JRT* | *Journal of Religious Thought* |
| *JSOT* | *Journal for the Study of the Old Testament* |
| JSOTSup | Journal for the Study of the Old Testament: Supplement Series |
| *Jub.* | *Jubilees* |
| NAC | New American Commentary |
| NIBC | New International Biblical Commentary |
| NICOT | New International Commentary of the Old Testament |
| *NIDOTTE* | *New International Dictionary of Old Testament Theology and Exegesis.* Edited by W. A. VanGemeren. Grand Rapids: Zondervan, 1997 |
| NRSV | New Revised Standard Version |
| OTL | Old Testament Library |
| *OtSt* | *Oudtestamentlische Studien* |
| *Paed.* | *Paedagogus* |
| PIASH | Proceedings of the Israel Academy of Sciences and Humanities |
| *Pirke R. El.* | *Pirke Rabbah Eliezer* |
| *Pol.* | *Politica* |
| *QG2* | *Questions and Answers on Genesis 2* |
| R. | Rabbi |
| SAAS | State Archives of Assyria Studies |
| *Sanh* | *Sanhedrin* |
| SOTSMS | Society for Old Testament Studies Monograph Series |
| *TDOT* | *Theological Dictionary of the Old Testament.* Edited by G. Kittel and G. Friedrich. Translated by G. W. Bromiley. 10 vols. Grand Rapids: Eerdmans,1964–1976 |

| TOTC | Tyndale Old Testament Commentaries |
|------|-----------------------------------|
| *VT* | *Vetus Testamentum* |
| WBC | Word Biblical Commentary |
| Wehr | Wehr, H. A. *A Dictionary of Modern Written Arabic.* Edited by J. M. Cowan, 4th ed. Weisbaden: Otto Harrassowitz, 1979 |
| *WUS* | *Das Wörterbuch der ugaritischen Sprache*, J. Aistleitner. Edited by O. Eissfeldt, 3d ed. Berlin: Akademie-Verlag, 1967 |
| *ZAW* | *Zeitschrift für die alttestamentliche Wissenschaft* |

CHAPTER 1

INTRODUCTION

## Thesis of the Study

This book is primarily an exegetical critique of views on (a) the nature of Ham's offense[1] and (b) the possible fulfillment of Noah's curse and blessing. Regarding the views on the former, we argue against sexual understanding which manifests itself as any of the following three readings: heterosexual (incest), homosexual, and the voyeuristic view.[2]

Instead, we argue for a two-part non-sexual understanding of Ham's action. The first act, which we will contend was not part of the offense, was Ham accidentally seeing his father naked. Even though visual by nature, this aspect of Ham's action should not be considered synonymous with voyeurism since there is no textual evidence that Ham derived sexual gratification or enjoyment from looking at the nakedness of his father. The second act, which we argue constituted the offense, was his decision to disclose to his brothers what he had seen rather than cover the nakedness of his father.

---

[1] For an abbreviated treatment of the nature of Ham's sin, see my 2013 article [Nicholas Odhiambo, "The Nature of Ham's Sin," *Bibliotheca Sacra* 170 (April-June 2013)].

[2] Even though the dictionary defines a voyeur in sexual ("a person who obtains sexual gratification by looking at sexual objects or acts") and non-sexual terms ("a person who derives exaggerated or unseemly enjoyment from being an observer") (Sol Steinmetz, ed. *Webster's American Family Dictionary* (NY: Random House, 1989)., the voyeuristic view, as propagated by Randall Bailey, assumes a sexual understanding (Randall C. Bailey, " They're Nothing but Incestous Bastards: The Polemical Use of Sex and Sexuality in Hebrew Canon Narratives," in *In Reading from This Place*, ed. Fernando F. Segovia and Mary Ann Tolbert, vol. 1, Social Location and Biblical interpretation in the United States ( Minneapolis: Fortress, 1994).

1

His siblings' reaction when they heard the report serves as a literary foil and the model response to unintentional nakedness. How the disclosure was carried out or the form that it took is not discussed by the text. For this reason we will plead that suggestions such as Ham's report took the form of laughter, jeer, or mockery be considered as reading too much into the text and therefore eisegetical.

The most probable fulfillment of Noah's curse is (1) the servitude of the Gibeonites; (2) the enslavement of the Canaanites following the conquest; or (3) the dominance of Rome and Greece over Tyre and Carthage, respectively. The first two correspond to the aspect of the curse utterance that pertains to the enslavement of Canaan by Shem. The last suggestion relates to the enslavement of Canaan by Japheth. Each of these three views meets the textually-based three-fold test of servitude as the outworking of the curse, Canaanite ancestry as the object of the curse, and Shemite and Japhethite ancestries as the beneficiaries of the servitude. Having said this, we admit to the awkwardness of a later fulfillment of the enslavement of Canaan by Japheth because the expectation would be that both the enslavement of Canaan by Shem and the enslavement of Canaan by Japheth should occur contemporaneously.

The events or phenomena least associated with the curse, in our view, are the following: (1) the service of the four kings in Gen 14 under Chedorlaomer and the King of Tidal; (2) the subjection of the Egyptians and Babylonians by the Persians; (3) the forced corvée service of the Egyptians by Pharaoh; (4) the triumph of Israel over Egypt during the Exodus; (5) the enslavement of the Africans; and (6) the African's dark skin color.

As for Noah's blessing, we will contend that none of the proposals pertaining to the phrase וְיִשְׁכֹּן בְּאָהֳלֵי־שֵׁם ("let him dwell in the tents of Shem") correlate well with the exegesis of the blessing remarks. Those proposals are: (1) the conversion of the Gentiles who are equated with the Japhethites; (2) dispersion of the Jews by the Romans in the second century; and (3) the cooperation between the Hebrew invaders from the East and the Pelasgic invaders (Philistines) invaders from the West against the settled population of Canaan. The first suggestion fails to correlate with the spatial connotation behind the phrase "dwelling in the tents." The second is unacceptable on the basis of the fact that the negativity attached to the idea of displacement does not harmonize well with the positive attribute of a blessing utterance. The third does not fit the fulfillment since the table of nation lists the Philistines under Ham, not Japheth (cf. Gen 10:14).

As regards proposals related to the enlargement of Japheth we have a viable candidate among the "non-spiritual" group of views but none within the "spiritual" group. The "spiritual" group consist of two suggestions: (1) the response of the Japhethites to the gospel; and (2) rebuilding of the temple in accordance with Cyrus' decree. The former suggestion lacks merit since the preferable meaning of יפת is "to enlarge," not "to persuade." The requirement that any proposal on the fulfillment of the blessings on Japheth constitute spatial enlargement disqualifies the view regarding rebuilding of the temple.

As a whole, the "non-spiritual" views consist of the following aspects: political dominance, intellectual promotion, intellectual conquest, spread of civilization, colonization of the rest of the world, and geographical expansion enhanced by vast population. With the exception of the last aspect, all of the others lack either the attribute of positivity or spatiality—both of which are inherent in the verb יפת and the context in which it sits. Thus the viable candidate among the "non-spiritual" group of views is "geographical expansion," a proposal made by, among others, John Lange (1884), Arthur C. Custance (1975), and Geerhadus Vos (1977).[3]

## The Need for the Study

### The Need to Critique the Sexual Interpretation of Ham's Sin (Gen 9:22–24)

Requiring constant scrutiny is the view that Ham's infraction against Noah was sexual in nature. First presented in a rabbinic debate between Rav and Samuel approximately one-and-a-half millennia ago,[4] this reading has attracted more and more supporters in recent years.[5] Besides a substantial increase of advocates, this interpretation merits the attention of scholarship for yet another reason: its appeal to other parts of Scripture to argue for its position.

There are three forms of this reading. The first understands Noah as a victim of voyeurism. This view distinguishes voyeurism from a sexual act that may have been performed on Noah. Contemporary proponents of this understanding include Randall

---

[3] Geerhardus Vos, *Biblical Theology: Old and New Testaments* (Grand Rapids, MI: Wm.B. Eerdmans Publishing Company, 1948; reprint, 1977)., 58; Arthur C. Custance, *Noah's Three Sons: Human History in Three Dimensions*, vol. 1, 8 vols., The Doorway Papers (Grand Rapids, MI: Zondervan Publishing House, 1975)., 28; and John Peter Lange, *Genesis, or the First Book of Moses, Together with a General Theological and Homiletical Introduction to the Old Testament*, trans. Tayler Lewis and A. Gosman, 5th ed., vol. 1, A Commentary on the Holy Scriptures: Critical, Doctrinal, and Homiletical, with Special Reference to Ministers and Students, ed. Johann Peter Lange and Philip Schaff (New York: Charles Scribner's Sons, 1884)., 337.

[4] One of the pair remarked, "He (Ham) sodomized him (רבעו)" (*Sanh.* 70a).

[5] For a listing of some of the subscribers see nn. 3 and 4 on p. 21 of chapter 2 below.

Bailey and H. H. Cohen.[6] The second defines the offense as incestuous. Current advocates

include Frederick Bassett, William Brunk, John Bergsma, and Scott Hahn.[7] The third

considers the offense to have been homosexuality. Contemporary supporters include

Anthony Philips and O. Palmer Robertson.[8]

As for their respective arguments, the voyeuristic view rules out the possibility of

a sexual act on the basis of the text's meticulous description of the effort taken by Shem

and Japheth not to look at their father. Proponents of both the homosexual and incest

views argue for a metaphorical meaning of the expression רָאָה עֶרְוַת in Gen 9:22. Other

passages in the Pentateuch (Lev 18 and 20), it is observed, use the term עֶרְוָה in

conjunction with either רָאה (Lev 20:17a) or גלה (Lev 18:6–11, 15-19; 20:17b) as a

reference to sexual sin. Based on the Leviticus usage, the conclusion is drawn that the

offense in Gen 9:22 is sexual in nature. In summary, the popularity of the view that the

infraction against Noah was of a sexual nature and its appeal to other parts of Scripture to

argue for its position demand some type of exegetical appraisal.

Granted, we would not be the first to offer such an appraisal. Others have done

exactly that and that in an able fashion. These include Nzash Lumeya, Allen Ross, Gene

---

[6] Randall C. Bailey, " They're Nothing But Incestuous Bastards: The Polemical Use of Sex and Sexuality in Hebrew Canon Narratives," in *In Reading from This Place*, ed. Fernando F. Segovia and Mary Ann Tolbert, vol. 1, Social Location and Biblical interpretation in the United States ( Minneapolis: Fortress, 1994).

[7] William A. Brunk, "The Action of Ham against Noah: Its Nature and Result (Gen 9:18–27)" (M.Div. thesis, Western Conservative Baptist Seminary, 1988), 48–68; Frederick W. Bassett, "Noah's Nakedness and the Curse on Canaan: A Case of Incest?" *VT* 21 (1971): 232–37; and John Sietze Bergsma and Scott Walker Hahn, "Noah's Nakedness and the Curse of Canaan (Genesis 9:20–27)," *JBL* 124, no. 1 (2005): 26, 34–39.

[8] O. Palmer Robertson, "Current Critical Questions Concerning the 'Curse of Ham'," *JETS* 41 (1998): 179; Anthony Phillips, "Uncovering the Father's Skirt," *VT* 1 (1980): 38–43.

Rice, Umberto Cassuto, Victor Hamilton, and John Hartley.[9] However, these works have had their own limitation and thus offer room for a new work. For instance Ross, Rice, Cassuto and Hamilton only interact with Bassett's interpretation of the offense as incestuous in nature and fail to address the homosexual and the voyeuristic views. Part of the reason, of course, is that their works pre-date those of contemporary advocates of the homosexual and voyeuristic readings. Moreover, as long as the sexual view is rehearsed over and over again, and more and more works embrace it, there will always be the need to revisit its argument.

The Need to Critique Certain Interpretations of<br>Noah's Utterances (vv. 25–27)

Certain suggestions of fulfillment of the Noachian utterances have yet to be evaluated for conformity with not only Gen 9:18–29, but the rest of the Scriptures. Two examples will suffice. First is the view that associates the phrase "dwelling in the tents" with the conversion of the Gentiles. The problem of allegorization aside, the peculiarity of this suggestion lies with its compositional understanding of the term "Gentile": Japhethites minus the Hamites.

Luther, for example, suggested at one point that by the utterance concerning the dwelling of Japheth in the tent of Shem, God revealed to Noah, "that even the poor *Gentiles* are to dwell in the tents of Shem, that is, that they are to share in the benefits that

---

[9] Nzash U. Lumeya, "The Curse on Ham's Descendants: Its Missiological Impact on Zairian Mbala Mennonite Brethren" (Ph.D. diss., Fuller Theological Seminary, 1988), 53–54; Allen Paul Ross, "The Table of Nations in Genesis" (Ph.D. diss., Dallas Theological Seminary, 1976), 347; Gene Rice, "The Curse That Never Was (Genesis 9:18–27)," *JRT* 29 (1972): 12; Umberto Cassuto, *From Noah to Abraham: A Commentary on Genesis vi. 9–xi. 32*, trans. Israel Abrahams (Jerusalem: Magnes Press, 1964), 2: 151–52; Victor P. Hamilton, *The Book of Genesis: Chapters 1–17*, NICOT, ed. R. K. Harrison (Grand Rapids: Eerdmans, 1990), 323; and John E. Hartley, *Genesis*, NIBC: Old Testament Series, ed. Robert L. Hubbard Jr. and Robert K. Johnson (Peabody, MA: Hendrickson Publishers, 2000), 113.

the Son of God brought into this world, namely, the forgiveness of sins, the Holy Spirit, and life eternal."[10] But when it came to the particularized fulfillment of the utterance, he only spoke of the gospel shining in Germany. Similarly, Calvin associated the utterance with the response of the Jews and the Gentiles to the gospel, and narrowly defined the Gentiles as "the progeny of Japheth."[11]

In 1773, Elisha Fish echoed this narrow understanding of Gentiles. Pointing to examples of Gentile converts in the Book of Acts, Fish conveniently ignored examples of Hamitic converts such the Ethiopian eunuch. Instead, he chose to highlight exclusively the example of Cornelius who "seems evidently to come from Europe, where Japheth's posterity dwell."[12]

Present-day subscribers to this narrow definition of "Gentile" include Arthur Custance and Bruce Waltke. The former agreeably draws attention to the traditional tendency to reserve the term "Gentile" for the children of Japheth.[13] The latter prefers to equate the Gentiles with the Japhethites on the grounds that the majority of the Gentiles during the apostolic age were Japhethites living in Anatolia and Greece.[14]

---

[10] *Lectures on Genesis Chapters 6–14*, trans. George V. Schick, vol. 2, Luther's Works, ed. Jaroslav Pelikan (St. Louis: Concordia Publishing House, 1960), 184, 186.

[11] John Calvin, *Commentaries on the First Book of Moses Called Genesis*, trans. John King, (Grand Rapids: Eerdmans, 1948), 1: 309.

[12] Elisha Fish, *Japheth Dwelling in the Tents of Shem or Infant Baptism Vindicated in a Discourse, the Substance of which was Delivered at Upton, January 5, 1772, with Objections Answered* (Boston: Thomas and John Fleet, 1773), 10–11.

[13] Arthur C. Custance, *Noah's Three Sons: Human History in Three Dimensions*, The Doorway Papers, vol. 1 (Grand Rapids: Zondervan Publishing House, 1975), 17, 23.

[14] Bruce K. Waltke, *Genesis: A Commentary* (Grand Rapids: Zondervan Publishing House, 2001), 153.

Our contention is that there is no justification for excluding the Hamites from the definition of Gentiles. Granted, the Hamites and particularly the people of African descent may have fallen outside the imaginative purview of the reformers. Nevertheless, these earlier writers should not have assumed that only the Japhethites could be converted by bringing to bear second century examples of conversions of the non-Japhethic Gentiles. One such example is the Ethiopian eunuch.[15] As for recent subscribers such as Custance, it is difficult to reconcile their position and the fact that, by the time they penned their works (i.e., 1970's), the gospel had already spread to Hamitic lands such as Africa where the Christian population was over 117 million.[16] In the case of Waltke, there were a sufficient number of historians who had traced the evidence of Christianity and Christian converts in Africa as far back as the second century by the time he published his 2001 commentary on Genesis. Mark Shaw's *Kingdom of God in Africa*, for instance, speaks of late second century Christianity in Egypt, which, he reminds us, is an "African country."[17] Similarly Adrian Hastings points to a third century Coptic translation of parts

---

[15] The geographical origin of the eunuch is debated. The most recent scholarship prefers to locate the eunuch's motherland in Meroe (Edwin M. Yamauchi, *Africa and the Bible* [Grand Rapids: Baker Academic, 2004], 161–81). Regardless of whether the eunuch hailed from Ethiopia or Aithopia, the fact still remains that these two regions were located in Africa and the racial identity of the eunuch was most probably Negroid (Ibid., 213; cf. Irenaeus *Haer.* 3.12.8; Eusebius *Hist. Eccl.* 2.1.13–14).

[16] According to David Barrett, the approximate number of Christians in Africa in 1970 was about 117, 070, 000 (*World Christian Encyclopedia: A Comparative Survey of Churches and Religions in the Modern World*, ed. David B. Barrett, George T. Kurian, and Todd M. Johnson, vol. 1 [The World by Countries: Religionists, Churches, Ministries], 2 vols. [New York: Oxford University Press, 2001], 12).

[17] Mark Shaw, *The Kingdom of God in Africa: A Short History of African Christianity* (Grand Rapids: Baker Books, 1996), 22, 27. Shaw discusses four eras of Christianity in Africa: Early African Christianity (100–600); Medieval African Christianity (600–1700); African Christianity in the eighteenth and nineteenth centuries; and African Christianity in the twentieth century.

of the Bible and the role of Copts such as Anthony and Pachom in mass conversions of

Egyptians as evidence of Christianity among Africans in the third century.[18]

Also in need of evaluation is the perspective that associates the enlargement with

the exportation of civilization by the Japhethites,[19] or endowment of the Japhethites with

intellectual superiority.[20] Even though this view is rather dated, the fact that no scholarly

work that we are aware of has offered a rebuttal calls not only for pause but also an

evaluation however belated. Our preliminary evaluation is that the view is somewhat

prejudicial in the sense that, by implication, it renders the non-Japhethite races as less

civilized or intellectually inferior.

But even in the case of suggestions of fulfillment that have been dismissed on the

grounds of their inaccuracies, those views still persist on record. A classic example is the

suggestion that the curse utterance found fulfillment in the oppression of the African

through slavery,[21] or the creation and enforcement of color bar policies.[22] There is no

---

[18] Adrian Hastings, *The Church in Africa (1450–1950)* (Oxford: Clarendon Press, 1994), 9. Other works that address the history of African Christianity include: Elizabeth Allo Isichei, *A History of Christianity in Africa: From Antiquity to the Present* (Grand Rapids: Eerdmans, 1995); Thomas Spear, "Toward the History of African Christianity," in *East African Expressions of Christianity*, ed. Thomas Spear and Isaria N. Kimambo, East African Studies (Athens, OH: Ohio University Press, 1999); and Ogbu U. Kalu, "African Christianity: An Overview," in *African Christianity: An African Story*, ed. Ogbu U. Kalu, Perspective on Christianity Series ed. O. U. Kalu, J. W. Hofmeyer, and P. J. Maritz, vol. 3 (Pretoria, South Africa: Business Print Center, 2005).

[19] For example, Lange, *Genesis, or the First Book of Moses, Together with a General Theological and Homiletical Introduction to the Old Testament*, 337.

[20] For instance, J. G. Murphy, *A Critical and Exegetical Commentary on the Book of Genesis: With a New Translation* (Boston: W. H. Halliday, 1868), 214.

[21] Names linked to this line of interpretation include Josiah Priest and particularly his remark that God "decreed the Negroes' enslavement by the whites of Japheth's race . . ." (Josiah Priest, *Bible Defense of Slavery; or the Origin, History, and Fortunes of the Negro Race* [Glasgow, KY: W. S. Brown, 1853], 289).

[22] Color bar policies were especially prevalent in pre-independent South Africa. According to H. F. Stander several rightist groups in South Africa held to the tripartite syllogistic belief that (a) God had

doubt whatsoever that this view has been thoroughly analyzed and properly rebutted.[23]

One only need glance at works on history of interpretation such as those of Thomas

Peterson,[24] Stephen Haynes,[25] and the book *Illusions of Innocence*,[26] to conclude that these

works have bequeathed to scholarship valuable insight into the thinking and

rationalization of white Southerners in regards to their outlook on the people of African

descent.

Peterson's dissertation is an American study of white culture between 1831 and

1861. One of the work's assertions is that white Southerners utilized the myth of Ham to

resolve the tension between their racial values and their most fundamental religious

---

cursed Ham, (b) blacks are the descendants of Ham, and (c) all blacks are destined to be servants. Armed with this kind of reasoning, the non-African minority went about maltreating the African majority convinced that their actions bore a biblical mandate (H. F. Stander, "The Church Fathers on the Cursing of Ham," *Acta patristica et byzantina* 5 [1994]: 113).

[23] A listing of a few opponents will suffice: Robertson, "Current Critical Questions Concerning the 'Curse of Ham'," 177; Franz Delitzsch, *A New Commentary on Genesis*, trans. Sophia Taylor, vol. 1, Clark's Foreign Theological Library (Edinburgh: T. & T. Clark, 1899), 294–95; Derek Kidner, *Genesis: An Introduction and Commentary*, TOTC, ed. D. J. Wiseman (Downers Grove, IL: Intervarsity Press, 1967), 104; Robert Brow, "The Curse of Ham—Capsule of Ancient History," *CT* (October 1973): 8; Lumeya, "The Curse on Ham's Descendants: Its Missiological Impact on Zairian Mbala Mennonite Brethren," 77.

[24] Thomas Virgil Peterson, *Ham and Japheth: The Mythic World of Whites in the Antebellum South*, ATLA Monograph Series, vol. 12 (Metuchen, NJ: The Scarecrow Press and the American Theological Library Association, 1978), 1, 5.

[25] Stephen R. Haynes, *Noah's Curse: The Biblical Justification of American Slavery*, Religion in America, ed. Harry S. Stout, vol. 20 (New York: Oxford University Press, 2002), 9.

[26] Richard T. Hughes and C. Leonard Allen, *Illusions of Innocence: Protestant Primitivism in America, 1630–1875* (Chicago, IL: University of Chicago Press, 1988), 198–99; cf. John Patrick Daly, "The Divine Economy: Evangelicalism and the Defense of Slavery, 1830–1865" (Ph.D. diss., Rice University, 1993), 265. Other studies on slavery and the antebellum period include David F. Ericson, *The Debate over Slavery: Antislavery and Proslavery Liberalism in Antebellum America* (New York: University Press, 2000); Edward Riley Crowther, "Southern Protestants, Slavery and Secession: A Study in Religious Ideology, 1830–1861" (Ph.D. diss., Auburn University, 1986); Evando de Morais Camara, "A Flight into Utopia: The Proslavery Argument of the American South in Social-Hermeneutical Perspective" (Ph.D. diss., University of Notre Dame, 1986); and G. Whit Hutchison, "The Bible and Slavery, a Test of Ethical Method: Biblical Interpretation, Social Ethics, and the Hermeneutics of Race in America, 1830–1861" (Ph.D. diss., Union Theological Seminary, 1996).

beliefs. The myth, for them, supplied the divine mandate that they sought to carry on their enslavement with good conscience.

Like Peterson's work, Haynes' book also focuses on the antebellum period. Its unique contribution is in demonstrating the role of the twin concepts of honor and shame in the antebellum readings of Noah's curse. Further reiteration of the South's utilization of the story of Ham and its regard of Noah as a prototype for the patriarchal structure of plantation life and as primal man is made by Richard T. Hughes and C. Leonard Allen.[27]

Despite such exposure and rebuttal, one still finds today the reference that the object of the curse was Ham or the Hamites.[28] Considering that the individual cursed in the text was Canaan, the view that the African enslavement was a fulfillment of the curse does not hold. Neither does the reading that Ham or the Hamites were cursed.

## Methodology

As would be expected of any critique, this work, first of all, will surface the various interpretations surrounding the issues of the nature of Ham's sin and fulfillment of the Noachian utterances. Following the cataloging of interpretations, which in this instance will take the form of history of interpretation, we will examine the readings for

---

[27] Hughes and Allen, *Illusions of Innocence: Protestant Primitivism in America, 1630–1875,* 198–99.

[28] Works that consider Ham and the Hamites the object of the curse include "Ham," in *Nelson's Illustrated Bible Dictionary: An Authoritative One-Volume Reference Work on the Bible, with Full-Color Illustrations,* ed. Herbert Lockyer (Nashville, TN: Thomas Nelson Publishers, 1986), 454; Paul R. House, *Old Testament Theology* (Downers Grove, IL: Inter-varsity Press, 1998), 70; Ralph L. Smith, *Old Testament Theology: Its History, Method, and Message,* (Nashville, TN: Broadman & Holman Publishers, 1993), 172; Custance, *Noah's Three Sons: Human History in Three Dimensions,* 26; and Henry Morris, *The Genesis Record: A Scientific and Devotional Commentary on the Book of Beginnings* (Grand Rapids: Baker Book House, 1976), 241–42.

their exegetical soundness. Since we intend to engage in exegesis, we will do well to reveal our hermeneutical approach.

Unlike Stephen Haynes,[29] whose reader-response approach obligates him to place great significance on the meanings that readers make, our interest in what the readers make of the text is limited primarily to surfacing and then critiquing those different readings. Meaning, for us, lies not with the readers, but with the author of the text. The goal then should be to capture the biblical author's "intended meaning." What do we mean by "intended meaning"? Norman Geisler isolates four possible meanings of "intention." Intention may mean: (1) plan; (2) purpose; (3) thought in one's mind; or (4) expressed meaning.[30] By "intention," we do not imply any of the first three options. If intention were to be regarded as any of these, then the task of pursuing authorial intent would be quite elusive. If, for instance, intent were regarded as the thoughts in an author's mind, how would we be expected to know this, especially if the author has already exited the scene, as is the case with classical authors? Such a psychologistic[31]

---

[29] "Readers—whatever their qualifications, background, or official status—make the meaning of biblical texts and the meanings they make, however foreign they appear to minds conditioned by biblical literalism or the historical-critical method, are significant in their own right" (Haynes, *Noah's Curse: The Biblical Justification of American Slavery*, ix). An earlier proponent from whom Haynes must be taking his cue is Gadamer who argued that the meaning of a text is produced when the "horizon of understanding" of a reader encounters and responds to the "horizon" of the text, resulting in a "fusion" of horizons (Warnke, *Gadamer: Hermeneutics, Tradition, and Reason* [Stanford, CA: Stanford University Press, 1987], 69, cf. John P. Newport, "Contemporary and Philosophical, Literary, and Sociological Hermeneutics," in *Biblical Hermeneutics: A Comprehensive Introduction to Interpreting Scripture*, ed. Bruce Corley et al. [Nashville, TN: Broadman & Holman Publishers, 1996], 138). Contrary to Gadamer, we advocate for the need of the reader to attempt to penetrate into the text's linguistic and historical horizon and once having determined the intended meaning apply this meaning into his own present horizon.

[30] Norman Geisler, "The Relation of the Purpose and Meaning in Interpreting Scripture," *GTJ* 5 (1984): 238.

[31] Schleiermacher is the individual that is primarily associated with the psychologistic perspective of hermeneutics. In *Hermeneutics,* he states that "before the art of hermeneutics can be practiced, the interpreter must put himself both objectively and subjectively in the position of the author"

understanding of authorial intent renders the whole exercise of hermeneutics untenable. We, on the other hand, define authorial intent as expressed meaning. But as much as the expressed meaning is the author's, its locus lies in the text, not the author's mind.[32]

Granted, the goal of capturing the meaning of the text is not free from the taint of presupposition. As a matter of fact, we owe a great deal to the proponents of the reader response approach for shinning a spotlight on the peril of prejudice.[33] We all come to the text with excess baggage or *Weltanschauung* so much so that it would be a great misnomer for any sober exegete to suppose that we engage the text at neutral gear. In the words of Martin Heidegger, interpretation is grounded in "something we have in advance— in a *vorhabe* (or fore-having)."[34] Thus we need to be constantly aware of our limitation to understanding the text brought about by preunderstandings. Additionally, we agree with Grant R. Osborne that we must allow good hermeneutical principles to control our tendency to read our prejudice into the text.[35]

---

(D. E. Schleiermacher, *Hermeneutics: The Handwritten Manuscripts*, ed. Heinz Kimmerle [Missoula, MT: Scholars Press, 1977], 99). Implicit in this concern is the apparent psychologistic association of meaning with author. Hirsch would later echo Schleiermacher's position: "Meaning is not restricted to conceptual meaning. It is not even restricted to mental 'content,' since, on my description, it embraces not only content of mind represented by written speech but also the effects and values that are necessary correlative to such a content. Defined in Husserl's terms, 'meaning' embraces not only intentional objects but also the species of intentional acts which sponsor those intentional objects...an intentional object cannot be disseverted from a species of intentional act, that subjective feeling, tone, mood and value, are constitutive of meaning in its fullest sense" (E. D. Hirsch, *The Aims of Interpretation* [Chicago: University of Chicago Press, 1976], 8).

[32] Geisler, "The Relation of the Purpose and Meaning in Interpreting Scripture," 238.

[33] According to Gadamer, to deny the reality of prejudice is to exhibit "prejudice against prejudice" (Hans Georg Gadamer, *Truth and Method*, trans. Joel Weinsheimer and Donald G. Marshall [New York: Continuum, 1994], 167).

[34] Martin Heidegger, *Being and Time*, trans. John Macquarrie and Edward Robinson (New York: Harper, 1962), 191.

[35] Incidentally one of those principles happens to be the hermeneutical approach that we are adopting here, viz., selecting the meaning that best fits the context (Grant R. Osborne, *The Hermeneutical*

Speaking of the text, our main concern will be with the text as we now have it and not how it came about. Now, we recognize that there are various schools of thought on the process by which the text came down to us. One example is Source Criticism[36] and its offshoots, the Documentary Hypothesis[37] and New Supplementary Hypothesis.[38] The approach attributes the shape of the present canon to a redactor(s) who compiled varied textual sources. In its deliberation, this approach utilizes these sources, whether they be J (850 B.C.), E (750 B.C.), D (625 B.C.), or P (540 B.C.) as the basis of its discussions. Traditional criticism (*Überlieferungsgeschichte*) is another example. It attempts to describe the earlier oral and written stages of the material found in the biblical texts. It investigates about the community or group responsible for the shaping and transmission of a particular tradition. Such groups would include the priesthood, the levites, and the wise men.[39] Then there is form criticism.[40] Discussions on the formulation of the text are

---

*Spiral: A Comprehensive Introduction to Biblical Interpretation*, 2d ed. [Downers Grove, IL: IVP Academics, 2006], 518–19).

[36] Source criticism is concerned about whether a text is the work of one author or several, whether literary sources have been used, and whether editors have reworked the text in some way. It deals with groups of readings that were presumably created at an earlier stage, that of the literary growth of the books. It is assumed that large-scale differences displaying a certain coherence were created at the level of the literary growth of the books by persons who considered themselves actively involved in the literary process of composition (Norman C. Habel, *Literary Criticism of the Old Testament*, Guides to Biblical Scholarship, Old Testament Series, ed. Gene M. Tucker [Philadelphia: Fortress Press, 1971], 6).

[37] An example of a Documentary theorist is Van Selm who dates v. 26 as post-mosaic on the basis of the occurrence of JHWH in that verse (A. Van Selms, "The Canaanite in the Book of Genesis," in *Studies on the Book of Genesis*, ed. B. Gemster, Oudtestamentische Studien, vol. 12 [Leiden, E. J. Brill, 1958], 186).

[38] Commonly associated with Van Seters, this hypothesis differs from the Documentary hypothesis in three ways: (a) it envisions only 3 documents (D, J, and P); (b) there are no redactors; and (c) each author—after the first— expanded the Pentateuchal tradition by supplementation.

[39] One example of this type of criticism at work is Gerhard von Rad's discussion of the development of the final form of the Hexateuch. According to him the final form was the outgrowth and intricate elaboration of early brief credos or confessional creeds such as those found in Deut 26:5b–9; 6:20–24; and Josh 24:2b–13. These creeds were comprised of historical traditions focusing on (i) the patriarchs to whom the land was promised, (ii) the exodus from Egypt, and (iii) the settlement in the

not limited to biblical critics. R. K. Harrison, a conservative, identifies eleven tablets that he opines Moses would have utilized in his compilation of the book of Genesis.[41]

Nevertheless, our interest remains with the final form of the text for two reasons. First, the authoritative nature of the text lies with its final form. This is certainly Eugene Merrill's point in his comment concerning the composition of the Pentateuch: "though there no doubt had been an unbroken oral (and perhaps written) tradition about their origins, history, and purpose, it was not until Moses gathered these traditions and integrated them into the corpus now known as the Torah that a comprehensive and *authoritative* (emphasis mine) synthesis emerged."[42] Second, our hermeneutical approach (viz., contextual exegesis) precludes the need to interact with theories pertaining to the preliterary phase except in instances when some of their conclusion conflict with the findings of our exegesis. For instance, on the question of the role of the phrase אֲבִי כְנָעַן, (Gen 9:19), the harmonization theory presented by Herman Gunkel[43] (a form critic),

---

promised land. To these traditions were then added the primeval history (Gen 1–11) as a preface and the Sinai tradition (See further K. C. Hanson, ed., *From Genesis to Chronicles: Explorations in Old Testament Theology, Gerhard Von Rad* [Minneapolis: Fortress Press, 2005], 1–58).

[40] Differing from source criticism because it concentrates on primary categories of form rather than on documents, form criticism, nevertheless, still deals with an earlier preliterary phase. It identifies and classifies units of (oral) material and relates them to their presumed sociological milieu (*sitz im leben*) in the earlier life of the community (Gene M. Tucker, *Form Criticism of the Old Testament*, Guides to Biblical Scholarship, Old Testament Series, ed. J. Coert Rylaarsdam [Philadelphia: Fortress Press, 1971], 1)

[41] R. K. Harrison, *Introduction to the Old Testament: With a Comprehensive Review of Old Testament Studies and a Special Supplement on the Apocrypha* (Grand Rapids: Eerdmans, 1969; reprint, Peabody, MA: Prince Press, 1999), 499, 547–553.

[42] Eugene H. Merrill, "A Theology of the Pentateuch," in *A Biblical Theology of the Old Testament*, ed. Roy B. Zuck (Chicago: Moody Press, 1991), 8.

[43] Hermann Gunkel, *Genesis*, trans. Mark E. Biddle, Mercer Library of Biblical Studies, ed. John Blenkinsopp and Walter Brueggemann (Macon, GA: Mercer University Press, 1997), 79.

Gerhard von Rad[44] (a tradition critic), and Van Seters[45] (a source critic) should not be preferred over the textually established use of the phrase, "the father of so-and-so," to foreground an individual in a narrative.

This focus on the final canonical form is very reflective of Brevard Child's canonical approach to Old Testament Theology. Indeed we are in agreement with his assertion that the materials for theological reflection (in our case, exegesis) are not the events or experiences behind the text, or apart from the construal in Scripture by a community of faith and practice."[46] The material for exegesis should be the final authoritative text by which every reading can then be measured and critiqued.

To elaborate further on our hermeneutics, there are two equally important hermeneutical factors that we should bring into play. First, we need to try to make sense of the text's syntax. Secondly, since words, in and of themselves, are polysemantic, we need to pursue the meaning of the terms employed within the literary context.[47] In other words, meaning is best derived from contextual exegesis since meaning is context-based.

---

[44] Gerhard von Rad, *Genesis: A Commentary*, trans. John H. Marks, OTL, ed. G. Ernest Wright et al. (Philadelphia: Westminster Press, 1961), 135.

[45] John Van Seters, *Prologue to History: The Yahwist as Historian in Genesis* (Louisville, KY: John Knox Press, 1992), 179.

[46] Brevard S. Childs, *Old Testament Theology in a Canonical Context* (Philadelphia: Fortress Press, 1985), 6.

[47] To this end we agree with the statement, "words only have meaning in sentences, and for the most part biblical sentences only have meaning in relation to the preceding and succeeding sentences" (Gordon D. Fee and Douglas Stuart, *How to Read the Bible for All Its Worth: A Guide to Understanding the Bible*, 2nd ed. (Grand Rapids: Zondervan Publishing House, 1993), 23. The importance of being mindful of the context in the process of determining meaning is underscored by, among others, Tremper Longman (*Making Sense of the Old Testament: Three Crucial Questions*, ed. Grant R. Osborne and Richard J. Jones [Grand Rapids: Baker Books, 1998], 32–39); Walter M. Dunnett (*The Interpretation of Holy Scripture* [Nashville: Thomas Nelson Publishers, 1984], 99–101); and Milton S. Terry (*Biblical Hermeneutics: A Treatise on the Interpretation of the Old and New Testaments* [Grand Rapids: Zondervan Publishing House, 1974], 219).

One criterion for determining the exegetical soundness of an interpretation, therefore, is the extent to which it is sensitive to the context. Indeed this criterion will serve as a cornerstone of our evaluation. Looking ahead, it will be our determination that the sexual reading, for instance, disregards the context in its assertion that the construction ראה עֶרְוַת carries a sexual meaning in Gen 9:22. Similarly disregarding the context are certain interpretations of the Noachian utterance. These include: (1) the equation of the beneficiaries of the curse with Canaan's brothers; (2) the association of the fulfillment of the curse with the forced corvée labor of the Egyptians by Pharaoh, the triumph of Israel over Egypt during the Exodus, or the enslavement of people of African descent; and (3) the linkage between the blessing utterance with the salvation of the Japhethites, intellectual superiority of the Japhethites, or the dispersion of the Jews by the Romans in the first century A.D.

The critique, however, will be offered in the context of a thorough analysis of the whole pericope. Aspects of this analysis will include (a) the role of vv. 18–19; (b) Noah's state leading up to the infraction (vv. 20–21); (c) Ham's action and his siblings' reaction (vv. 22–23); and (d) analysis of the Noachian utterances and evaluation of the proposed fulfillments.

## Organization of the Study

Following the introduction in chapter one, chapter two will offer a brief history of interpretation of the two primary aspects that constitute the heart of the book: the nature of the offense against Noah and the suggestions of fulfillment together with the perceived meaning of the Noachian utterances. The need for brevity arises from the fact that the work is not exclusively a history of interpretation. The downside is that our coverage of the history of interpretation is bound to be more representative than exhaustive.

In the process of cataloging the history of the interpretation, we will resist offering any exegetical critique as much as possible. That will have to await chapter four, the critique-proper section of the book. The critique itself will rely on the exegetical findings of chapter three, the exegesis section of our work. Our summary and conclusions will be offered in chapter five.

## Anticipated Readers of the Study

Considering the thoroughness with which we have treated the nature of Ham's offense and the meaning of Noah's words, we hope that this study will serve as a reference for Old Testaments students, professors and commentators. Additionally, we hope that people of color will appreciate the contribution we have made in as far as critiquing readings of Gen 9:18–27 that are or have been prejudicial to individuals of African descent.

## The Limitation of the Study

Unable to find any suggestion pertaining to the fulfillment of the phrase וְיִשְׁכֹּן בְּאָהֳלֵי־שֵׁם ("let him dwell in the tents of Shem") that matches the exegetical findings of this aspect of the blessing remarks, this study stopped at only debunking the various suggestions that have been proposed and did not attempt to offer any new proposal. We leave this aspect of research to others who, hopefully, will take note of our exegetical conclusions regarding this phrase.

Also, the study has not attempted to evaluate the various explanations of why Noah directed the curse to an apparently innocent individual, viz., Canaan. All we have done is list the seven proposals. Briefly those views are: (1) some curse-resistant phenomenon that is thought to have shielded Ham from the curse; (2) some sin or vice on the part of Canaan that served as rationale for the curse; (3) Canaan was either a co-offender with Ham or the sole offender in the story; (4) Canaan should be understood figuratively, namely, synecdoche of part for the whole; (5) the principle of *lex talionis* is at work in the cursing of Canaan; (6) the curse is an outworking of the principle of children suffering for the sins of their parents; and (7) Canaan was cursed in order to stop Ham from passing on the sexually acquired "potency of leadership" to him.[48]

---

[48] For an elaboration of the seven proposals, see the appendix.

# CHAPTER 2

# A BRIEF HISTORY OF INTERPRETATION

This chapter covers interpretations that have been offered in reference to the twin issues of the nature of the infraction against Noah and suggested fulfillments of the Noachian utterances.

## The Nature of the Infraction against Noah

It is our understanding that there are five different views on the nature of the infraction against Noah. They are: (a) sexual; (b) sight; (c) disclosure; (d) unfilial irreverence; and (e) castration. The sexual view is further categorized into homosexuality (or sodomy), incest and voyeurism.[1] The "unfilial irreverence" view can be further categorized into mockery, laughter, and jeering.

### Sexual View

Whereas the pervasiveness of the sexual reading in the antebellum period is debated,[2] beyond the 1800's, not only has the sexual interpretation continued to enjoy

---

[1] Even though voyeurism would fit under the "sight" view, we are inclined to place it under the "sexual" category because of sexual intent in the peering. The "sight" view does not carry the connotation of sexual pleasure in the way that "voyeurism" does.

[2] There is disagreement between Stephen Haynes and Thomas Peterson as to the pervasiveness of the sexual reading during this period. The latter considers the reading rather pervasive and enumerates some examples (Thomas Virgil Peterson, *Ham and Japheth: The Mythic World of Whites in the Antebellum South*, ATLA Monograph Series, vol. 12 [Metuchen, NJ: The Scarecrow Press and the American Theological Library Association, 1978], 78). Proslavery writers who constitute Peterson's listing are as follows: Nathan Lord, *A Northern Presbyter's Second Letter* [Boston: Little, Brown, 1855], 42, 57, James Sloan, *The Great Question Answered* [Memphis: Hutton, Galaway, 1857], 17, and John Fletcher, *Studies on Slavery* [Natchez, MS: Jackson Warner, 1852], 17, 222.

The former maintains that after reviewing more that fifty primary documents from the antebellum period, he could not find a single reference that explicitly charged Ham or Canaan with sexual misconduct (Stephen Haynes, *Noah's Curse: The Biblical Justification of American Slavery*, vol. 20, Religion in America, ed. Harry S. Stout [New York: Oxford University Press, 2002], 246, n. 13).

endorsement, but its supporters have also grown considerably in number. Indeed, beginning in the 1960's and extending to the present, scholarship has witnessed what may rightly be considered a new wave of acceptance for the sexual interpretation based on the large number of works that subscribe to it. Even though the majority of these subscribers stop at simply labeling the offense as sexual,[3] there are those who offer accompanying argumentation.[4] Among the latter, three types of sexual acts are discernable.

### Incest

One suggestion is that the offense was of an incestuous nature. This interpretation finds espousal as far back as the antebellum period in the person of Josiah Priest (1843):

> It is believed by some, and not without reason, that (the crime of Ham) did not consist alone in the seeing his father's nakedness as a *man*, but rather in the abuse and actual *violation* of his own mother.

---

[3] Arthur Frederick Ide, *Noah and the Ark: The Influence of Sex, Homophobia and Heterosexism in the Flood Story and Its Writing* (Las Colinas, TX: Monument, 1992), 51; Regina M. Schwartz, *The Curse of Cain: The Violent Legacy of Monotheism* (Chicago: University of Chicago Press, 1997), 106; Eugene F. Roop, *Genesis* (Scottdale, PA: Herald Press, 1987), 77; H. Hirsch Cohen, *The Drunkenness of Noah* (Tuscaloosa, AL: University of Alabama Press, 1974), 18–19; Walter Brueggemann, *Genesis*, Interpretation: A Bible Commentary for Teaching and Preaching, ed. James Luther Mays (Atlanta: John Knox Press, 1982), 91; Laurence A. Turner, *Genesis*, Readings: A New Biblical Commentary, ed. John Jarick (Sheffield: Sheffield Academic Press, 2000), 56; Edmund Leach, *Genesis as Myth and Other Essays*, Cape Editions, ed. Nathaniel Tarn, vol. 39 (London: Jonathan Cape, 1969), 19; Haynes, *Noah's Curse: The Biblical Justification of American Slavery*, 209; Wayne Perryman, *The 1993 Trial on the Curse of Ham*, ed. Hattie Greenhouse, Simone Williams, and Peter P. Parker (Bakersfield, CA: Pneuma Life Publishing, 1994), 28; Robert L. Cohn, "Narrative Structure and Canonical Perspective in Genesis," *JSOT* 25 (1983): 5; Bruce K. Waltke, *Genesis: A Commentary* (Grand Rapids: Zondervan, 2001), 148–49.

[4] Anthony Phillips, "Uncovering the Father's Skirt," *VT* 1 (1980): 38–43; O. Palmer Robertson, "Current Critical Questions Concerning the 'Curse of Ham'," *JETS* 41 (1998): 179; Randall C. Bailey, "They're Nothing but Incestuous Bastards: The Polemical Use of Sex and Sexuality in Hebrew Canon Narratives," in *In Reading from This Place*, ed. Mary Ann Tolbert, vol. 1, *Social Location and Biblical Interpretation in the United States* (Minneapolis: Fortress, 1994), 134; William A. Brunk, "The Action of Ham against Noah: Its Nature and Result (Genesis 9:18–27)" (M.Div. thesis, Western Conservative Baptist Seminary, 1988), 79; Adin Steinsaltz, *Tractate Sanhedrin: Part V*, trans. Rabbi David Strauss, The Talmud: The Steinsaltz Edition, vol. 19 (New York: Random House, 1999), 25; Frederick W. Bassett, "Noah's Nakedness and the Curse on Canaan: A Case of Incest?," *VT* 21 (April, 1971): 233–35; Isaac M. Kikawada and Arthur Quinn, *Before Abraham Was: The Unity of Genesis 1–11* (Nashville: Abingdon Press, 1985), 102–103; Seth Daniel Kunin, *The Logic of Incest: A Structuralist Analysis of Hebrew Mythology*, JSOTsup, ed. David J. A. Clines and Philip R. Davies, vol. 185 (Sheffield: Sheffield Academic Press, 1995), 174; John Sietze Bergsma and Scott Walker Hahn, "Noah's Nakedness and the Curse of Canaan (Genesis 9:20–27)," *JBL* 124, no. 1 (2005): 26, 34–39.

This opinion is strengthened by a passage found in Leviticus xviii. 8, which reads as follows, "The nakedness of thy father's wife shalt thou not uncover: it is thy *father's* nakedness." On account of *this* passage, it has been believed that the crime of Ham did not consist alone of seeing his father in an improper manner, but rather of his own mother, the wife of Noah, and violating her.

If this was so, how much horrible, therefore appears the character of Ham, and how much more deserving of the *curse,* which was laid upon him and his race, of whom it was foreseen that *they* would be like *this,* their lewd ancestor.[5]

Two elements are observable from Priest's citation. First, he proffered a cause-and-effect relationship between Ham's sexual sin and the African's supposed "animal–like sensuality."[6] Second, he brought an exegetical argument to bear.

Later advocates offer similar, if not more elaborate, exegetical argumentation. Brunk (1988), for instance, argues that Gen 9:22 parallels Lev 20:17 in the sense that both verses feature of the expression ראה ערוה and both mark the only instance where this expression is used in reference to people. Building on this supposed parallelism, he reasons that since the clause ראה ערוה in Lev 20:17 clearly carries a sexual meaning, by virtue of its parallelism to the clause גלה ערוה ("uncover nakedness"), Gen 9:22 must similarly carry a sexual connotation.[7] Bassett (1971), on the other hand, bases his argumentation on the construct form עֶרְוַת ("nakedness of"). Since this particular

---

[5] Josiah Priest, *Slavery, as It Relates to the Negro, or African Race, Examined in the Light of Circumstances, History and the Holy Scriptures; with an Account of the Origin of the Black Man's Color, Causes of His State of Servitude and Traces of His Character as Well in Ancient as in Modern Times*, vol. 1, Anti-Movements in America, ed. Gerald N. Grob (Albany, NY: C. Van Benthuysen, 1843; reprint, New York: Arno Press, 1977), 152.

[6] Peterson, *Ham and Japheth: The Mythic World of Whites in the Antebellum South*, 74–75. Peterson's observation is that the white southerners utilized the story of Ham to underline their views on the attributes of the Blackman.

[7] Brunk, "The Action of Ham against Noah," 48; cf. Brueggemann, *Genesis*, 90–91.

construct appears in Lev 18 (vv. 7, 8, 14, 16) with a sexual connotation, he argues, it must have the same meaning in Gen 9:22.[8]

Kikawada and Quinn (1985) offer additional arguments in favor of the incest reading.[9] One, alcohol was one of the recognized libido stimuli of the ancient Near East and is even cited in relationship to romance in the Song of Songs 7:9. Two, the chiastic connection between the story about the sons of God in Gen 6:1–5 and Noah's story suggests that the object of the curse in Gen 9 (i.e., Canaan) was a product of an illicit union in the same way that the illicit union in Gen 6 (i.e., the mighty and renowned men of old) was cursed through the agency of the flood. Three, the occasion of Canaan's conception is the moment of incestuous activity between Ham and his mother, "after his father is rendered incapacitated by drink (and after Noah arouses the mother but proves incapable of satisfying her)." Four, the phrase "his tent" (אָהֳלֹה) (9:21) is a questionable translation; the noun has an ending that suggests "her tent."

Substituting the word "homosexuality" with "paternal incest" as opposed to "maternal incest," John Bergsma and Scott Hahn (2005) argue for the latter along the following lines: (a) No combination of the terms ערוה, ראה, and/or גלה is found associated with homosexual relations anywhere in the Bible; (b) understanding Ham's deed as maternal incest offers a viable rationale for Canaan's curse, viz., Canaan is cursed because his origin was a vile, taboo act on the part of his father; and (c) the relationship between Gen 9:20–27 and Gen 19:30–38, as well as Gen 6:1–4; Lev 18:1–8;

---

[8] Bassett, "Noah's Nakedness and the Curse on Canaan: A Case of Incest?" 235.

[9] Kikawada and Quinn, *Before Abraham Was*, 102–103.

Deut 23:1; and 27:20, all support the implication of sexual violation of Noah's wife by her son.[10]

## *Voyeurism*

According to Bailey (1994), the meticulous description of the effort taken by Shem and Japheth not to look at their father should cause the reader to dismiss the suggestion that some sexual act was committed against Noah. Instead the reader should consider the possibility that the offense may have been voyeurism on Ham's part.[11]

## *Homosexuality*

The earliest mention of the homosexual interpretation appears in *Sanhedrin* (A.D. 500–550). In a debate to which we have already alluded, Rav and Samuel advanced contrasting opinions on the nature of Ham's offense against Noah. Of pertinence is a remark by one of the two rabbis to the effect that "he (Ham) sodomized him" (רבעו).[12] In other words, Ham subjected Noah to a homosexual act. Noteworthy is the absence of any exegetical argument.

Unlike the Talmud's *a priori* assertion that Ham's infraction was homosexuality, Robertson (1998), a later advocate, appeals to verses such as Lev 20:17, 18, and 19. According to him, the phraseology of these prohibitions in Leviticus concerning sexual relations approximates very closely the language used to describe the sin of Ham. "Looked on the nakedness of his father," in Genesis, parallels "look on (a woman's)

---

[10] Bergsma and Hahn, "Noah's Nakedness and the Curse of Canaan (Genesis 9:20–27)," 35–36.

[11] Bailey, "They're Nothing but Incestuous Bastards: The Polemical Use of Sex and Sexuality in Hebrew Canon Narratives," 134.

[12] *Sanh.* 70a. The contrasting opinion is that Ham castrated Noah.

nakedness" or "uncover (a woman's) nakedness" in Leviticus. Ham, therefore, should be understood as having initiated a homosexual relationship with his drunken father. [13]

## Sight View

Even though the "sight" view is similar to the voyeurism view, in as far the viewing is concerned, its intent, unlike voyeurism, is non-sexual. The view appears in the work of Clement of Alexandria (A.D. 150–215). [14] There he identified the offense simply as beholding what was forbidden. This same understanding seems to be reflected by current commentators who insist on limiting the misdemeanor to just seeing. [15]

In an apparent rebuttal to a society that plays down the seriousness of seeing the nakedness of another individual, Ross (1976), an advocate of the "sight" view, makes the following points: (a) to see someone uncovered was to bring dishonor and to gain advantage for potential exploitation; (b) within the boundaries of honor, seeing the nakedness was considered shameful and impious; (c) nakedness in the Old Testament was from the beginning a thing of shame for fallen man; (d) to be exposed meant to be unprotected; this can be seen by the fact that the horrors of the exile are couched in the image of shameful nakedness (Hab 3:13; Lam 1:8; 4:21); and (e) there seems to be a taboo in the Old Testament against a look that suggests an overstepping of the set limits

---

[13] Robertson, "Current Critical Questions Concerning the 'Curse of Ham'," 179; cf. Phillips, "Uncovering the Father's Skirt," 38–43; Donald J. Wold, *Out of Order: Homosexuality in the Bible and the Ancient Near East* (Grand Rapids: Baker Books, 1998), 65–76; Kunin, *The Logic of Incest: A Structuralist Analysis of Hebrew Mythology*, 174.

[14] Clement, *Paed.* 2.6.

[15] Umberto Cassuto, *From Noah to Abraham (Genesis vi. 9–xi, 32)*, trans. Israel Abrahams, vol. 2, A Commentary on the Book of Genesis (Jerusalem: Magnes Press, 1964), 151–52; Nzash U. Lumeya, "The Curse on Ham's Descendants: Its Missiological Impact on Zairian Mbala Mennonite Brethren" (Ph.D. diss., Fuller Theological Seminary, 1988), 64; Victor P. Hamilton, *The Book of Genesis: Chapters 1–17*, NICOT, ed. R. K. Harrison (Grand Rapids: Eerdmans, 1990), 323; John E. Hartley, *Genesis*, NIBC: Old Testament Series, ed. Robert L. Hubbard Jr. and Robert K. Johnson (Peabody, MA: Hendrickson Publishers, 2000), 113.

by identification with the object seen (Gen 19:26; Exod 33:20; Judg 13:22;

1 Sam 6; 19).[16]

## Disclosure View

Disclosure assumes that an individual has seen something and then reports what

he or she has seen. The view was expressed within the patristic era by among others

Augustine and Lactantius.[17] The view is also present in Jewish literature particularly in

the *Genesis Rabbah* (fifth century A.D.) where R. Nehemiah described Canaan's offense

as כנען ראה והגיד להן (seeing and then informing others).[18] Later advocates of the

"disclosure" view included Thomas Whitelaw (1900),[19] George Bush (1860),[20] and Elisha

Fish (1772).[21]

## Unfilial Irreverence View

As in the case with disclosure, unfilial irreverence emphasizes the reaction upon

seeing something.[22] Whereas the reaction in disclosure is reporting what one has seen, the

---

[16] Allen P. Ross, "The Table of Nations in Genesis" (Ph.D. diss., Dallas Theological Seminary, 1976): 230–31; cf. Clyde T. Francisco, "The Curse on Canaan," *CT* 8 (1964): 8–9.

[17] Augustine (A.D. 354–430) (*Civ.* 5.16.1) and Lactantius (third century A.D.) (*Inst.* 2.14).

[18] *Gen. Rab.* 37.7.3e (fifth century A.D.). See also Jubilees, which understands the offender as Ham (*Jub.* 7.9) (161–140 B.C.).

[19] Whitelaw regarded the offense as both rejoicing and disclosing (Thomas Whitelaw, *Genesis*, new ed., vol. 1, *The Pulpit Commentary*, ed. H. D. M. Spence and Joseph S. Exell [London: Funk & Wagnalls Company, 1900], 149).

[20] George Bush, *Notes Critical and Practical on the Book of Genesis: Designed as a General Help to Biblical Reading and Instruction*, 26th ed. (New York: Ivison, Phiney & Company, 1860), 161.

[21] Elisha Fish, *Japheth Dwelling in the Tents of Shem or Infant Baptism Vindicated in a Discourse, the Substance of Which Was Delivered at Upton, January 5, 1772, with Objections Answered* (Boston, New England: Thomas and John Fleet, 1773), 4.

[22] The term "unfilial" as a description of Ham's behavior is utilized by M. M. Kalisch (*Genesis*, English ed., Historical and Critical Commentary: The Old Testament with a New Translation [London: Longman, Brown, Green, Longman, and Roberts, 1858], 154); Robert S. Candlish (*The Book of Genesis: Expounded in a Series of Discourses* [Edinburgh: Adam and Charles Black, 1868], 1:158–159);

reactions characterized as "unfilial irreverence" have the common intent of shaming the victim.

## Mockery

In the context of a discussion on the significance of the four trees mentioned in the Judg 9:8-15 allegory, Methodius (d. A.D. 311) made the point that "the fruit of the vine (i.e., the wine) represented the precept given to Noah at the time of the deluge *because, when overpowered by wine, he was mocked*" (emphasis mine).[23] The idea of mockery or ridicule is present in Philo's work (20 B.C.–A.D. 50)[24] and in Pirke de Rabbi Eliezer (A.D. 750–850).[25] The former describes Ham's offense as reporting the involuntary evil of his father "with ridicule in his very words, making a jest of what ought not to have been treated with laughter and derision, but shame and fear mingled with reverence." The latter depicted Ham as not having taken to heart the duty of honoring (one's father) when he preferred instead to tell "his brothers in the market, making sport of his father."

## Laughter

According to Chrysostom's (A.D. 347–407) Homily VI of the *Gospel of Matthew*, there are only two instances when laughing is mentioned in the Scriptures. One instance involves Sarah "when she is blamed." The other pertains to "the son of Noe, when for a

---

Arthur W. Pink (*Gleanings in Genesis* [New York: Our Hope, 1922], 1:126); and W. H. Griffith Thomas (*Genesis: A Devotional Commentary* [Grand Rapids: Eerdmans, 1946], 96).

[23] Methodius, *The Banquet of the Ten Virgins* 10.2; cf. Justin Martyr, *Dial.* 136.

[24] Philo, *QG* 2.70.

[25] *Pirke De Rabbi Eliezer: According to the Text of the Manuscript Belonging to Abraham Epstein of Vienna*, trans. Gerald Friedlander, 4th ed., The Judaic Studies Library, vol. 6 (New York: Sepher-Hermon Press, 1981), 170.

freeman he became a slave."[26] Other patristic writers who shared the "laughter" view

included Origen (A.D. 185–254), Ambrose of Milan (A.D. 340–397), Vincent of Lerins

(d. A.D. 450),[27] and the Book of Adam and Eve (fifth and sixth century A.D.).[28] The

laughter view appears in the writings of Josephus (A.D. 37–100) who identified Ham's

offense as laughingly disclosing Noah's nakedness.[29] The view was expressed also during

the Reformation. According to Luther (A.D. 1483–1586), not only did Ham "laugh at his

father as a fool," he broadcasted his father and made sport of him.[30]

### Jeering

Calvin Goodspeed and D. M. Welton (1909) assert that "Ham's sin lay not in his

seeing his father's nakedness, which might have been accidental, but in the evidently

unfilial and jeering pleasure with which he saw and reported the same to his brethren."[31]

Other advocates include Delitzsch who describes the offense as "scornful merriment,"

and B. Jacob (1974), who remarks that Ham "first glanced into the tent from the outside

and frivolously enjoyed his father's commencing drunkenness; he entered when the

---

[26] Chrysostom, *Hom. Matt.* 6.8.

[27] Origen, *Hom.Gen.* 16; Ambrose, *On the Duties of the Clergy*, 1.18.79; Vinicent of Lerins, *A Commonitory*, 7.19.

[28] Even though the *Book of Adam and Eve* is not a patristic work, we include it here simply because it is by nature a Christian work thought to be written by a pious and orthodox Egyptian (*The Book of Adam and Eve, Also Called the Conflict of Adam and Eve with Satan: A Book of the Early Eastern Church, Translated from the Ethiopic, with Notes from the Kufale, Talmud, Midrashim, and Other Eastern Works*, trans. S. C. Malan [London: Williams and Norgate, 1882], 160).

[29] *Ant.*1.6.3.

[30] *Lectures on Genesis Chapters 6–14*, trans. George V. Schick, vol. 2, Luther's Works, ed. Jaroslav Pelikan (St. Louis: Concordia Publishing House, 1960), 167–68, 173; cf. John Calvin, *Commentaries on the First Book of Moses, Called Genesis*, trans. John King (Grand Rapids: Eerdmans, 1948), 2: 302.

[31] Calvin Goodspeed and D. M. Welton, *The Book of Genesis*, An American Commentary on the Old Testament (PA: American Baptist Publication Society, 1909), 96.

drunken man became unconscious, gloatingly ran out to let the brother's participate in the spectacle, insensitively assuming that they would enjoy this too."[32]

## Castration View

This view appears exclusively in the Jewish literature where we find both implicit suggestion and explicit assertion that the offense was actually the involuntary castration of Noah. The implicit suggestion is found in *Genesis Rabbah's* (fifth century A.D.) accusatory remark, which it attributes to Noah following his resolution to secure for himself an aide in his sunset years through fathering a son upon boarding the ark. The exact remark is that Ham had stopped his father from producing a young son to take care of him (*R. Berekhiah*) or as worded by *R. Huna*, Ham had stopped his father from "doing something that is done in darkness."[33] Explicit assertion that the offense was, indeed, castration is made by the *Sanhedrin* (A.D. 500–550), *Pirke R. Eli.*, and *Zohar* (thirtenth century). According to *Sanh.* either Rav or Samuel said: "He (i.e., Ham) castrated him (סרסו) . . ."[34] As for *Pirke R. Eli.* "Canaan entered and saw the nakedness of Noah, and he bound a thread (where the mark of) the Covenant was, and emasculated him after which

---

[32] Franz Delitzsch, *A New Commentary on Genesis*, trans. Sophia Taylor, vol. 1, Clark's Foreign Theological Library (Edinburgh: T. & T. Clark, 1899), 293; Benno Jacob, *The First Book of the Bible: Genesis*, trans. Ernest I. Jacob and Walter Jacob (New York: Ktav Publishing House, 1974), 67.

[33] Gen. Rab. 36.7.4c.

[34] *Sanh.* 70a. Ginzberg's rehearsal of this view could not have been any clearer: "In the drunken condition Noah betook himself to the tent of his wife. His son Ham saw him there, and he told his brothers what he had noticed, and said: 'The first man had but two sons, and one slew the other; this man Noah has three sons, yet he desires to beget a fourth besides.' Nor did Ham rest satisfied with these disrespectful words against his father. He added to this sin of irreverence the still greater outrage of attempting to perform an operation upon his father designed to prevent procreation" (Louis Ginzberg, *Bible Times and Characters from the Creation to Jacob*, trans. Henrietta Szold, *The Legend of the Jews*, vol. 1 [Philadelphia: The Jewish Publication Society of America, 1937], 168).

he went forth and told his brethren."[35] Lastly, *Zohar* suggested that "Canaan seized the opportunity to work his will by removing from that righteous man the mystical symbol of the covenant; for this, according to tradition, is what he did."[36]

## Summary

There are essentially five views on the nature of Ham's offense. The first view is that the offense was of a sexual nature. Advocates of this view can be further categorized into those who consider the sexual offense to be incest, those who regard Ham's act to have been of a homosexual nature, and those who consider the offense to have been voyeurism. The other four views are sight, disclosure, unfilial irreverence, and castration, respectively.

## The Meaning and Possible Fulfillment of the Noachian Utterances

### The Meaning and Fulfillment of the Curse (vv. 25, 26b, 27b)

Views on the original meaning and ultimate fulfillment of the curse utterance by Noah fall into two groups. One group, the "Canaan" view, understands Canaan or the Canaanites as the object of the curse. The other considers Ham or the Hamites as the object of the curse; thus the label, the "Ham" view.

### *Canaan View*

Church Fathers

The church fathers were more hesitant to offer opinions on fulfillment than they were willing to associate Canaan with the curse. For instance, among four church fathers

---

[35] *Pirke de Rabbi Eliezer (the Chapters of Rabbi Eliezer the Great): According to the Text of the Manuscript Belonging to Abraham Epstein of Vienna*, 170.

[36] Zohar, *Noah* 73b.

who regarded Canaan as the individual who was cursed,[37] only two ventured an opinion regarding the possible occasion of the fulfillment of the utterances, viz., Justin Martyr (ca. A.D. 153) and Chrysostom (A.D. 347–407). For the former, the unfolding of the Noachian curse utterance took place when Israel invaded the territory of the sons of Canaan by the will of God and possessed it. The possession was not final, however, since Israel suffered invasion by the sons of Japheth who dispossessed her of the land from which she had driven Canaan away.[38] Like Justin Martyr, Chrysostom also saw the fulfillment of the curse in the subjugation of the Canaanites by Israel. Specifically, though, he proffered that Noah's utterances pertaining to Canaan "came to pass in the Gibeonites, Canaan's descendants."[39] So, while these writers consider the object of the curse to be an individual, they seem to have people groups in view in their discussions of fulfillment.

Jewish Works

Suggestions of possible fulfillment of the curse utterance are even scarcer, if not altogether absent, among Jewish works. The hermeneutical comments among the Jewish works, however, are noteworthy. Rashi (A.D. 1040–1105), for instance, interpreted "brothers" in v. 25 literally. Thus the recipients of Canaan's servitude were the sons of Ham, viz., Cush, Mizraim and Put. As regards the meaning of v. 27b, Rashi explained,

---

[37] Justin Martyr, *Dial.* 139; Lactantius, *Inst.* 2.14; Chrysostom, *Hom. Matt.* 6.8; and Augustine, *Doctr. chr.* 4.21.45.

[38] Justin Martyr, *Dial.* 139.

[39] Chrysostom, *Hom. Matt.* 6.8. The servitude of the Gibeonites as an aspect of the fulfillment is entertained later by Samuel Sewall (*The Selling of Joseph: A Memorial*, ed. Sydney Kaplan [Amherst, MA: University of Massachusetts Press, 1969], 13).

"even after the descendants of Shem are exiled, some of the descendants of Canaan will be sold to them as slaves."[40]

Also noteworthy is Ibn Ezra's (A.D. 1089–1164)) interpretation of v. 26b and 27b. Reading the suffix מוֹ— at the end of verse 26 as plural, Ibn Ezra perceived its antecedent to be God and Shem. Thus the recipients or beneficiaries of Canaan's servitude were both God and Shem. To circumvent the critique that he would be advocating that God made Canaan his slave, Ibn Ezra clarified that it was actually Shem who would force Canaan to worship God. As regards the meaning of verse 27b, Ibn Ezra explained that Canaan would be a slave to Shem and to Japheth.[41]

Nineteenth Century to the Present

Association of the curse with the conquest in the nineteenth century onwards is reminiscent of the view held by both Justin Martyr and Chrysostom. Figures in this time frame envisage the domination of the Canaanites following the conquest as the fulfillment of Noah's curse.[42] Unique to this period, however, is the need to account for both the utterance concerning the enslavement of Canaan by Shem and the enslavement of Canaan by Japheth. Concerning the subjugation by the Shemites, two historical

---

[40] *Genesis: A New English Translation, Translation of Text, Rashi, and Other Commentaries*, trans. Rabbi A. J. Rosenberg (New York: Judaica Press, 1993), 1:129. Rashi's literal interpretation of "brothers" in v. 25 is echoed later on by, among others Claus Westermann. Following his referencing of Gen 27:29 and 27:40, where brother is to serve brother, he asserts that, "the curse upon the son who dishonored his father does not refer to the political status of a particular people among others. It refers rather to the state of servitude of one brother to his brothers which has become possible because of the outrage committed and not the people groups that these brothers represent" (Claus Westermann, *Gen 1–11*, trans. John J. Scullion, Genesis: A Commentary, vol. 1 [Minneapolis: Augsburg Publishing House, 1984], 492).

[41] Abraham ben Meir Ibn Ezra, *Genesis*, trans. H. Norman Strickman and Arthur M. Silver, vol. 1, Ibn Ezra's Commentary on the Pentateuch (New York: Menorah Publishing Company, 1988), 129–30.

[42] E.g., Joseph P. Thompson, *Teaching of the New Testament on Slavery* (New York: Joseph H. Ladd, 1856), 9.

occasions feature in the discussions of fulfillment. One is the episode recorded in Genesis 14 where five kings are depicted as serving Chedorlaomer. Convinced that this episode ought to be regarded as the fulfillment of the aspect of the curse concerning the enslavement of Canaan by Shem, Cassuto (1964) argues as follows:

> Here it is stated that Canaan would be a slave of Shem; that means that the children of Canaan would be in bondage to the children of Shem. Now further on, in chapter x (v. 22), we are told who the children of Shem are, and that the first of them is *Elam*. In the same chapter (v. 19) the borders of the Canaanites are defined, and they are said to extend *in the direction of* SODOM, GOMORRAH, ADMAH *and* ZEBOIIM, *as far as Lasha*, that is to say, that all these cities were included in the territory of the Canaanites . . . These cities—Sodom, Gomorrah, Admah and Zeboiim—are again listed together in chapter xiv, where the relations between the kings of the *Canaanite* cities and Chedorlaomer, king of *Elam*, are described. Now the relationship was that *they had served Chedorlaomer* (xiv. 4), that is, the children of *Canaan* served him who ruled over the first of the peoples of the children of *Shem. They had served* . . . exactly what we are told here: *and let Canaan be his* SLAVE. There can be no doubt that it is to this historic episode that our verse refers.[43]

The other occasion is during the tenures of Joshua and Solomon. Under Joshua, Canaanites were partly exterminated and partly reduced to the lowest form of slavery by the Israelites, who belonged to the family of Shem (Josh 9:23; Judg 1:28, 30, 33, 35). The remaining Canaanites were further reduced to slavery during the reign of King Solomon (1 Kgs 9:20, 21).[44]

Just as the fulfillment of the subjugation of Canaan by Shem is variously perceived, so is the fulfillment of the subjugation of the Canaanites by the Japhethites. For Cassuto, the fulfillment lies with one, King Tidal, who was part of the group of kings who reimposed the yoke of servitude upon the Canaanite cities in the Jordan plain (Gen

---

[43] Cassuto, *From Noah to Abraham (Genesis vi. 9–xi. 32)*, 168.

[44] Goodspeed and Welton, *The Book of Genesis*, 97; George Woosung Wade, *The Book of Genesis* (London: Hodder Brothers, 1896), 218; Kalisch, *Genesis*, 55.

14).[45] The moment of fulfillment, according to Delitzsch (1899), was the period when the Canaanite people of Tyre and Sidon were subjugated by the Greek and the Roman empires. The subjugation by the Greeks took place during the reign of Alexander the Great. The subjugation by the Romans followed the destruction of Carthage in 146 B.C.[46] Some commentators, however, express doubt whether the fulfillment of Canaan's enslavement by Japheth can actually be historically determined.[47]

### *Ham view*

Not all have regarded Canaan or the Canaanites as the sole object(s) of the Noachian curse. Some consider Ham as the target. Others regard the Hamitic people as the object. The "Ham" view constitutes four aspects.

Ham as the Object of the Curse

One aspect concludes that Ham was the object of the curse in lieu of Canaan on the basis of textual emendation, social customs, or Ham's offense. The earliest manifestation of textual emendation appears in a set of Greek Byzantine texts in which the proper name in Gen 9:25 is substituted with Χαμ.[48] Similar emendation is evident in the Old Latin text of Ambrose (fourth century A.D.), which reads *et dixit maledictus*

---

[45] Cassuto, *From Noah to Abraham*, 168.

[46] Delitzsch, *A New Commentary on Genesis*, 294–95.

[47] Herbert E. Ryle, *The Book of Genesis in the Revised Version, with Introduction and Notes by Herbert E. Ryle* (Cambridge, England: University Press, 1914), 128; cf. Ross, "The Table of Nations in Genesis," 369.

[48] The critical apparatus of *Biblia Hebraica* draws attention to the existence of such manuscripts (*Biblia Hebraica*, ed. Rudolf Kittel [Stuttgart: Württembergische Bibelanstalt, 1951], 13). The manuscripts themselves, however, are listed by John Wever (*Genesis*, ed. John William Wevers, Septuaginta: Vetus Testamentum Graecum Auctoritate Academiae Scientiarum Gottingensis Editum, vol. 1 [Göttingen: Vandenhoeck & Ruprecht, 1974], 131); cf. John William Wevers, *Notes on the Greek Text of Genesis*, Septuagint and Cognate Studies Series, ed. Leonard J. Greenspoon, vol. 35 (Atlanta: Scholars Press, 1993), 124.

*Cham*,[49] and Irenaeus' second century work *On the Apostolic Preaching*.[50] Support for this revised reading appears later within the quarters of eighteenth century proslavery advocates. One such advocate is Bishop Thomas Newton who, in a 1759 work, argued that the text of Genesis 9:25 was corrupted and should be read, "cursed be *Ham the father of* Canaan."[51]

Appeal to social customs is apparent in the works of Saadia Gaon (d. A.D. 942) and Arthur Custance (1975). The former suggests that the phrase "cursed be Ham" be read in the place of "cursed be the father of Canaan," based on an Arabic custom of calling a father by the name of the best-known son.[52] The latter envisions the "primitive" habit of indirectly referring to a father that is at play in the conversation between Saul and his general in 1 Sam 17 to be also at play in Gen 9. In 1 Sam 17, Saul's ultimate intent in inquiring about David's father was to honor the father "according to social custom."[53] In the same way, Noah had Ham in mind when he pronounced a curse upon Ham's son.

The declaration that Ham's offense led to him being subjected to the curse was made by two patristic figures. Irenaeus (b. ca. A.D. 150), who, as already indicated,

---

[49] *Genesis*, ed. Bonifatius Fischer, vol. 2, Vetus Latina, ed. Petrus Sabatier (Freiburg: Herder, 1951), 131.

[50] Irenaeus *Epid.* 20. We owe it to David Goldenberg's book for making us aware of both the Vetus Latina and Irenaeus' *On the Apostolic Preaching* (David M. Goldenberg, *The Curse of Ham: Race and Slavery in Early Judaism, Christianity, and Islam, Jews, Christians, and Muslims from the Ancient to the Modern World*, ed. R. Stephen Humphreys, William Chester Jordan, and Peter Schäfer [Princeton: Princeton University Press, 2003], 340, n. 1). The latter is a recently discovered work in which Bishop Irenaeus (A.D. 177) presents the faith chronologically, from the creation of the world to the death of Christ.

[51] Thomas Newton, *Dissertations on the Prophecies, Which Have Remarkably Been Fulfilled, and at This Time Are Fulfilling in the World* (London: J. F. Dove, 1830), 18–19.

[52] Saadia, *Perushei R. Saadya Gaon li-Bereshit*, ed. Moshe Zucker (New York, 1984), 353; cited by Ibn Ezra, *Genesis*, 130.

[53] Arthur C. Custance, *Noah's Three Sons: Human History in Three Dimensions*, The Doorway Papers, vol. 1 (Grand Rapids: Zondervan Publishing House, 1975), 26.

preferred the emended form of Gen 9:25, quoted a presbyter's injunction: "with respect to those misdeeds for which the Scriptures themselves blame the patriarchs and prophets, we ought not to inveigh against them, nor become like Ham, who ridiculed the shame of his father, and so fell under a curse …"[54] Concerning Ham, Sulpitius Severus (d. ca. A.D. 420) said, "Because he had mocked his father when senseless with wine, he incurred his father's curse."[55]

Hamites Cursed via Canaan

Unlike the first aspect, which considers Ham the object of the curse in lieu of Canaan, the second aspect draws the rest of the Hamites into the circle of the curse. Thus Canaan is still considered cursed. But the scope of the curse extends beyond the Canaanites and covers the whole Hamitic people group. How the whole Hamitic group came to be included in the curse against Canaan is explained variously. According to Candlish (1868), "the posterity of Canaan, mixing themselves by dispersion and by colonization with the other descendants of Ham, may have carried with them, wherever they went, their liability to the curse, and may have involved in it, more or less, the people among whom they happened to settle."[56] For Dominick M'Causland (1872), the absence of a blessing on Ham served as a basis for assuming that the curse of Noah on Canaan attended the steps of the whole family.[57] The rationale for considering the whole Hamitic familiy as cursed even though the text identifies only Canaan as the object of the

---

[54] Irenaeus, *Haer.* 4.31.1.

[55] Sulpitius Severus, *The Sacred History* 1.4.

[56] Candlish, *The Book of Genesis: Expounded in a Series of Discourses*, 162.

[57] Dominick M'Causland, *Adam and the Adamite*, 3d ed. (London: Richard Bentley and Son, 1872), 224.

curse include the following: (a) the curse originated with Canaan[58]; (b) Canaan

figuratively stood for the Hamites[59]; and (3) Canaan was the progenitor of the Canaanite

tribes with whom Israel specially had to deal in the land of Canaan.[60]

Hamites cursed via Ham

The third aspect considers Ham, and by extension his descendants, the object of

the curse. Pachomius (d. A.D. 346/7),[61] for instance, asserted that Ham was cursed along

with his descendants. Unlike the first aspect, the issue here is not whether Canaan should

be substituted as the object of the curse. Canaan is simply not contemplated as the object

of the curse. Also, unlike the second aspect, Canaan is not considered the beginning point

of the curse from whom the effect of the curse then spread to the rest of the Hamites. It is

Ham who is considered to have drawn down the curse to his descendants.[62] In certain

instances, though, the Hamites are presented as cursed without any indication that Ham

was the beginning point.

Luther's work serves as an example of such an instance.[63] Prior to Luther, Tabari

(A. D. 838–923), a Persian historian, documented the same view. He spoke of a prayer by

Noah to the effect that Ham's descendants "would be slaves to the children of Shem and

---

[58] Justin Martyr, *Dial.* 139.1.

[59] Samuel Davies Baldwin, *Dominion; or the Unity and Trinity of the Human Race with the Divine Political Constitution of the World, and the Divine Rights of Shem, Ham, and Japheth* (Nashville: E. Stevenson and F. A. Owen, 1858), 53.

[60] M. A. Zimmerman, *Studies in Genesis*, 2d ed. (Menasha, WI: Fellowship of Protestant Lutherans, 1979), 102.

[61] *The Letters of Saint Pachomius* (trans. Armand Veilleux in *Pachomian Koinonia: The Lives, Rules, and Other Writings of Saint Pachomius and His Disciples* (Kalamazoo, MI: Cistercian Publication, 1980–82), 3.5.5.

[62] Vincent of Lerins, *The Commonitory*, 7.

[63] *Lectures on Genesis Chapters 6–14*, 176.

Japheth." Similarly the father of Ibn Ata (A.D. 647–732) said: "wherever his (Ham's)

descendants met the children of Shem, the latter would enslave them."[64]

Particular Non-Canaanite Hamites
as the Object of the Curse

The fourth aspect associates the curse with some particular non-Canaanite

Hamitic groups. Specifically the groups are Egyptians and Africans (Cushites). That

Origen (d. ca. A.D. 253) envisioned a link between the Egyptians and the curse of slavery

is evident in the following citation:

> But Pharao easily reduced the Egyptian people to bondage to himself, nor is it
> written that he did this by force. For the Egyptians are prone to a degenerate life
> and quickly sink to every slavery of the vices. Look at the origin of the race and
> you will discover that their father Cham, who had laughed at his father's
> nakedness, deserved a judgment of this kind, that his son Chanaan should be a
> servant to his brothers, in which case the condition of bondage would prove the
> wickedness of his conduct. Not without merit, therefore, does the discolored
> posterity imitate the ignobility of the race [*Non ergo immerito ignobilitatem
> generis decolor posteritas imitatur*].[65]

Luther drew a similar association between the Egyptians and the curse when he labeled

the exodus as the fulfillment of the "curse that Ham and all his descendants had regarded

with arrogant contempt and unbelief for so long."[66]

As for the association of the African with the curse, this tendency finds

representation in some unnamed party whom Ibn Ezra (A.D. 1089–1164) dismissed for

suggesting that it was the Cushites (Africans) who were cursed. "Those who say that the

---

[64] *The History of Al-Tabari*, ed. Ehsan Yar-Shater, trans. William M. Brinner (Prophets and Patriarchs), vol. 2, Suny Series in Near Eastern Studies, ed. Said Amir Arjomand (Albany, New York: State University of New York Press, 1987), 14, 21.

[65] *Origen: Homilies on Genesis and Exodus*, trans. Ronald E. Heine, The Fathers of the Church: A New Translation, ed. Hermigild Dressler et al, vol. 71 (Washington, D.C: Catholic University of America Press, 1982), 215.

[66] *Lectures on Genesis Chapters 6–14*, 176.

Cushites are enslaved because Noah cursed Ham have forgotten that the first king to rule after the flood was a Cushite."[67] That there existed a party that perceived the African as a cursed people as early as Ibn Ezra's time should not be surprising considering that, prior to Ibn Ezra, a number of works were already presenting certain physiognomical aspects of Ham and his seed (particularly the Africans) as resulting from either the curse or some punitive measures taken against Ham for an offense he is thought to have committed.

The punitive association of Ham and his seed with a somatic aspect other than skin color was present in Midrash, *Tanhuma Yelammedenu Noah*, 13, according to which three aspects of Ham's physiognomy were punitively affected almost in a *quid pro quo* fashion: (a) his eyes became red for glancing at the nakedness of his father; (b) the hair of his head and beard was singed because he turned his face away (ignored his father's condition); and (c) he went about naked with his prepuce extended (*nimshekhah ayin orlato*) because he neglected to cover his naked father. Regarding the physiognomical descriptions here, Goldenberg is of the opinion that *Tanhuma* has the African in mind. The reason for this conclusion is that its remarks compare well with Muslim and Greco-Roman literatures, which definitely have the African in view.[68] Indeed there are examples of Islamic citations that employ physiognomical terms very similar to that of *Tanhuma* and would most probably be alluding to the African. One example is the remark by the father of Ibn Ata to the effect that Ham begat all those who are black and curly-haired

---

[67] Ibn Ezra, *Genesis*, 129.

[68] Goldenberg, *The Curse of Ham: Race and Slavery in Early Judaism, Christianity, and Islam*, 192–93.

and that Noah prayed that the hair of Ham's descendants would not grow beyond their ears.[69]

Punitive association of Ham and his seed with dark skin color is found in certain Jewish works. In *Genesis Rabbah* (36.7.4d, 5a), a third century rabbinic work of Tannaitic tradition, the offense was castration and it was Ham's seed, which experienced the darkening of skin color (*mefuham*). In *Midrash Tanhuma Yelammedenu* 2.12 and *bSanhedrin* 108b, the offense was sexual activity between Ham and his wife at a time when sex was banned in the ark. Unlike *Genesis Rabbah*, it is Ham who experienced the darkening of skin color.

Punitive association of the Hamites and skin color is also found among Muslim authors one of whom shares the sex-in-the ark tradition with *Tanhuma* and *bSanhedrin*. According to Ibn Hisham (d. A.D. 828 or 833), despite the placement of women in isolation, Ham still managed to have intercourse with his wife. When Noah knew of Ham's sexual engagement, he asked that Allah would blacken the face of Ham and his descendants. Consequently, Ham's wife had a black son and he named him Kusha.[70]

The rest of the Islamic literature attributed the darkening of skin simply to Noah's curse as opposed to Noah's reaction against Ham's engagement in sex while in the ark. Moreover, they became more specific as to who the dark descendants of Ham were and a couple of them even went so far as to propose that the Noachian curse of slavery was applicable to the African.

---

[69] *The History of Al-Tabari*, 21.

[70] Abd alMalik Ibn Hisham, *Kitab al-tijan an fi muluk Himyar* (Haydarabad, 1928–29), 24, cited in Goldenberg, *The Curse of Ham: Race and Slavery in Early Judaism, Christianity, and Islam*, 106. The translation is by von Schlegel.

For Kab al-Akhbar (d. A.D. 652), the descendants of Ham include Nubians, Negroes (*zanj*), Berbers, Sindhis, Indians, and all the blacks (*Sudan*). His attribution of dark skin was housed in the retort of Ham's wife following her husband's denial that her black boy and girl were actually his: "they are yours . . . for the curse of your father is upon us."[71]

In the case of Wahb Ibn Munabbih (d. ca. A.D. 730), a South Arabian convert to Islam,

> Ham the son of Noah was a white man, with a handsome face and fine figure, and the Almighty changed his color and the color of his descendants in response to his father's curse. He went away, followed by his sons, and they settled by the shore, where God increased and multiplied them. They are the blacks. Their food is fish, and they sharpened their teeth like needles, as the fish stuck to them. Some of his children went to the West (*maghrib*). Ham begat Cush ibn Ham, Canaan ibn Ham, and Fut ibn Ham. Fut settled in India and Sind and their inhabitants are his descendants. Kush and Kanaan's descendants are the various races of blacks: Nubians, Zanj, Qaran, Zaghawa, Ethiopians, Copts, and Berbers.[72]

Lastly, Ibn Khaldun, a Tunisian historian of the fifteenth century, though a figure later than Ibn Ezra, identified the "Negroes" as the children of Ham who were not only "singled out to be black as a result of Noah's curse, which produced Ham's color," but were targets of the slavery God inflicted upon Ham's descendants.[73]

The period between the nineteenth century and the present has also had its share of commentators who envision an association between the curse and the African. The

---

[71] *The Tales of the Prophets of Al-Kisai*, trans. W. M. Thackston, Library of Classical Arabic Literature, ed. Ilse Lichtenstadter, vol. 2 (Boston: Twayne Publishers, 1978), 107–8.

[72] *Kitab al-Maarif*, ed. Tharwat Ukasha, 2d ed. (Cairo, 1969), 26, cited in Bernard Lewis, *Race and Slavery in the Middle East: An Historical Enquiry* (New York: Oxford University Press, 1990), 124–25.

[73] *Ibn Khaldun: The Muqaddimah, an Introduction to History*, trans. Franz Rosenthal, Bollingen Series, vol. 2 (New York: Bollingen Foundation, 1958), 169–70.

event mostly associated with the curse is the enslavement[74] of the Africans in the Americas and Europe. Priest, for instance, was of the opinion that "the fulfillment of (the) curse was found in the subjection of Africans by the inhabitants of America (descendants of Japheth) with God's permission and blessing."[75] Baldwin (1858) related the fulfillment of the Noachian curse to the "services of Ham to Japheth in the Southern States, in the islands, and in South America."[76] Philip Schaff (1861) spoke of the Negro being a servant during his time.[77] J. G. Murphy (1868) pointed to the nations of Europe engaging in the trading of African slaves.[78] Keil and Delitzsch (1951) traced the outworking of the curse from enslavement of the Canaanites by the Israelites through the Japhetic subjection of the Phoenicians, Carthagians and the Egyptians, and finally the sighing of the Negro beneath the yoke of the most crushing slavery in the New World.[79] Last but not least, Custance (1975) wrote that innate genetics and divine leading would guarantee that the subjugation of the Hamites would occur in fulfillment of the Noachian declarations.[80]

---

[74] The rationale for the degradation of the Africans in English America, according to Winthrop Jordan, included demand for cheap labor, the powerlessness of the Africans and the differentness (cultural, religious, and physiognomical) of the African (Winthrop D. Jordan, *The White Man's Burden: Historical Origins of Racism in the United States* [London: Oxford University Press, 1974], 50–54).

[75] Josiah Priest, *Bible Defense of Slavery; or the Origin, History, and Fortunes of the Negro Race* (Glasgow, Kentucky: W. S. Brown, 1853), 289.

[76] Baldwin, *Dominion; or the Unity and Trinity of the Human Race with the Divine Political Constitution of the World, and the Divine Rights of Shem, Ham, and Japheth*, 17.

[77] Philip Schaff, *Slavery and the Bible: A Tract for the Times* (Chambersburg, PA: M. Kieffer, 1861), 6.

[78] J. G. Murphy, *A Critical and Exegetical Commentary on the Book of Genesis: With a New Translation* (Boston: W. H. Halliday and Company, 1868), 211–12.

[79] C. F. Keil and F. Delitzsch, *The Pentateuch*, trans. James Martin, Biblical Commentary on the Old Testament, vol. 1 (Grand Rapids: Eerdmans, 1951), 158.

[80] Custance, *Noah's Three Sons: Human History in Three Dimensions*, 12.

These latter-day appeals to the Noachian curse as justification for the thralldom and oppression of the people of African descent in nineteenth century America and twentieth century South Africa[81] are thought to find their matrix in pre-Ibn Ezra perspectives. The question, however, has been whether the provenance of these later anti-black stances is Jewish literature or Islamic writings.

Those who consider rabbinic literature as the matrix of the Hamitic myth include Thomas Gossett, Cain Hope Felder, and Charles B. Copher. Copher (1991) labels the remarks by these Jewish writings "the Old Hamite view" which holds that "Ham was turned black as a result of Noah's curse and his descendants were doomed to bear the same."[82] According to Gossett (1965), the racist association of the Negro with the Genesis story concerning Ham and Canaan first appears in the oral traditions of the Jews collected in the Babylonian Talmud from the second century to the sixth century A.D.[83] Similarly,

---

[81] Jerrold Packard explains the extent of the so-called "Black Codes" that were applied to the freed "Blacks" after the end of the civil war. The codes required public transportation to segregate facilities for blacks. Thousands of theatres, parks, hotels, restaurants, and shops were closed to blacks under the Codes. The Codes also excluded the blacks from schools (Jerrold M. Packard, *American Nightmare: The History of Jim Crow* [New York: St. Martin's Press, 2002], 42–43). Segregation in the schools did not become illegal until the 1954 landmark Supreme Court ruling (*Brown vs. Board of Education*) about a case involving a seven-year-old African American girl named Linda Brown who had been denied admission to a White elementary school near her home in Topeka, Kansas (Martha Minow, "Surprising Legacies of *Brown V. Board*," in *Legacies of Brown: Multiracial Equity in American Education*, ed. Dorinda J. Carter, Stella M. Flores, and Richard J. Reddick [Cambridge, MA: Harvard Educational Review, 2004], 10).

What Jim Crow's system of segregation was to America, apartheid was to South Africa. Apartheid limited contact between the Afrikaners and the blacks. This involved the creation of separate amenities such as restaurants, hotels, hospitals, beaches, sports clubs, buses, trains, and so forth. It also involved outlawing interracial sex and marriage (P. Eric Louw, *The Rise, Fall, and Legacy of Apartheid* [Westport, CT: Praeger, 2004], 50).

[82] Charles B. Copher, "The Black Presence in the Old Testament," in *Stony the Road We Trod: African American Biblical Interpretation*, ed. Cain Hope Felder (Minneapolis: Fortress Press, 1991), 147.

[83] Thomas F. Gossett, *Race: The History of an Idea in America* (New York: Schocken Books, 1965), 5.

Felder (1991) maintains that the Midrash and the Talmud offer fuel for latter-day racism by their demeaning outlook on black people.[84]

Islamic literature is considered the provenance of the "Hamitic" myth by, among others, Stephen Haynes, David Goldenberg, and David Aaron.[85] Haynes (2002) is convinced that it was in the Muslim Near East world that slavery was first closely allied with color, that black Africans first gained a slavish reputation, and that the so-called Hamitic myth was first invoked as a justification for human thralldom. It appears, he argues, that race and slavery were consciously combined in the reading of Gen 9 first by Muslim exegetes during the ninth and tenth centuries.[86] Like Haynes, Goldenberg (1997) is also of the opinion that the justification for social structures that subjugated the blacks in the nineteenth and twentieth centuries was spurred by the identification of blacks with the slave class in the Islamic world of the seventh century. This is not to say that rabbis did not envision a link between black skin and the curse. Their reference to the black skin simply exhibits their aesthetic preference for their own skin color. Such ethnocentrism, however, should not be equated with racism.[87]

Incidentally, preference for lighter skin is also evident among the blacks themselves. Their aesthetic attribute of varied shades of skin colors turns out to be the Achilles' heel. Fair-skinned blacks regard darker skin as somehow aberrational and ugly.

---

[84] Cain Hope Felder, "Race, Racism, and the Biblical Narratives," in *Stony the Road We Trod: African American Biblical Interpretation*, ed. Cain Hope Felder (Minneapolis: Fortress Press, 1991), 129–32.

[85] David H. Aaron, "Early Rabbinic Exegesis on Noah's Son, Ham and the So-Called 'Hamitic Myth'," *JAAR* 63 (1995): 721–59.

[86] Haynes, *Noah's Curse: The Biblical Justification of American Slavery*, 7.

[87] David M. Goldenberg, "The Curse of Ham: A Case of Rabbinic Racism?," in *Struggles in the Promised Land: Toward a History of Black-Jewish Relations in the United States*, ed. Jack Salzman and Cornel West (New York: Oxford University Press, 1997), 26, 35.

Thus dark-skinned individuals are teased or put down for their color. In the case of a family consisting of both fair and dark-skinned children, fair-skinned children are considered prettier than their dark-skinned siblings. Evidence that families tend to view dark skin differently and dark skinned individuals express dissatisfaction with their skin color has been empirically established.[88] The individual believes that he or she is unattractive, wishes that he or she were fair-skinned and in certain instances goes about to correct the "ugliness" through the bleaching of the skin.

The Meaning and Fulfillment of the Enlargement of
the Blessing Utterance (v. 27)

### The Meaning and Fulfillment of the Enlargement of Japheth

Our discussion here will highlight the three meanings that have been attached to the verbal form יַפְתְּ, and the ensuing opinions of possible fulfillment of the phrase יַפְתְּ אֱלֹהִים לְיֶפֶת (v. 27aα). The suggestions of fulfillment can be categorized as spiritual and non-spiritual.

The Meaning of יַפְתְּ

The meaning that has been mostly attached to the form יַפְתְּ is "enlarge" from the homonymous III-ה root פתה.[89] Two other meanings, however, are attested. Considering

---

[88] Stephanie Irby Coard, Alfiee M. Breland, and Patricia Raskin, "Perceptions of and Preferences for Skin Color, Black Racial Identity, and Self-Esteem among African Americans," *JASP* 31 (2001): 2260–2269; cf. Selena Bond and Thomas F. Cash, "Black Beauty: Skin Color and Body Images among African-American College Women," *JASP* 22(1992): 874–885; T. L. Robinson and J. V. Ward, "African American Adolescents and Skin Color," *JBP* 21 (1995): 256–274; Joni Hersch, "Skin Tone Effects among African Americans: Perceptions and Reality," *American Economic Review Papers and Proceedings* 96, no. 2 (2006): 251–55.

[89] Justin Martyr, *Dial.* 139; Iranaeus, *Haer.* 3.5; Augustine, *Civ.* 5.16.2; Goodspeed and Welton, *The Book of Genesis*, 98.

the root as I-י, Targum Jonathan adopted the resulting meaning "beautify" (יפה).[90]

Rejecting both Targum Jonathan's יפי and the meaning "enlarge" whose root he thought was פתח, Luther settled, instead, for the meaning "persuade or deceive with kindly words" (from the root פתה).[91] Like Luther, Calvin also opted for the reading "persuade."[92] Luther's choice finds subsequent support in John Trapp[93] and Baldwin.[94] This reading, however, has not been without its critics.

Bush, for instance, remains unconvinced about its legitimacy for three reasons: (a) פתה, wherever it signifies to persuade or allure, is always, with perhaps the single exception of Jer 20:7, used in a bad sense implying that kind of persuasion which is connected with deception; (b) when thus used, it is always followed by the simple accusative of the object instead of the dative with a preposition as here; and (c) none of the more ancient versions give it the sense of persuading.[95]

Suggested Fulfillment

The nature of the suggested fulfillments can be categorized as spiritual and non-spiritual.

---

[90] J. W. Etheridge, *The Targums of Onkelos and Jonathan Ben Uzziel on the Pentateuch with the Fragments of the Jerusalem Targum from the Chaldee* (New York: Ktav Publishing House, 1968), 185.

[91] *Lectures on Genesis Chapters 6–14*, 182–84.

[92] Calvin, *Commentaries on the First Book of Moses Called Genesis*, 308.

[93] John Trapp, *Genesis to Second Chronicles*, ed. W. Webster and Hugh Martin,, A Commentary on the Old and New Testaments, vol. 1 (London: Richard Dickinson, 1865–1868; reprint, Eureka, CA: Tanski Publications, 1997), 43.

[94] Baldwin, *Dominion*, 76.

[95] Bush, *Notes Critical and Practical on the Book of Genesis*, 166.

*Spiritual fulfillment.* Predictably, suggestions of a spiritual nature arise in part from works that interpret יפת as "persuade." For instance, Luther linked the fulfillment to positive response to the Gospel. According to him, Noah's request was that

> the Lord may lovingly persuade him (Japheth), in the first place, not to begrudge his brother the honor and not be too impatient because this prerogative was taken from him and transferred to his brother. In the second place, because this pertains solely to the person of Japheth, Noah includes all his descendants and prays that although the promise was given to Shem alone, God would speak to them lovingly through the Gospel, in order that they, too, might be a יָפֵת and be persuaded by the voice of the gospel.[96]

Prior to Luther, Augustine and *Gen. Rab.* (36.7.1d) offered suggestions of fulfillment that similarly touched on the spiritual. The latter associated the enlargement of Japheth with Cyrus' decree to rebuild the temple, a symbol of Jewish spirituality. In the case of the former, the enlargement finds its manifestation in the "houses of Christ."[97]

*Non-spiritual fulfillment.* Suggestions of a non-spiritual nature are commonly found within the nineteenth and twentieth century period. Such suggestions include those of an 1892 anonymous work, which envisioned the fulfillment in terms of political dominance and intellectual promotion by the nations of Europe and America.[98] Noteworthy was the work's depiction of the Hamites, in the same breath, as inferior to the Japhethites. Like this work, John Lange (1884) too perceived the fulfillment in term of the Japhethites' expressed intellectual conquest of the world. Additionally, though, Lange included geographical expansion and spread of civilization as components of

---

[96] *Lectures on Genesis Chapters 6–14*, 182–84.

[97] Augustine, *Civ.* 5.16.2.

[98] *Practical Reflections Upon Every Verse of the Book of Genesis* (London: Longmans, Green, and Co., 1892), 52.

fulfillment.[99] Likewise, J. G. Murphy describes the fulfillment in terms of territorial conquest, multitudousness of the Japhethites, and their intellectual and active faculties.[100]

The suggestions of the fulfillment of the utterance concerning enlargement in the 1900's echo to a great extent those offered in the previous century. The suggestion of geographical expansion cited by Lange in the nineteenth century turns out to be the view held by twentieth century writers like Custance and Geerhardus Vos (1948).[101] In the case of Custance, expansion is only part of the fulfillment. The other is the element of technology.[102] W. H. Griffith Thomas (1946) also envisions domination as fulfillment. Specifically he defines the domination in terms of political control of human affairs by the Japhethites.[103]

### The Meaning and Fulfillment of the Dwelling of an Individual in the Tents of Shem (v. 27aβ)

The nature of the discussion surrounding the phrase וְיִשְׁכֹּן בְּאָהֳלֵי־שֵׁם ("may he dwell in the tents of Shem") is both hermeneutical and propositional. The hermeneutical aspect seeks to determine the antecedent of the 3ms subject and the meaning of "dwelling in the tent" of someone, while the propositional aspect attempts to conjecture the most likely fulfillment of the phrase.

---

[99] John Peter Lange, *Genesis, or the First Book of Moses, Together with a General Theological and Homiletical Introduction to the Old Testament*, trans. Tayler Lewis and A. Gosman, 5th ed., A Commentary on the Holy Scriptures: Critical, Doctrinal, and Homiletical, with Special Reference to Ministers and Students, ed. Johann Peter Lange and Philip Schaff, vol. 1 (New York: Charles Scribner's Sons, 1884), 337.

[100] Murphy, *A Critical and Exegetical Commentary on the Book of Genesis: With a New Translation*, 214.

[101] Geerhardus Vos, *Biblical Theology: Old and New Testaments* (Grand Rapids: Eerdmans, 1948; reprint, Grand Rapids: Eerdmans, 1977), 58.

[102] Custance, *Noah's Three Sons: Human History in Three Dimensions*, 28.

[103] Thomas, *Genesis: A Devotional Commentary*, 98.

The antecedent of the 3ms subject

The antecedent of the pronoun has been identified as either of two entities. One entity is God. Earlier representation of the view includes certain Jewish works[104] and Targum Onkelos to Genesis (first century A.D.), which reads: וְיַשְׁרֵי שְׁכִינְתֵּיהּ בְּמַשְׁכְּנֵי שֵׁם "may he cause his Shekhinah to rest in the tents of Shem."[105] The Targumic reading finds acceptance in a later work by Benjamin Foster dated 1779.[106]

Nineteenth and twentieth century representatives include among others Tayler Lewis (1884) and Walter Kaiser (1978). These two commentators are especially notable because, unlike any of the other representatives of the view that God is the antecedent, they advance exegetical arguments.

Lewis argues along three lines. First, he points to passages depicting God as dwelling in the tents of humanity (Exod 25:8; Deut 12:11; 1 Kgs 6:13; 8:29; Ps 90:1; Ezek 43:9; Zech 8:3; John 1:14) as a means of proving that the concept of God dwelling in the tents is not alien to the Old Testament. Second, the two verbs יַפְתְּ and יִשְׁכֹּן, joined by the conjunction, whether taken copulatively or disjunctively, must have the same grammatical subject unless a new one intervenes, or the context *necessarily* implies it. In other words, it would be irregular to make the object of the first verb the subject of the

---

[104] *Gen. Rab.* 36.7.1d; Jub. 7.12; and Ibn Ezra, *Ibn Ezra's Commentary on the Pentateuch: Genesis*, 130–31.

[105] *Targum Onkelos to Genesis: A Critical Analysis Together with an English Translation of the Text (Based on A. Sperber's Edition)*, trans. Moses Aberbach and Bernard Grossfeld (Denver: Ktav Publishing House, 1982), 68–69; cf. Bernard Grossfeld, *Targum Neofiti 1: An Exegetical Commentary to Genesis Including Full Rabbinic Parallels*, ed. Lawrence H. Schiffman (New York: Sepher-Hermon Press, 2000), 117.

[106] Benjamin Foster, *The Washing of Regeneration, or, the Divine Rite of Immersion, and a Letter to the Reverend Mr. Fish, on "Japheth yet Dwelling in the Tents of She"* (Boston: Draper and Folsom, 1779), 2.

second considering that there exists neither an explicit reference to a new subject nor implicit contextual support necessitating the supply of a new subject.[107]

Kaiser's arguments are similar to those of Lewis. For instance, Kaiser argues that the subject of the previous clause ought to be presumed to continue into the next clause since the subject is unexpressed. Kaiser similarly believes that there are no strong contextual reasons for making the indirect object of the previous line the subject of the next line. Unique to Kaiser, however, is the argument that the Hebrew phrase, "and he will dwell in the tents of Shem," could not be attributed to Japheth, for Japheth had already been granted the blessing of expansion.[108]

Opponents of the view that consider God as the antecedent include the co-authors, Goodspeed and Welton, and G. J. Spurrell (1887). According to the former, the problem with considering God as the antecedent is two-fold. First, the reading would substantially repeat the blessing already given to Shem and also restrict to Shem the blessing which the context shows would be restricted to Japheth. Second, it would contradict the fact that "his servant" at the end of the verse properly applies to Japheth (that is, to his descendants) only.[109] The latter's argument is that the construction וְהוּא יִשְׁכֹּן would be required if the reading were to stand.[110]

[107] Lange, *Genesis*, 341.

[108] Walter C. Kaiser, *Toward an Old Testament Theology* (Grand Rapids: Zondervan Publishing House, 1978), 82.

[109] Goodspeed and Welton, *The Book of Genesis*, 98; cf. Lange, *Genesis, or the First Book of Moses, Together with a General Theological and Homiletical Introduction to the Old Testament*, 337.

[110] G. J. Spurrell, *Notes on the Hebrew Text of the Book of Genesis with Two Appendices* (Oxford: Clarendon Press, 1887), 88.

The alternative to God as the antecedent is Japheth. Earlier representatives of this alternate view consist of certain church fathers.[111] Among its later representatives are commentators such as Goodspeed, Welton and Lewis.[112] Charles Augustus Briggs (1886), also a later proponent, argues along the following lines. First, as Shem is the subject of the blessing, v. 26, so also will Japheth be the subject of the blessing, v. 27. Second, God's gracious presence with Shem is already contained in בָּרוּךְ יְהֹוָה אֱלֹהֵי שֵׁם. Third, the God of Shem, as distinguished from the God of Japheth, is called not אֱלֹהִים but יְהֹוָה. Fourth, the plural לְאֶחָי leads us to infer a collective idea as the subject, and the more so, that the statement that God would dwell in the אָהֳלֵי of Israel is elsewhere unconfirmed, because it is at variance with the unity of the place of worship. Fifth, in the circumstance that Japheth will have free hospitable access to Shem, whose God is Yahweh, and will dwell with him in brotherly fashion (Ps. 133:1) in common tents, will the delicate filial action jointly performed by Shem and Japheth find its corresponding final blessing.[113]

The Meaning of "Dwelling in the Tents"

The second hermeneutical issue pertains to the meaning of וְיִשְׁכֹּן בְּאָהֳלֵי (one "dwelling in the tent" of another). The concept of dwelling in another's tent has been interpreted as connoting hostility, peaceful coexistence, or the speaking of the Torah in the tents of Shem in the language of the Greeks (Japheth's language).

The interpretation that regards the phrase as connoting hostility finds representation as early as the second century (A.D.). Justin Martyr interpreted the phrase

---

[111] Justin Martyr, *Dial.* 139; Lactantius, *Inst.* 2.14; Augustine, *Civ.* 5.16.2.

[112] Goodspeed and Welton, *The Book of Genesis*, 98; cf. Lange, *Genesis*, 337.

[113] Charles Augustus Briggs, *Messianic Prophecy: The Prediction of the Fulfillment of Redemption through the Messiah* (Edinburgh: T. & T. Clark, 1886), 82.

to mean the despoiling of the Shemites by the Japhethites. This dispossession, according

to him, was unfolding during his own time.[114] Unlike Justin Martyr, who offered no

exegetical reasoning for his interpretation, Hermann Gunkel (1902) exegetically defended

the interpretation. First, he called for comparison with Ps. 78:55 and 1 Chron 5:10 where

dispossession is the obvious meaning. Second, he maintained that if friendly relations

were the intended meaning, either of two constructions would have been utilized: (a) the

verb יָגוּר ("may he sojourn as a guest"), would have been employed, or (b) יִשְׁכֹּן would

have had to have a modifier such as "in peace," "together," or the like, cf. Ps 78:55.[115]

Another 20th century writer who associates the phrase with hostility and dispossession is

Vos.[116]

The interpretation of the phrase as connoting the speaking of the Torah in the

language of the Japhethites was suggested in the fifth century A.D. by Bar Qappara in

*Genesis Rabbah*: "Let words of Torah in the language of Japheth (Greek) be spoken in

the tents of Shem." According to 2b, Rabbi Yudan embraced this reading and interpreted

it as offering permission for the Scripture to be rendered into other languages.[117]

---

[114] Justin Martyr, *Dial.* 139. A new translation of Justin's work comments that Justin had in mind the Romans here (*St Justin Martyr: Dialogue with Trypho*, ed. Michael Slusser, trans. Thomas B. Falls, Selections from the Fathers of the Church [Washington, D.C.: The Catholic University of America Press, 2003], 208).

[115] Hermann Gunkel, *Genesis: Translated and Interpreted by Hermann Gunkel*, trans. Mark E. Biddle, Mercer Library of Biblical Studies, ed. John Blenkinsopp and Walter Brueggemann (Macon, GA: Mercer University Press, 1997), 82.

[116] Vos, *Biblical Theology: Old and New Testaments*, 58; cf. J. Hoftijzer, "Some Remarks to the Tale of Noah's Drunkenness," in *Studies on the Book of Genesis*, ed. B. Gemster, Oudtestamentische Studien, vol. 12 (Leiden, E. J. Brill, 1958), 25.

[117] *Gen. Rab.* 36.7.2a, b; cf. Mendele Mocher Sforim, "Shem and Japheth on the Train (1890)," in *Modern Hebrew Literature*, ed. Robert Alter, trans. Walter Lever, Library of Jewish Studies ed. Neal Kozodoy (New York: Behrman House, 1975), 38.

The interpretation of the phrase as connoting peaceful co-existence is the most recent of the three interpretations. Proponents of this perspective are mainly nineteenth-twentieth century figures.[118]

The Conversion of the Gentiles as Fulfillment

Much as there are other suggestions of fulfillment that have been offered by those who consider Japheth the antecedent,[119] we isolate the one pertaining to the conversion of the Gentiles for further elaboration due to its parochial nature.

This suggestion appears as early as the patristic era in a work by Irenaeus. In his *Against Heresies*, he considers the fulfillment to have come about with the bringing together of the Jews and the Gentiles in accordance with Ephesians.[120]

During the Reformation Period, the fulfillment was not only equated with the conversion of the Gentiles, the Gentiles were now equated with only the Japhethites. Following an explicative association of the phrase "dwelling in the tents of" with the idea of Gentiles sharing "in the benefits that the Son of God brought into this world," Luther, for instance, conjectured the fulfillment of the "prophecy about Japheth" to be the shining of the Gospel in Germany.[121] Like Luther, Calvin both associated the "prophecy" with the

---

[118] Goodspeed and Welton, *The Book of Genesis*, 98; Spurrell, *Notes on the Hebrew Text of the Book of Genesis with Two Appendices*, 88; Murphy, *A Critical and Exegetical Commentary on the Book of Genesis*, 214; Kalisch, *Genesis*, 155; and Ryle, *The Book of Genesis*, 129.

[119] These include: (a) banishment of the Jews from Jerusalem in the second century A.D. (Justin Martyr, *Dial.* 139) (b) subjugation of Shemitic territory by the Greeks and the Romans (Vos, *Biblical Theology*, 58) (c) territorial occupation of the same land by both the Shemites and the Japhethites (Gerhard Von Rad, *Genesis: A Commentary*, trans. John H. Marks, The Old Testament Library, ed. G. Ernest Wright et al. [Philadelphia: The Westminster Press, 1961], 135) (d) cooperation between the Hebrew invaders from the East and the Pelasgic invaders (Philistines) invaders from the West against the settled population of Canaan (A. Van Selms, "The Canaanite in the Book of Genesis," in *Studies on the Book of Genesis*, ed. B. Gemster, Oudtestamentische Studien, vol.12 [Leiden, E. J. Brill, 1958], 187).

[120] Irenaeus, *Haer.* 3.5.3; cf. Augustine, *Civ.* 16.3.

[121] *Lectures on Genesis Chapters 6–14*, 184, 186; cf. Calvin, *Commentaries on the First Book of Moses Called Genesis*, 309.

response of the Jews and the Gentiles to the gospel and narrowly defined the Gentiles as "the progeny of Japheth."[122]

Further conjoining of the two elements of the conversion of the Gentiles and the limited understanding of who composes the Gentiles appears in writings spanning the period after the Reformation to the present times. Such works include Elisha Fish's 1773 book, which pointed to the record of the conversion of the Gentiles in the book of Acts as the beginning of the fulfillment. As for the definition of a Gentile, Fish pointed to the example of Cornelius, a Roman officer, and his friends, "who seem evidently to come from Europe, where Japheth's posterity dwell."[123] Further evidence of the work's narrow definition of a Gentile can be gleaned from its supposition of the nature of the utterance's continued fulfillment:

> The spread of the gospel from the apostolic age to this day, through those countries where it is most evident that the seed of Japheth dwell, agreeable to that expression, concerning the posterity of Japheth, "By these were the isles of the Gentiles divided in their lands" Gen. x. 5. And the waters of the sanctuary, under the Gospel, have had special flow, from the eastern parts of, through Europe, and from thence to America, among the Christian inhabitants; the body of these people, in both countries being justly esteemed the posterity of Japheth, and by whom the Gospel is in an eminent manner enjoyed at this day.[124]

The conjoint elements found expression in the nineteenth and twentieth centuries through figures such as Cowles, Delitzsch, and A. B. Simpson. Cowles is cited as having associated the fulfillment of the utterance with the coming of the Gentile races of Japheth to the Hebrew communion through proselytization and also the rise of the Protestant

---

[122] Ibid.

[123] Fish, *Japheth Dwelling in the Tents of Shem*, 10–11.

[124] Ibid., 22.

Christendom of Japheth's line through spiritual grafting.[125] Delitzsch echoed Bar Qappara (*Gen. Rab.*) when he claimed that "the language of the New Testament is the speech of Javan dwelling in the tents of Shem, the gospel is the proclamation of salvation translated from Semitic into Japhethic."[126] Like Cowles he claimed, "Gentile Christians are for the most part Japhethites dwelling in the tents of Shem."[127] Simpson (1888) similarly equated the Gentiles with the Japhethites in his linkage of fulfillment of the utterance about dwelling in the tents with "the fact that the Gentiles have superseded the family of Shem in their religious privileges and have entered their tents as the heirs of their covenant blessing."[128]

Present-day advocates of the dual perspectives include Arthur Custance and Talbert Swan. Custance dates the commencement of the fulfillment to when the Jewish people committed national suicide by rejecting Jesus and endorses the traditional limitation of the term Gentiles to the Japhethites.[129] Swan (2003) upholds the perspective that "dwelling in the tents" implies the Japhethites becoming believers.[130]

---

[125] Goodspeed and Welton, *The Book of Genesis*, 98.

[126] Delitzsch, *A New Commentary on Genesis*, 298.

[127] Ibid. Other commentators who adopt the narrow definition of a Gentile include the following: Spurrell, *Notes on the Hebrew Text of the Book of Genesis with Two Appendices*, 88; Lange, *Genesis*, 337; and Pink, *Gleanings in Genesis*, 128.

[128] A. B. Simpson, *Genesis and Exodus*, vol. 1, Christ in the Bible, ed. A. B. Simpson (New York: Word, Work and World, 1888), 98; cf. Ernest Shufelt, "Noah's Curse and Blessing, Gen 9:18–27," *CTJ* 17 (1946): 741.

[129] Custance, *Noah's Three Sons: Human History in Three Dimensions*, 17, 23. It may just be that the tendency to equate the Gentiles with Japheth stems from interpretation of the phrase (אִיֵּי הַגּוֹיִם) in Gen 10:5 as meaning "Gentiles or Nations"; cf. B. Oded, "The Table of Nations (Genesis 10)— A Socio-Cultural Approach," *ZAW* 98 (1986): 30.

[130] Talbert W. Swan, *No More Cursing: Destroying the Roots of Religious Racism* (Indian Orchard, MA: Trumpet in Zion Publishing, 2003), 49.

## Summary/Conclusion

This section on the history of interpretation sought to present the different interpretative views on the questions of the nature of the offense and the suggestions of possible fulfillment of Noah's utterances. Our interest was simply to present the views, not interact exegetically with them.

Beginning with the offense, its nature has been understood as any of the following: sexual, sight, disclosure, castration, or unfilial irreverence. The sexual interpretation consists of three variations: incest, voyeurism, and homosexuality. "Unfilial irreverence" can be further categorized as mockery, laughter, and jeering.

Regarding the sexual view, a plot of the number of adherents against time reveals a steep rise in the number of advocates is evident beginning in the 60's. Supporters include Josiah Priest, Walter Brueggemann, Bruce Waltke, H. Cohen, Stephen Haynes, Anthony Phillips, O. Palmer Robertson, Randall Bailey, William Brunk, Frederick Bassett, John Bergsma, and Scott Hahn. More than just regarding the offense as sexual, the view does advance exegetical rationales. Those arguments include the following: (1) in light of its parallelism elsewhere with גלה עֶרְוָה or עֶרְוַת (cf. Lev 18: 7, 8, 14, 16), the clause ראה עֶרְוָה in Gen 9:22 connotes that Ham engaged in an incestuous act with Noah's wife; (2) voyeurism on Ham's part should be entertained since the text rules out the possibility of a sexual act; (3) the clause ראה עֶרְוָה elsewhere (cf. Lev 20:17, 18, 19) connotes sexual activity between the subject (Ham) and the object (Noah); (4) the chiastic connection between the story about the sons of God in Gen 6:1–5 and Noah's story suggests that the object of the curse in Gen 9 (i.e., Canaan) was a product of an illicit union in the same way that the illicit union in Gen 6 (i.e., the mighty and renowned men of old) was cursed through the agency of the flood; (5) the phrase "his tent" (אָהֳלֹה)

(9:21) is a questionable translation; (6) the noun has an ending that suggests "her tent";

and (7) the relationship between Gen 9:20–27 and Gen 19:30–38, as well as Gen 6:1–4;

Lev 18:1–8; Deut 23:1; and 27:20, all support the implication of sexual violation of

Noah's wife by her son.

Before recapitulating the discussion on the meaning and possible fulfillment of

Noah's utterances, we would like to reiterate the distinction between the sexual view and

the other four views and rehash the definitions of each of the four views. The sight view

should not be mixed up with voyeurism. Unlike the latter, the former is non-sexual in its

intent. The disclosure view has to do with an individual seeing something and then

reporting what he or she has seen. Whereas the reaction in disclosure is reporting what

one has seen, the reactions characterized as unfilial irreverence have the common goal of

shaming the victim. The castration view needs no further definition since it is self-

explanatory.

The suggestions of fulfillment of the curse utterance are classifiable into views

that consider Canaan or the Canaanites as the object(s) of the curse and those that regard

Ham or the Hamites as the target(s) of the curse. Advocates of the "Canaan" view include

Justin Martyr, Chrysostom, Ibn Ezra, Cassuto, and Delitzsch. Exegetical comments

associated with the view include: a literal understanding of "brothers" in Gen 9:25 and

the suffix מוֹ at the end of verse 26 and 27 is plural. Suggestions of fulfillment that fall

under this category are subjugation of the Canaanites by the Israelites following the

conquest and during the reign of King Solomon, subjugation of the Gibeonites by the

Israelites, Canaanite kings serving Chedorlaomer and Tidal in Gen 14, and the subjugation of Tyre and Sidon by the Greeks and Romans.

The "Ham" view, which can be classified into four sub-views (viz., "Ham as the object of the curse," "Ham cursed via Canaan," "Hamites cursed via Ham," and "particular non-Canaanites Hamites as the object of the curse") considers Ham the object of the curse on the basis of textual emendation, certain biblical references or social customs, absence of a blessing on Ham, figurative meaning of "Canaan," or Ham's offense. Advocates include Irenaeus, Sulptius Severus, Pachomius, Origen, Midrash, Saadia Gaon, Luther, Josiah Priest, Bishop Thomas Newton, Philip Schaff, and Arthur Custance. Suggestions of fulfillment include Pharaoh's subjection of the Egyptians to bondage, the exodus, physiognomical aspects of the Africans, apartheid policies in South Africa, and the enslavement of the Africans in the Americas and Europe.

Discussions surrounding the blessing utterance entail the meaning of the verbal form יַפְתְּ and the phrase וְיִשְׁכֹּן בְּאָהֳלֵי־שֵׁם. Three meanings have been associated with יַפְתְּ. They are "enlarge," beautify," and "persuade." Regarding the phrase וְיִשְׁכֹּן בְּאָהֳלֵי־שֵׁם, two hermeneutical issues have come to the forefront of the discussion. The first issue concerns the antecedent of the 3ms subject of the verb יִשְׁכֹּן. Some consider the antecedent to be God. Proponents of this interpretation include Ibn Ezra, Jubilees, *Genesis Rabbah*, Targum Onkelos to Genesis, Benjamin Forster, Tayler Lewis, and Walter Kaiser. Arguments for this view include: God is depicted as dwelling in the tents of humanity; the two verbs יַפְתְּ and יִשְׁכֹּן, joined by the conjunction, whether taken copulatively or disjunctively, must have the same grammatical subject unless a new one intervenes, or the context *necessarily* implies it; the subject of the previous clause ought to be presumed to continue into the next clause since the subject is unexpressed; there are no strong contextual reasons for making the indirect object of the previous line the subject of the next line; and the Hebrew phrase, "and he will dwell in the tents of Shem," could not be attributed to Japheth, for Japheth had already been granted the blessing of expansion.

The alternative interpretation is that the antecedent is Japheth. Advocates include Justin Martyr, Lactantius, Augustine, Goodspeed, Welton and Lewis, and Charles Augustus Briggs. Arguments advanced in favor of this view are as follows. First, as Shem is the subject of the blessing, v. 26, so also will Japheth be the subject of the blessing, v. 27. Second, God's gracious presence with Shem is already contained in בָּרוּךְ יְהֹוָה אֱלֹהֵי שֵׁם. Third, the God of Shem, as distinguished from the God of Japheth, is called not אֱלֹהִים but יְהֹוָה. Fourth, the plural לְאָחָיו leads us to infer a collective idea as the subject, and the more so, that the statement that God would dwell in the אָהֳלֵי of Israel is elsewhere unconfirmed, because it is at variance with the unity of the place of worship. Fifth, in the circumstance that Japheth will have free hospitable access to Shem, whose God is Yahweh, and will dwell with him in brotherly fashion (Ps 133:1) in common tents, will the delicate filial action jointly performed by Shem and Japheth find its corresponding final blessing.

The second hermeneutical issue pertains to the meaning of וְיִשְׁכֹּן בְּאָהֳלֵי־. Three interpretations have been offered: hostility, peaceful coexistence, or the speaking of the Torah in the tents of Shem in the language of the Greeks (Japheth's language). Advocates of the "hostility" view include Justin Martyr, Vos and Herman Gunkel. Exegetical rationales for this reading are as follows. First, the phrase occurs in Ps 78:55 and 1 Chron 5:10 where dispossession is the obvious meaning. Second, if friendly relations were the intended meaning, either of two constructions would have been utilized: (a) the verb יָגוּר ("may he sojourn as a guest"), would have been employed, or (b) יִשְׁכֹּן would have had to have a modifier such as "in peace," "together," or the like, cf. Ps 78:55. Advocates of the interpretation that the phrase as connotes the speaking of the Torah in the language of the Japhethites include *Genesis Rabbah*. Proponents of the view that the phrase refers to peaceful co-existence compose Spurrell, Murphy, Ryle, Kalisch, Goodspeed, and Welton.

Suggestions of fulfillment of the blessing utterance consist of response to the Gospel by the Gentiles who are equated with the Japhethites, Cyrus' decree to rebuild the temple, political domination and intellectual promotion by America and Europe, geographical expansion of the Japhethites, and the spread of civilization by the Japhethites.

Now that we have enumerated the views and their exegetical rationales, we are ready to offer a critique (chap. 4) that will be prefaced by an exegetical section (chap. 3). Even though we are splitting these two sections, the critique-proper part of our work will depend entirely on our exegetical findings in its evaluation of the various views. In many ways, then, the critique-proper section will be a juxtaposition of the various views on the nature of the offense and possible fulfillments of Noah's utterances against a contextual exegesis of Gen 9:18–29. All to say that the sole basis for determining the acceptability of a view will be how well it measures against the text.

# CHAPTER 3

## EXEGETICAL STUDY OF GEN 9:18–29

### Determining the Primary and Secondary
### Contexts of the Pericope

This section consists of a macro-analysis of the pericope. Such a bird's eye view

is bound to inform the microanalysis of the text. Moreover, such an analysis will clearly

reveal the functional and textual relationship between Gen 9:18–29 and its general ontext

which spans the *Urgeschichte, Vatergeschichte*, and the Pentateuch as a whole.

### Determining the Primary Context

Establishing the context of a passage, whether primary or secondary, requires a

determination of the larger parameters of the text. Where does the surrounding context of

Gen 9:18–29 begin? One clue lies with the phrase, "went out of the ark,"[1] which looks

back to the narrative captured in 6:1–9:17. The subject of this most immediate anterior

context is primarily the flood and its aftermath. So pervasive was sin during Noah's

generation that the holy God decided to annihilate all that He had created as a

manifestation of His judgment. But in order not to reverse the product of creation and

nullify it altogether, He chose to preserve a portion of life by embarking on a preservation

process wherein a portion of life would be spared from the destruction. The chosen

facilitator of this rescue mission was Noah. The plan to salvage life involved the

construction of an ark into which a portion of life would enter and thus be saved from the

flood. This flood motif that permeates the most immediate context receives mention,

---

[1] Unless otherwise stated, all Bible citations are from NRSV.

albeit tersely, in the Gen 9:18–29 pericope and thus serves as an element of continuity between the two sections. The motif finds explicit mention in v. 28 and is implied in two phrases, viz., "went out of the ark" (v. 18) and "from these the whole earth was peopled." (v. 19).

The other clue resides in the closing verses of the passage, viz., verses 28 and 29. These two verses constitute a genealogical formula that typically consists of 3 parts: (a) when personality "a" had lived "x" number of years, "a" became the father of individual(s) "A"; (b) personality "a" lived after the birth of individual(s) "A" for "y" number of years, and he had others sons and daughters; (c) thus all the days of personality "a" were "x+y" years; and he died.[2] Verses 28 and 29 of Gen. 9 only make up parts "b" and "c" of the genealogical formula. Part "a" is found in 5:32.

Not only are Gen 5:32 and 9:28–29 formulaically associated, but the intervening material (6:9–9:18) is also considered by some to be a unit on the basis of its chiastic or palistrophic structuring.[3] Besides the chiasmus, part of which includes the repetition of the list of Noah's three sons at the beginning and end of the flood story (6:10; 9:18), this intervening section is also held together by a *toledot* formula in 6:9. Indeed the various *toledot* formulas serve as break markers. The superimposition of the *toledot* formulae in Genesis upon the outline of the book reveals a match between the verses that house the

---

[2] The formula appears elsewhere in 5:3–5, 6-8, 9–11, 12–14, 15–17, 18–20, 21–24 (the last part of "c" has been substituted by the concept of being taken away), 25–27, 28–31; 11:10–11 (lacks part "c"), 12–13 (lacks part "c"), 14–15 (lacks part "c"), 16–17 (lacks part "c"), 18–19 (lacks part "c"), 20–21 (lacks part "c"), 22–23 (lacks part "c"), 24–25 (lacks part "c"), 26–32.

[3] For a depiction of the chiasm of the flood story see Bernhard W. Anderson, "From Analysis to Synthesis: The Interpretation of Genesis 1–11," *JBL* 97 (1978): 38 (cf. Bruce K. Waltke, *Genesis: A Commentary* [Grand Rapids: Zondervan, 2001], 125; Gordon J. Wenham, *Genesis 1–15*, WBC, ed. David A. Hubbard and Glenn W. Barker, vol. 1 [Waco, Texas: Word Books, 1987], 156; and David A. Dorsey, *The Literary Structure of the Old Testament: A Commentary on Genesis—Malachi* [Grand Rapids: Baker Books, 1999], 52).

formula and the breaks in the book. For instance, the formula in 2:4 coincides with the break between 1:1–2:3 and 2:4–25. The formula in 5:1 coincides with the break between 4:1–26 and 5:1–32. The formula in 11:10 coincides with the break between 11:1–9 and 11:10–26, etc. Structurally, then, it is legitimate to argue that Gen 5:32, at the very least, serves as one of the anterior parameter markers of our pericope.

Is Gen. 5:32 the furthermost anterior parameter marker? The answer is in the negative for three reasons. First, repetition of phrases and ideas found in Gen 9 confirm that the anterior parameter marker lies much further back.[4] The phrase, "be fruitful and multiply, and fill the earth," in 9:1 first appears in 1:28 in reference to man. The dietary comment (9:3) recalls 1:29. The concept of *imago Dei* (9:6) echoes 1:26.

Second, Gen 5:1–2, which is prefatorially linked to 5:3–32,[5] consists of phrases that recall the succinct creation story of man in Gen 1. The phrase, "male and female he created them and he blessed them," appears in both 5:1 and 1:27–28a. The generic term אָדָם appears in 5:2 and 1:26–27. The term דְּמוּת appears in 5:1 and 1:26.

Third, there exists a striking parallelism, in as far as terms are concerned, between our pericope and both the story of the fall (Gen 2–3) and the story of Cain and Abel (4:1–16). The parallelism takes the form of a narrative technique known as *recursion*,

---

[4] Practitioners of literary criticism have established the role of matching themes and theme-words in integrative reading. Matching themes and words, they would argue, signify some type of literary connection between the two units (see Laurence A. Turner, *Genesis*, Readings: A New Biblical Commentary, ed. John Jarick [Sheffield: Sheffield Academic Press, 2000], 16; Jack M. Sasson, "The 'Tower of Babel' as a Clue to the Redactional Structuring of the Primeval History [Gen. 1–11:9]," in *The Bible World: Essays in Honor of Cyrus H. Gordon*, ed. Gary Rendsburg et al. [New York: Ktav Publishing House, 1980], 218; Gary A. Rendsburg, *The Redaction of Genesis* [Winona Lake, IN: Eisenbrauns, 1986], 5).

[5] Genesis 5:32 must be considered part and parcel of the list of interconnected progenitor-focused genealogical formulae that commence in verse 3. Each of the formulae is connected to the previous formula via a name overlap. The son-name in one formula reappears as a father-name in the next formula.

which is defined by John Sailhamer as "the author's deliberate shaping of narrative events so that key elements of one narrative are repeated in others."[6] As envisioned by Sailhamer, the repetitions, for instance, between Gen 2-3 and our pericope are as follows: (a) 2:8 ("And the Lord God planted a garden … and there put the man") and 9:20 ("Noah … plant a vineyard"); (b) 3:6 ("She took of its fruit and ate") and 9:21 ("He drank some of the wine and became drunk"); (c) 3:7 ("And they knew that they were naked") and 9:21 ("And he lay uncovered in his tent"); (d) 3:7 ("and made loincloths for themselves") and 9:23 ("and covered the nakedness of their father"); (e) 3:7 ("Then the eyes of both were opened, and they knew that they were naked") and 9:24 ("When Noah awoke from his wine and knew what his youngest son had done to him"); and (f) 3:14 ("cursed are you") and 9:25 ("Cursed be Canaan").[7] The beginning of Genesis, therefore, serves as the furthermost anterior parameter marker of our pericope.

Now that we have determined the furthermost anterior parameter marker, what is the furthermost posterior parameter marker of our pericope? As much as the *toledot* formula in 10:1 marks the beginning of a new section,[8] the break introduced by the formula is not absolute. A look at our pericope vis-à-vis the next two chapters reveals

---

[6] John H. Sailhamer, "Genesis," in *A Complete Literary Guide to the Bible*, ed. Leland Ryken and Tremper Longman (Grand Rapids: Zondervan Publishing House, 1993), 112.

[7] Ibid., 114. The parallelism between 9:18–27and 4:1–16 is illustrated by among others Sasson ("The 'Tower of Babel' as a Clue to the Redactional Structuring of the Primeval History [Gen. 1–11:9]," 218), Rendsburg (*The Redaction of Genesis*, 13–15); Gary V. Smith ("Structure and Purpose in Genesis 1–11," *JETS* 20 [1977]: 317); and Robert L. Cohn ("Narrative Structure and Canonical Perspective in Genesis," *JSOT* 25[1983]: 5). The argument that Gen 2–3 is as much a counterpart of 9:18-27 as 4:1–16 is presented by Anthony J. Tomasino ("History Repeats Itself: The 'Fall' and Noah's Drunkenness," *VT* 42 [1992]: 129–130; cf. Waltke, *Genesis: A Commentary*, 127–28).

[8] Breaks indeed, but these breaks would have to be considered minor. The broadly accepted bifurcation of Genesis is the *Urgeschichte* (1–11) and the *Vatergeschichte* (12–50).

evidence of elaborative and formulaic connections.[9] The elaborative connection is observable between the laconic statement, "from these the whole earth was peopled" (9:19), and the more detailed Table of Nations (chap. 10). The formulaic connection between our pericope and chapter eleven is evident in the resumption of the genealogical formula (11:10–26), which was last seen at the end of chapter nine and can be traced as far back as chapter 5.

In conclusion, then, the primary contextual parameters of the Gen 9:18–29 pericope constitute the whole of the *Urgeschichte*, which spans the first eleven chapters of the book.[10]

## Determining the Secondary Context

The secondary context of the pericope spans not just the *Vatergeschichte*, but also the rest of the Pentateuch if not the whole Tanakh. This assertion is based on several demonstrable linkages, first between the *Urgeschichte* and the *Vatergeschichte*, and then between the *Vatergeschichte* and rest of the Pentateuch. One such linkage constitutes the genealogical formula of 11:10–26, which initially serves as the bridge between the person of Shem and Abraham. Abraham, of course, is the *de facto* subject of the Abraham cycle (11:27–25:11).[11] The Abraham cycle is in turn linked to the Jacob cycle (25:19–35:29) through kinship and repetition of the dual promise of land and countless descendants

---

[9] Bruce Waltke considers the whole pericope a transition to 10:1–11:9 (*Genesis: A Commentary*, 124).

[10] According to Baumgart, the following verses have been suggested as marking the end of the Urgeschichte: 9:29; 11:9; 11:9; 11:26; 11:32; 12:9. The vast majority of commentators, he notes, considers 11:26 as the marker for the bifurcating break (Nobert Clemens Baumgart, "Das End der biblischen Urgeschichte in Gen 9, 29," *BN* 82 [1996]: 49).

[11] We say *de facto* with John Goldingay since, strictly speaking, the section constitutes a Terah story even though Abraham is the prominent character (John Goldingay, "The Patriarchs in Scripture and History," in *Essays on the Patriarchal Narratives*, ed. A. R. Millard and D. J. Wiseman [Winona Lake, IN: Eisenbrauns, 1983], 7).

(12:7; 13:15, 16// 26:3, 4; 28:13, 14). Similarly, the Jacob cycle (37:1–50:26) is linked to the Joseph cycle via kinship and promise (26:3, 4; 28:13, 14// 48:3, 4; 50:24). The dual promises of land and countless descendants, which interconnect the three cycles together, in turn link the *Vatergeschichte* to the rest of the Pentateuch in so far as their fulfillment is concerned.[12] The land aspect of the dual promise, for instance, serves as part of the motivation for the exodus (Exod 3:8, 17; 6:4; Lev 25:38) and finds fulfillment in the conquest as described in the books of Numbers (trans-Jordan conquest) and Joshua-Judges (cis-Jordan conquest).[13] The population aspect of the dual promise experiences partial fulfillment with the unstoppable surge in Israelite population in Egypt and is presented as completely fulfilled in Deut 10:22.

Another linkage pertains to 10:16–19, which describes the territorial boundaries of Canaan and enumerates the people groups that constitute the progeny of Canaan, the object of Noah's curse in 9:25–27. The land cited in 10:16-19 turns out to be the location where much of the drama described in the *Vatergeschichte* unfolds. To this land the calling of Abraham leads him (Gen 11:31; 12:5). There he lived, died, and was buried (13:12, 25:10). Similarly Isaac lived, died, and was buried in Canaan (35:29). Except for the time he was in exile, Jacob also lived, died, and was buried in Canaan (37:1; 50:13). We have already seen how the land component of the promise to Abraham features beyond the *Vatergeschichte* in as far as the fulfillment of land inheritance is concerned.

---

[12] David Clines adds divine-human relationship to this list and considers these three the delineation of the promise (to the patriarch) whose partial fulfillment constitutes the theme of the Pentateuch (David J. A. Clines, "The Theme of the Pentateuch," in *JSOTSup*, ed. David J. A. Clines, Philip R. Davies, and David M. Gunn, vol. 19 [Sheffield: University of Sheffield, 1978], 29).

[13] For further discussion on the promise of the land, see Walter Brueggemann, *The Land: Place as Gift, Promise, and Challenge in Biblical Faith*, 2d ed. Overtures to Biblical Theology (Minneapolis: Fortress Press, 2002).

As for the Canaanite people group cited in 10:16–19, their presence in the land is noted a couple of times (12:6; 13:7). Though living in juxtaposition with the Canaanites in the land, the patriarchs express the desire to not intermarry (24:37; 28:1, 6, 8). Their mention in conjunction with promise of the land implies that they had been marked out as objects of dispossession, for it would take their dispossession for Israel to possess the land (cf. Exod 33:2; Josh 3:10). This dispossession, of course, occurred rather imperfectly as the aftermath of the conquest.

## Text, Exegetical Outline, and Exegesis of Gen 9:18–29

### The Text of Gen 9:18–29

[18]The sons of Noah who went out of the ark were Shem, Ham, and Japheth. Ham was the father of Canaan. [19]These three were the sons of Noah; and from these the whole earth was populated. [20]Noah, a farmer, was the first to plant a vineyard. [21]He drank some of the wine and became drunk, and he lay uncovered in his tent. [22]Now Ham, the father of Canaan, saw the nakedness of his father, and told his two brothers outside. [23]Then Shem and Japheth took a garment, laid it on both their shoulders, and walked backward and covered the nakedness of their father; their faces were turned away, and they did not see their father's nakedness. [24]When Noah awoke from his wine and realized what his youngest/younger son had done to him, [25]he said, "Cursed be Canaan; lowest of slaves shall he be to his brothers." [26]He also said, "Blessed by the LORD my God be Shem; and let Canaan be his slave." [27]May God make room for Japheth, and let him live in the tents of Shem; and let Canaan be his slave." [28]After the flood Noah lived three hundred fifty years. [29]All the days of Noah were nine hundred fifty years; and he died.

### Exegetical Outline of Gen 9:18–29

Exegetical Idea: Noah utters a curse and a blessing following what had transpired while he was in a drunken stupor (9:18–29)

    A. Introduction: The sons of Noah, one of whom is highlighted, are reintroduced as survivors of the flood and progenitors of the new generation (9:18–19).

    B. Noah uncovers himself in his tent after partaking of the wine and getting drunk (9:20–21)

C. In contrast to his two brothers, Ham looked at the nakedness of his drunk father (9:22–23)

D. Upon coming to an awareness of the actions of his sons while he lay naked and drunk in his tent, Noah utters curses and blessings (9:24–27)

E. Conclusion (9:28–29)

Exegesis of Gen 9:18–29: with Special Attention to the
Nature of the Offense and Suggestions of Fulfillment

Our exegesis will focus on the twin issues of the nature of the offense and the meaning of the Noachian utterances for two reasons. First, the sexual interpretation touches on the question of the nature of the offense. Second, the basis of the evaluation of suggested fulfillments is the meaning of the Noachian utterances. Additionally, our insistence that the nature of the offense be determined via contextual exegesis will result in our having to address the attendant issues, viz., the role of verses 18 and 19, Noah's state leading up to the infraction (20, 21) and the reaction of Ham's siblings (22–24).

*Contextual Exegesis of the
Nature of the Offense*

The task here is to determine what answer the exegesis of the text yields in response to the question: "Was the infraction against Noah of a sexual nature or otherwise?" In order to be true to our commitment to contextual exegesis we shall not merely focus on the term עֶרְוָה ("nakedness") or the phrase וַיַּרְא . . . אֵת עֶרְוַת אָבִיו ("he saw the nakedness of his father"). Proper exegesis does not engage in determination of meaning at the expense of the surrounding context. Rather, it recognizes the relationship between the signification of a term or phrase and the surrounding data; thus our insistence on the exegesis of the *text* as opposed to merely the exegesis of v. 22. *Text* for us spans vv. 18–24.

## The Role of vv.18–19

Verses 18 and 19 mark a break from the preceding narrative by virtue of the fact that they contain a new agenda. In and of themselves the two verses are linked together via the following chiasm:

A the sons of Noah were    B Shem, Ham and Japheth

B These three                A were the sons of Noah

The newness of the agenda lies neither with the mere mention of the three sons of Noah nor the underscoring that they were indeed survivors of the flood catastrophe.[14] The appearance of the sibling listing here marks the fourth time the sons of Noah are mentioned. The first mention appears in Gen 5:32 in the context of a progenitor-focused genealogical formula. The second record appears in Gen. 6:10 in the midst of a *toledot* formula. The third occurrence appears in Gen. 7:13 where a comprehensive listing of all the people who entered the ark is offered.[15] That the sons of Noah survived the flood is first related in chapter eight (v. 16) when Noah and his family receive the instruction to step out of the ark and onto the now dry land.

---

[14] The survival element is depicted by the relative (attributive) participle הַיֹּצְאִים and the genitival construction מִן־הַתֵּבָה. The function of the article in the articular form הַתֵּבָה in Gen 6:14β is clearly to point back to the aforementioned inarticulate noun תֵּבַת (Gen 6:14α). Between this verse and Gen 9:18, there are 24 occurrences (6:15, 16, 18, 19; 7:1, 7, 9, 13, 15, 17, 18, 23; 8:1, 4, 6, 9a, 9b, 10, 13, 16, 19; 9:10, 18) of the noun תבה all of which are articular. The function of the article in all these occurrences could be viewed as identical to the function of the article attached to the noun in Gen 6:14, viz., pointing to the aforementioned noun. Alternatively the article could be viewed as functioning to express definiteness. The genitive is the object of the preposition.

[15] The question still remains, however, why the sibling names are repeated here in Gen 9:18. Our supposition is that, in offering us the names of Noah and the sons, the narrator is supplying the reader with the listing of what Jean-Marc Heimerdinger terms "topical participants" (Jean-Marc Heimerdinger, *Topic, Focus and Foreground in Ancient Hebrew Narratives*, JSOTsup, ed. David J. A. Clines and Philip R. Davies, vol. 295 [Sheffield: Sheffield Academic Press, 1999], 106). In other words these are the individuals who will constitute the narrative about to unfold. The fact that their wives are not mentioned implies that they are not meant to play any role in the narrative.

Rather, the newness of the agenda resides partly in the progenitorial role attributed to Noah's three sons. Granted, a command to be fruitful, multiply, and fill the earth had been directed to Noah and his family (9:1). Here, though, the report is given that the trio had indeed fulfilled their progenitorial role—a role captured by the genitival construction מֵאֵלֶּה and the verbal clause נָפְצָה כָל־הָאָרֶץ.[16]

Why does the narrator see the need to bring up the motif of progenitorship (19b) here when it rightly belongs to chapter 10? What role does this motif, however tersely cited, play in the narrative that is about to unfold? Our answer is that the motif plays a supportive role in its structural parallelism with 18b. That 18b is structurally parallel to 19b is deducible from the fact that both phrases lie outside the chiasm of vv. 18–19 and can only be seen as parallelistic to each other. The pictorial presentation of the parallel relation between these two phrases within the context of verses 18 and 19 is as follows:

A the sons of Noah were      B Shem, Ham and Japheth

C Ham was the father of Canaan

B These three      A were the sons of Noah

C´ from these the whole …

To recapitulate, the reason the narrator stops at a cursory reference of the motif of progenitorship is because his interest at this point lies more in utilizing this theme as a supporting parallel[17] to a second topic of interest than in laying out a full-blown stemma

---

[16] The form is parsed Qal perfect 3fs from the root form נפץ (translated "disperse or scatter") (cf. BDB, 659, *DCH* 5:724; *HALOT* 2:711). GKC (§67dd), however, parses the form differently, i.e., niphal perfect 3ms from פוץ ("be scattered").

[17] By supportive role, we mean that the progenitorial theme affords the narrator the logic of pinpointing the fatherhood of Ham.

of Noah's three sons. The narrator's second topic of interest is comprised in the

parenthetical[18] phrase חָם הוּא אֲבִי כְנָעַן (18b) and consists of three parts.

The first part is the highlighting of the person of Ham. The intent to accent Ham

is signaled by two textual components. One is the syntactical arrangement: nominative

absolute (חָם)[19]-resumptive pronoun (הוּא) - predicate (אֲבִי כְנָעַן). The resumptive pronoun,

in particular, casts the spotlight on the subject in view by virtue of its emphasizing role.

In the words of Muraoka, "the force of the copula in this pattern is often *selective-*

*exclusive,* and emphatic in that sense. The element to be emphasized is the subject, which

is singled out and contrasted with other possible or actual alternative(s)."[20] The other

textual component that signals the highlighting of Ham is the presence of a disjunctive

accent (*zaqef magnum*) on the first constituent (חָם) in the nominative absolute-pronoun-

predicate syntactical pattern.[21]

The second part is the pinpointing the fatherhood of Ham through the predicate

אֲבִי כְנָעַן. We have already shown how the narrator parallels the whole identifying clause,

חָם הוּא אֲבִי כְנָעַן,[22] with the theme of progenitorship for the purpose of utilizing the latter

theme as a license for introducing the former.

---

[18] The parenthesis is denoted by the phrase's non-standard construction, viz., a *waw* followed by a non verb (= Subject) + supplied verb "to be."

[19] Cf. *IBHS*, 298.

[20] T. Muraoka, *Emphatic Words and Structures in Biblical Hebrew* (Leiden: E. J. Brill, 1985), 72; cf. A. B. Davidson, *Introductory Hebrew Grammar: Hebrew Syntax*, 3d ed. (Edinburgh: T. & T. Clark, 1912), 149. The construction appears elsewhere in Deut 12:23; Lev 1:13, 17, etc.

[21] See Joüon-Muraoka for further discussion on the occurrence of a disjunctive accent with the first constituent in the S(ubject)-P(ronoun)-P(redicate) pattern (Paul Joüon, *Syntax*, trans. T. Muraoka, vol. 2, *A Grammar of Biblical Hebrew* (Rome: Editrice Pontificio Istituto Biblico, 1991), §154i.

[22] A clause is identifying if the predicate is definite. The predicate אֲבִי כְנָעַן is definite on the basis of the definite absolute.

The third part is the foregrounding of Canaan via אֲבִי כְנַעַן, the genitive of family relationship. We envision a foregrounding here due to the narrator's exclusive interest in only one son when in the actual sense Ham had three others sons (cf. 10:6). The function of the foregrounding is to anticipate the later mention of Canaan in the narrative. If Canaan were not mentioned at this point, the reader would be at a loss as to his identity in v. 25 since the text would not be able to answer the question, "Now who is Canaan?" Similar foregrounding of narrative characters through the employment of the "the father of so-and-so" construction is attested elsewhere in Gen 33:19. There, even though Hamor had other sons, the construction אֲבִי שְׁכֶם suggests a foregrounding of Shechem in light of the central role he ends up playing in the story that is about to unfold.

By embracing an anticipative role as part of the function of verse 18b, we agree with earlier proponents like Rashi[23] and later scholars like Calvin Goodspeed, D. M. Welton,[24] and Allen Ross.[25] At the same time we disagree with those who dismiss verse 18b as a gloss[26] (e.g. Gerhard von Rad,[27] Hermann Gunkel,[28] and John Van Seters[29])

---

[23] Rashi remarked that "the reader would not know whether Canaan was the son of Ham if the phrase were to be omitted altogether since until now the generations of Ham were not written" (A. J. Rosenberg, *Genesis: A New English Translation*, trans. of text , Rashi, and other Commentaries by A. J. Rosenberg [New York: Judaica Press, 1993], 124).

[24] According to them the emphasis is owing probably to his being the subject of the curse (Calvin Goodspeed and D. M. Welton, *The Book of Genesis*, An American Commentary on the Old Testament [Philadelphia: American Baptist Publication Society, 1909], 96).

[25] Allen P. Ross, "The Table of Nations in Genesis" (Ph.D. diss., Dallas Theological Seminary, 1976), 167.

[26] The author of the phrase has been identified as either of two personalities. Either he is the same as the author who wrote the narrative or he is a separate entity, possibly a redactor (or a compiler). The understanding that the phrase emerges from a hand different from the author of the narrative is typical of the period when the Bible was being read through the prism of historical criticism. Commentators associated with this perspective uniformly define the purpose of the phrase as harmonization. The need for the harmonization is based on the theory that verses 20–27 belong to a much older and more limited tradition, which von Rad labels *Palestinian* and which identifies Noah's children as Shem, Japheth and Canaan.

and those who envision a function of 18b other than foregrounding Canaan, highlighting

Ham, or pinpointing his fatherhood. The function of the phrase is not to highlight the

sinfulness of both the father and the son as claimed by Philo[30] and Ibn Ezra.[31]

As regards the view that "father of" in v. 18b is a gloss, the confusion in regards

to the identity of Canaan that the absence of the construction would create implies very

strongly that the construction is the work of the original author.

Noah's State Prior to the Infraction (vv. 20, 21)

*Activities preceding the state*. Even though Noah's state *per se* is not depicted

until verse 21, the preceding verse and part of v. 21 lay out a couple of activities in which

Noah engaged that brought about his condition. To understand the first activity requires

---

[27] According to him, the harmonization succeeded only in bringing the narrative into external agreement with the *ecumenical* scheme; its inner orientation toward Canaan and the *Palestinian* sphere remained (Gerhard von Rad, *Genesis: A Commentary*, trans. John H. Marks, OTL, ed. G. Ernest Wright et al. [Philadelphia: Westminster Press, 1961], 135).

[28] Gunkel argues that: (a) Noah, "the farmer" and vintner, who lies drunk in his tent, seems to be an entirely different figure compared to the righteous and pious Noah of the flood legend; (b) whereas in the flood narrative Noah's sons are married, here they are still so young that they live with their father in his tent; moreover Canaan's behavior is not that of a grown man; (c) making Ham the offender introduces some textual difficulty since it is Canaan who is cursed; (d) Ham appears second in the name sequence of v. 18; yet v. 24 labels the offender the "youngest" son; and (e) Canaan is mentioned as the brother of Shem and Japheth. Sensing the inconsistency between the preceding flood story, which enumerates the sons of Noah as Shem, Ham and Japheth, and vv. 20–27, which considers the sons to be Shem, Japheth, and Canaan, the redactor, in the name of harmonization, inserted into v. 18 and v. 22 the words "Ham, the father of" before the name "Canaan" (Hermann Gunkel, *Genesis*, trans. Mark E. Biddle, Mercer Library of Biblical Studies, ed. John Blenkinsopp and Walter Brueggemann [Macon, GA: Mercer University Press, 1997]. 79).

[29] According to Van Seters, "it was the Yahwist who took this rather limited local tradition and fitted it into his more universal perspective by making it the story of Noah and his three sons, Shem, Ham, and Japheth, instead of Canaan and Eber" (John Van Seters, *Prologue to History: The Yahwist as Historian in Genesis* [Louisville, KY: John Knox Press, 1992], 179).

[30] According to him, Canaan and Ham were mentioned together in order to highlight the sinfulness of both the father and the son and thus offered a justification of Canaan's displacement from the land by the Israelites (Philo *QG* 2.65).

[31] According to him, the phrase "teaches that both Ham and Canaan were wicked, and as a father does, so do the children" (Abraham ben Meir Ibn Ezra, *Genesis*, trans. H. Norman Strickman and Arthur M. Silver, Ibn Ezra's Commentary on the Pentateuch, vol. 1 [New York: Menorah Publishing Company, 1988], 126).

that we make sense of the syntax and phraseology of verse 20. Specifically we need to

make a determination of the following: (a) the syntactical relationship between נֹחַ and

אִישׁ; (b) the meaning of the phrase אִישׁ הָאֲדָמָה; and (c) the syntactical relationship

between וַיָּחֶל and וַיִּטַּע, and the import of the former verb.

We begin with the syntactical relationship between נֹחַ and אִישׁ. Two proposals

have been made. One proposal is that the relationship is appositional.[32] The other

proposal is that אִישׁ should be regarded as a subordinate noun.[33] A search for a

construction consisting of a verb followed by a proper noun followed by a construct noun

followed by an articular noun reveals sufficient appositional examples for us to conclude

that the syntactical relationship between נֹחַ and אִישׁ is indeed appositional.[34] As for the

assertion that אִישׁ could be regarded as a subordinate noun, GKC and *Davidson's*

*Introductory Hebrew Grammar*[35] are not convincing enough. Neither offers any other

parallel examples where a substantive functions subordinately. GKC even suggests that

the article attached to הָאֲדָמָה be omitted. If omitted the phrase אִישׁ הָאֲדָמָה would fail to

exhibit the necessary agreement in definiteness with the proper name "Noah."

---

[32] Goodspeed and Welton, *The Book of Genesis*, 96; G. J. Spurrell, *Notes on the Hebrew Text of the Book of Genesis with Two Appendices* (Oxford: Clarendon Press, 1887), 86; Clyde T. Francisco, "The Curse on Canaan," *CT* 8 (1964): 8–9; NRSV; NIV.

[33] RV ("Noah was the first tiller of the soil; he planted a vineyard"); cf. RSV; Herman Gunkel, *Genesis Übersetzt und Erklärt* Göttinger Handkommentar zum Alten Testament (Göttingen: Vandenhoeck und Ruprecht, 1902), 70; Von-Rad, *Genesis: A Commentary*, 131. A translation that interprets Noah's agricultural engagement as a new endeavor for him and classifies אִישׁ as a subordinated noun is KJV: "Noah began to be a husbandman, and he planted a vineyard" (cf. Darby, ASV, AV, Davidson, *Introductory Hebrew Grammar: Hebrew Syntax*, 115; GKC, § 120b).

[34] The appositional examples we have in mind are: Exod 9:1, 13; 10:3; Num 21:23; 27:16; Deut 3:1; 33:1; Judg 9:30; 15:6; 1 Kgs 11:15, 21; 2 Kgs 5:8; 11:2; Esth 2:15; Neh 3:31.

[35] See n. 33 above.

Next we turn to the meaning of אִישׁ הָאֲדָמָה. Two meanings have been assigned to the phrase. One understanding is that the phrase connotes a position or title. According to *Genesis Rabbah*, the phrase designated either that Noah was a "man of the earth," because, on his account the earth was saved, and also because his descendants covered the face of the earth, or that he was a "man of the earth" in the way in which the guard of the fortress bears the name of the fortress.[36] Similarly, Midrash *Tanhuma Buber* understood the phrase as designating to Noah the title "man of the land" just as a man is known as the son of man.[37] According to Rashi, the phrase should be interpreted as "master of the earth" in the same way that Elimelech is אִישׁ נָעֳמִי in Ruth 1:3.[38] Recent commentators who interpret the phrase as a title include Cassuto[39], Ross,[40] and Brunk.[41]

The second view is that the phrase designates an occupation. Chrysostom understood the phrase in this manner judging from his translation: "tiller of the soil."[42]

---

[36] *Gen. Rab.* 36.3.4.

[37] *Midrash Tanhuma Buber* 2.20.

[38] Thus just as Elimelech is depicted as having mastery over his wife, so should Noah be understood to have mastery over the earth (*Genesis: A New English Translation, Translation of Text, Rashi, and Other Commentaries*, 125).

[39] Cassuto prefers the meaning "sovereign of earth" in place of "tiller of soil" or "husbandman" (Umberto Cassuto, *From Noah to Abraham (Genesis vi. 9–xi. 32)*, trans. Israel Abrahams, A Commentary on the Book of Genesis, vol. 2 (Jerusalem: Magnes Press, 1964), 159-60.

[40] The translation he offers is "master of the earth" (Ross, "The Table of Nations in Genesis," 226).

[41] Brunk does not supply a specific rendering of the phrase. But he does envision the phrase as a designation of position (William A. Brunk, "The Action of Ham against Noah: Its Nature and Result (Genesis 9:18–27)" [M.Div. thesis, Western Conservative Baptist Seminary, 1988], 80).

[42] Chrysostom, *Hom. Gen.* 29.6.

Other proponents include Ibn Ezra, who offered the interpretation "skilled agriculturist,"[43] and certain nineteen and twentieth century works.[44]

In opposition to this second interpretation, Cassuto offers the following reasons why the Hebrew phrase in question should not be rendered "tiller of the soil": (a) the Hebrew equivalent of "tiller of the soil" is עֹבֵד אֲדָמָה; (b) unlike the term מִלְחָמָה, which, in and of itself, is the equivalent of the phrase אִישׁ מִלְחָמָה ("warrior"), אֲדָמָה alone is insufficient to convey the concept of עֹבֵד אֲדָמָה; and (c) the word אֲדָמָה does indeed denote at times cultivated ground specifically, but not necessarily so; at other times it simply means earth in general.[45]

We disagree with Rashi's[46] implication that the phrase אִישׁ נָעֳמִי in Ruth 1:3 carries the connotation of "master of." The usual word for master is either אָדוֹן or בַּעַל. We agree with Cassuto only in part. We accept his observation that the phrase עֹבֵד אֲדָמָה clearly means "tiller of the soil" (cf. Gen 4:2; Zech 13:5; Prov 12:11; 28:19). Our disagreement with him pertains to his denial of a parallelism between אִישׁ מִלְחָמָה and אִישׁ אֲדָמָה. We are of the opinion that the manner in which the frequently occurring phrase "man of war"[47]

---

[43] Ibn Ezra, *Genesis*, 127.

[44] Goodspeed and Welton, *The Book of Genesis*, 96; Spurrell, *Notes on the Hebrew Text of the Book of Genesis with Two Appendices*, 86; John Peter Lange, *Genesis, or the First Book of Moses, Together with a General Theological and Homiletical Introduction to the Old Testament*, trans. Tayler Lewis and A. Gosman, 5th ed., A Commentary on the Holy Scriptures: Critical, Doctrinal, and Homiletical, with Special Reference to Ministers and Students, ed. Johann Peter Lange and Philip Schaff, vol. 1 (New York: Charles Scribner's Sons, 1884), 335; George Bush, *Notes Critical and Practical on the Book of Genesis: Designed as a General Help to Biblical Reading and Instruction*, 26th ed. (New York: Ivison, Phiney & Company, 1860), 1:160; Herbert Edward Ryle, *The Early Narratives of Genesis: A Brief Introduction to the Study of Genesis 1–11* (London: Macmillan, 1892), 127; RV; KJV.

[45] Cassuto, *From Noah to Abraham (Genesis vi. 9–xi. 32)*, 159.

[46] See n. 38 on p. 75.

[47] The phrase appears a total of 21x (Num 31:28, 49; Deut 2:14, 16; Josh 5:4, 6; 6:3; 10:24; 1 Sam 18:5; 1 Kgs 9:22; 2 Kgs 25:4, 19; Jer 38:4; 39:4; 41:3, 16; 49:26; 51:32; 52:7, 25; Joel 4:9).

functions should inform the way we understand the *hapax* phrase "man of the soil." As it is, the phrase אִישׁ מִלְחָמָה is an abbreviation of the periphrastic expression, "one who engages in war." The same could be said of the phrase involving either "man" or "men" and the articular noun הָעִיר (cf. Gen 19:4; Josh 8:14; Judg 6:27, 28, 30; 8:17; 14:18; 19:22; 1 Sam 5:9; 2 Sam 11:17; 2 Kgs 2:19; 23:17). It is a condensed form of "one or those who inhabit a particular city."[48] Considering the weightiness of evidence that a construction involving either "men" or "man" and an articular noun serves as an abbreviation of an otherwise periphrastic concept, it should not be problematic to view אִישׁ אֲדָמָה as standing for "a man who tills the ground" or "husbandman."[49]

Lastly, we must make a determination of the syntactical relationship between וַיָּחֶל and וַיִּטַּע and the import of the former verb. The syntax has been understood as either a hendiadys[50] or non-hendiadys.[51] Based on the conclusion we have come to on the issue of the syntax of נֹחַ and אִישׁ, we can describe the syntactical relationship between וַיָּחֶל and וַיִּטַּע only as complementary or a hendiadys. The complementariness is needful since a

---

[48] Other examples of abbreviations involve the following articular nouns: הַשֵּׁם ("the name") (Gen 6:4), הַמָּקוֹם ("the place") (Gen 26:7; 29:22; 38:22; Judg 19:16), הַבַּיִת ("the house") (Gen 39:11), הָאָרֶץ ("the earth") (Lev 18:27), הַצָּבָא ("the army") (Num 31:21), הָאֱלֹהִים ("God") (Deut 33:1; Josh 14:6; Judg 13:6, 8; 1 Sam 9:7, 8, 10; 1 Kgs 12:22; 13:4, 5, 6, 7, 8, 11, 12, 14, 21, 26, 29, 31; 17:18; 20:28; 2 Kgs 1:9, 11, 12, 13; 4:7, 16, 21, 22, 25, 27, 40, 42; 5:8, 14, 15, 20; 6:6, 9, 10, 15; 7:2, 17, 18, 19; 8:2, 4, 7, 8, 11; 13:19; 23:16, 17; Jer 35:4; Ps 90:1; Ezra 3:2; Neh 12:24, 36; 1 Chr 23:14; 2 Chr 8:14; 11:2; 25:7, 9; 30:16), הָאִשָּׁה ("the woman") (Judges 20:4), הַמַּצָּבָה ("the Garrison") (1 Sam 14:12), הַבֵּנַיִם ("the champion") (1 Sam 17:4, 23), הַבְּלִיַּעַל ("the Belial") (1 Sam 25:25; 2 Sam 16:7; 1 Kgs 21:13), הַדָּמִים ("the blood") (2 Sam 16:7), הַחַיִל ("valor") (2 Kgs 24:16; Eccl 12:3), הָרוּחַ ("the spirit") (Hos 9:7), הַכִּכָּר ("the surrounding area") (Neh 3:22), הַמִּשְׁמָר ("the watch") (Neh 4:17).

[49] Davidson points out that this phrase is an exception to the rule that a definite genitive makes the whole expression definite. In the case of Gen 9:20 the construct remains indefinite (Davidson, *Introductory Hebrew Grammar*, 24; cf. *IBHS*, 241).

[50] Goodspeed and Welton, *The Book of Genesis*, 96; Spurrell, *Notes on the Hebrew Text of the Book of Genesis with Two Appendices*, 86; Francisco, "The Curse on Canaan," 8–9; NRSV; NIV.

[51] Lange, *Genesis*, 335; Bush, *Notes Critical and Practical on the Book of Genesis*, 160.

classification of the relationship between נֹחַ and אִישׁ as appositional leaves the verb וַיָּחֶל

incomplete in itself.

As for the import of the verb וַיָּחֶל, the suggestions made have ranged from limited

pioneering through unlimited pioneering to initial engagement in viniculture by Noah.

For instance, Midrash *Tanhuma Buber*[52] and Midrash *Tanhuma Yelammedenu*[53]

understood the term in conjunction with the phrase וַיִּטַּע כָּרֶם to mean that Noah was the

first one to plant a vineyard (unlimited pioneering). Philo, who dates prior to these two

Jewish works, qualified "first one" to mean the first to begin cultivation after the deluge,

viz., limited pioneering.[54] Later works that similarly see in the phrase a depiction of Noah

as the earliest vinedresser include E. A. Speiser,[55] von Rad,[56] Ross,[57] Nahum Sarna,[58] John

Hartley,[59] and certain Bible versions.[60] Not all later works, however, read etiology or

pioneering in the phrase in question. A third set of later works, which constitute several

---

[52] *Midrash Tanhuma Buber* 2.20.

[53] *Midrash Tanhuma-Yelammedenu* 2.14.

[54] Philo, *QG* 2.66.

[55] E. A. Speiser, *Genesis: Introduction, Translation and Notes*, AB, ed. William Foxwell Albright and David Noel Freedman, vol. 1 (Garden City, New York: Doubleday, 1964), 61.

[56] Von Rad refers to this verse as housing an "inventor-saga" (von Rad, *Genesis: A Commentary*, 132).

[57] Like Philo, Ross also understands "first one" more narrowly. Noah, according to him, was the first person to plant a vineyard after the flood (Ross, "The Table of Nations in Genesis," 226).

[58] Nahum M. Sarna, *Genesis*, The JPS Torah Commentary, ed. Nahum M. Sarna (Jerusalem: The Jewish Publication Society, 1989), 65.

[59] John E. Hartley, *Genesis*, NIBC: Old Testament Series, ed. Robert L. Hubbard Jr. and Robert K. Johnson (Peabody, MA: Hendrickson Publishers, 2000), 112.

[60] RV and NRSV.

Bible translations, interpret the phrase to mean that the cultivation of vine was a first but only in respect to Noah (initial engagement).[61]

The hiphil form of the verb חלל connotes the commencement of a certain activity. At the very least all would agree that verse 20 reports on Noah's commencement of a vinicultural project. Whether this commencement ought to be further classified as pioneering (or etiological) or a first for Noah can only be determined from the context. Indeed, in clear cases such as Gen. 10:8 and 1 Sam 22:15, the context provides the necessary clues to make the determination that חלל connotes pioneering and first time engagement respectively.[62] When it comes to Gen 9:20, there is no clue whatsoever that would allow us to read etiology. Additionally, evidence that the practice of winemaking predates Noah should caution the exegete from interpreting the verse etiologically. Basing her assertion on seeds of cultivated grapes unearthed at Tell esh-Shuna in the Jordan Valley, Michal Dayagi-Mendels states that "in the land of Israel, where the wild grapevine grew since Paleolithic times, some 800,000 years before the present, viticulture can be traced back to the Chalcolithic period, the 4th millennium B.C."[63] Based upon Eugene Merrill's calculations, Noah was born between the second and third millennium

[61] ASV, AV, KJV, NIV, Darby, and NET Bible.

[62] The presence of בָּאָרֶץ at the end of Gen. 10:8 clearly connotes etiology. That it was not the first time Ahimelech had inquired of the Lord on behalf of David is evident in the use of הַיּוֹם at the beginning of 1 Sam 22:15.

[63] Michal Dayagi-Mendels, *Drink and Be Merry: Wine and Beer in Ancient Times* (Jerusalem: Israel Museum, 1999), 15, cf.; Tim Unwin, *Wine and the Vine* (New York: Routledge, 1996), 63; Marvin A. Powell, "Wine and the Vine in Ancient Mesopotamia: The Cuneiform Evidence," in *The Origins and Ancient History of Wine*, ed. Patrick E. McGovern, Stuart J. Fleming, and Solomon H. Katz, Food and Nutrition in History and Anthropology ed. Solomon H. Katz, vol. 11 (Toronto, Canada: Gordon and Breach Publishers, 1996), 101.

B.C; in which case, the birth of viniculture pre-dated him by a thousand years.[64] As regards the perspective that Noah had never engaged in vine growing until now, the fact that no mention is made of prior vinicultural activity by Noah supports this suggestion. Thus the first of several activities in which Noah engaged in was winemaking. The second activity was partaking of the fruit of his agricultural endeavor, i.e., he drank some wine.[65]

*Noah's state of drunkenness.* Following the partaking of wine, which would be the natural thing for a vinedresser to do,[66] Noah experienced drunkenness[67] throughout the occurrence of the activities described in verses 22 and 23 after which the stuporous effects of the wine wore off according to v. 24a (וַיִּיקֶץ נֹחַ מִיֵּינוֹ).[68] The effect of the wine was partly loss of awareness and partly the second state that Noah entered into.

One would be hard-pressed to find an explicit condemnation of Noah of the caliber of Prov 23:20; 23:31; etc. There is no evidence of explicit chiding just like the

---

[64] Merrill dates the birth of Terah at 2296 B.C. Relying on the genealogy in Gen 11:11–26, we can place Noah somewhere between 2600 B.C and 3000 B.C. (Eugene H. Merrill, "Chronology," in *Dictionary of the Old Testament: Pentateuch*, ed. T. Desmond Alexander and David W. Baker [Downers Grove, Illinois: InterVarsity Press, 2003], 121).

[65] This rendering "drank some wine" accurately captures the twin ideas of drinking שתה and the partitive מִן preposition attached to the genitive form יַיִן.

[66] Partaking of the fruit of a vinicultural activity is depicted as a natural consequence in the Old Testament (cf. Deut 20:6; 2 Kgs 19:29; Isa 37:30; 65:21; Jer 31:5; Ezek 28:26; Amos 9:14; Zeph 1:13).

[67] The consequential relationship between drinking and getting drunk is evident is Gen 43:34, 2 Sam 11:13, and Jer 25:27. Structurally the element of consequence is expressed by the stringing together of two *wayyiqtols*.

[68] In all the instances where the verb יקץ appears in conjunction with the מִן preposition, this is the only time where the object of the מִן preposition is not שֵׁנָה ("sleep") (cf. Gen 28:16; Judg 16:14, 20). Instead we have the יַיִן, which could be classified as a metonymy of cause for effect. Delitzsch cites 1 Sam 1:14 and 25:37 as additional occurrences where the term "wine" is to be understood as designating the effect of wine (Franz Delitzsch, *A New Commentary on Genesis*, trans. Sophia Taylor, Clark's Foreign Theological Library, vol. 1 (Edinburgh: T. & T. Clark, 1899), 293; cf. Spurrell, *Notes on the Hebrew Text of the Book of Genesis with Two Appendices*, 87).

drunkenness by Joseph and his brothers in Gen 43:34 is not explicitly reproved. To this

end those who argue that the text is neutral[69] or does not show interest in evaluating the

drunkenness[70] are probably right. At the same time, one has to wonder whether the text is

being less neutral and more exonerating through its use of חלל and the partitive מִן

preposition. The verb חלל, we have suggested, carries the connotation that Noah's

engagement in viniculture was a first for him. If so, the Church Fathers (e.g., Clement,[71]

Jerome,[72] and Chrysostom[73]) and certain eighteenth to nineteenth century commentators

(e.g., Elisha Fish,[74] Lange,[75] Candlish,[76] and Bush[77]) would be right in their claim that

---

[69] Victor P. Hamilton, *The Book of Genesis: Chapters 1–17*, NICOT, ed. R. K. Harrison (Grand Rapids: Eerdmans, 1990), 321; cf. Derek Kidner, *Genesis: An Introduction and Commentary*, TOTC, ed. D. J. Wiseman (Chicago: Inter-varsity Press, 1967), 103; Johnson T. K. Lim, *Grace in the Midst of Judgment: Grappling with Genesis 1–11*, Beihefte zur Zeitschrift für die Alttestamentliche Wissenschaft, vol. 314 (Berlin: Walter de Gruyter, 2002), 176.

[70] John H. Walton, *Genesis*, The NIV Application Commentaries Series, ed. Terry Muck (Grand Rapids: Zondervan, 2001), 346; cf. Walter Brueggemann, *Genesis*, Interpretation: A Bible Commentary for Teaching and Preaching, ed. James Luther Mays (Atlanta: John Knox Press, 1982), 89.

[71] Clement of Alexandria (A.D.150–215) was unwilling to point an accusatory finger at Noah by placing the blame squarely on the intoxication and maintained that Noah the righteous was merely ignorant of the shameful effects of the wine (Clement, *Paedagogus* 2.6).

[72] Similarly Jerome (A.D. 331–420), in the context of making a case for the avoidance of wine in a letter (dated A.D. 384) to lady Eustochium, reasoned that perhaps Noah did not know the vine's power of inebriation since he lived in the rude age of the flood when the vine was first planted (*Select Letters of St. Jerome* 22).

[73] The very word "first," according to Chrysostom (A.D. 347–407), showed that Noah "made the first discovery of wine drinking; and through ignorance and inexperience of the proper amount to drink fell into a drunken stupor" (Chrysostom, *Hom. Gen.* 29.6).

[74] Fish perceives the phrase "began to be an husbandman" as possibly connoting ignorance of the effect of wine on Noah's part (Elisha Fish, *Japheth Dwelling in the Tents of Shem or Infant Baptism Vindicated in a Discourse, the Substance of Which Was Delivered at Upton, January 5, 1772. With Objections Answered* [Boston: Thomas and John Fleet, 1773], 3).

[75] Lange believes that Noah was oblivious of the effects of wine. Thus he "erred in ignorance and not in the form of conscious transgression" (Lange, *Genesis*, 336).

[76] According to Candlish, Noah's was an "unwonted offence" (Robert S. Candlish, *The Book of Genesis: Expounded in a Series of Discourses* [Edinburgh: Adam and Charles Black, 1868], 1:158).

[77] Bush reasons as follows: "Noah was perhaps the first who invented presses for extracting the juice of the grape, and making wine in this manner. If so, the increased quantities procured, or the

Noah was ignorant of the inebriating effects of wine. By the same token the מִן

preposition implies some type of restraint in the drinking of the wine by Noah even

though the final effect was nevertheless drunkenness. If exoneration be the thrust of vv.

20 and 21, then expressions critical of Noah's drunkenness (e.g. *Genesis Rabbah*,[78]

Talmud,[79] Luther,[80] John Calvin,[81] Delitzsch,[82] Morris[83]) would have to be dismissed as

---

augmented strength of the beverage, may account for the effect produced by drinking it upon Noah... It was very lawful for Noah to partake of the fruits of his labor, but he sinned in drinking to excess. He might not indeed have been aware of the strength of the wine, or his age might have rendered him sooner affected by it. At any rate, we have reason to conclude from his general character, that it was a fault of inadvertence, one of which he was overtaken, and of which he afterwards bitterly repented" (Bush, *Notes Critical and Practical on the Book of Genesis*, 160; cf. Goodspeed and Welton, *The Book of Genesis*, 96; Sarna, *Genesis*, 65; and von Rad, *Genesis*, 136).

[78] According to *Genesis Rabbah*, Noah's decision to engage in such an activity was both poor and defiling. The decision was poor since he possibly had the option of planting something valuable such as a young fig shoot or olive shoot. The decision was defiling on the basis of the rabbinical interpretation of the word *began*. Because the word for *began* (וַיָּחֶל) uses consonants that can produce the word for *become profane*, the rabbis interpreted the verse to mean: "He was made common (no longer holy) (נתחלל) and became profane (חולין)" (*Gen. Rab.* 36.3.1[cf. Rashi in *Genesis*, 125; *Midrash Tanhuma-Yelammedenu* 2.13]).

[79] The Talmud chides Noah for failing to appropriate the lesson of the first man in regards to the drinking of wine (*Sanh.* 70a).

[80] Luther was not convinced that Noah was unfamiliar with the nature of this juice. The truth of the matter, according to him, was that Noah simply drank too much and those who excuse the patriarch "dispense of their own accord with the comfort that the Holy Spirit considered necessary for the churches, namely, that even the greatest saints sometimes fall" (*Lectures on Genesis Chapters 6–14*, trans. George V. Schick, vol. 2, Luther's Works, ed. Jaroslav Pelikan [St. Louis: Concordia Publishing House, 1960], 166–67).

[81] Calvin labels Noah's drunkenness as "sin" (John Calvin, *Commentaries on the First Book of Moses Called Genesis*, trans. John King [Grand Rapids: Eerdmans, 1948], 1: 300).

[82] Franz Delitzsch labels the act as sinful (Delitzsch, *A New Commentary on Genesis*, 292; cf. Cornelius H. Edgar, *The Curse of Canaan Rightly Interpreted and Kindred Topics: Three Lectures Delivered in the Reformed Dutch Church, Easton, Pa* [New York: Baker & Godwin Printers, 1862], 4; Francisco, "The Curse of Canaan," 8).

[83] Morris maintains that Noah cannot be excused on the basis of his ignorance that the new wine would decay into intoxicating wine (Henry M. Morris, *The Genesis Record: A Scientific and Devotional Commentary on the Book of Beginnings* [Grand Rapids: Baker Book House, 1976], 234; cf. O. Palmer Robertson, "Current Critical Questions Concerning the 'Curse of Ham'," *JETS* 41 [1998], 178).

baseless. If Noah were to be faulted at all, it would be on the basis of overall biblical teaching on wine usage and not on the basis of Gen. 9:21.[84]

*Noah's state of nakedness.* The second state that Noah entered into and the significance of the adjoining locative phrase בְּתוֹךְ אָהֳלֹה has recently become a subject of alternative interpretation. Specifically, the debate centers on the meaning of the verbal form יִתְגַּל[85] and the ה at the end of the locative phrase. Excluded from the debate are two aspects of verse 21. First, the relationship between the drunkenness and the onset of this second state is agreeably causal. Drunkenness certainly played a role in the rise of this second state. Elsewhere we read about other acts with which drunkenness is consequentially associated. Drunkenness can lead to abnormal self-addressing (1 Sam 1:14), blurred judgment (2 Sam 11:13; Isa 28:7; 25:36; Prov 31:5), stumbling (Isa 28:7; 29:9), vomiting (Jer 25:27; 48:26), and self-stripping (Lam 4:21).[86] The *wayyiqtol* form of גלה preceded by the *wayyiqtol* form of שׁכר further clarifies the consequential relationship of the two acts. Thus Noah's drunkenness emerged from his drinking. His drunkenness then led to the second state.

Secondly, whatever the understanding of the second state, it came about in a private location.[87] By the nature of its very syntax the locative phrase בְּתוֹךְ אָהֳלֹה seeks to

---

[84] For a detailed study on wine and the Old Testament, see Carey Ellen Walsh, *The Fruit of the Vine: Viticulture in Ancient Israel*, Harvard Semitic Monographs, ed. Peter Machinist, vol. 60 (Winona Lake, IN: Eisenbrauns, 2000), 249–58.

[85] This is a *hapax* form that is parsed hithpael preterite 3ms from גלה. BDB offers the translation "he was uncovered"(*BDB*, 163). GKC (§75 bb) translates the form as "he uncovered himself."

[86] The correspondence between this Lamentation reference and our verse is rather striking. In both cases drunkenness is associated with cloth removal with the verb indicating removal of clothing being in the hithpael stem.

[87] The significance of observing the setting of a story has been widely documented. See Tremper Longman, *Literary Approaches to Biblical Interpretation*, Foundations of Contemporary Interpretation, ed. Moisés Silva, vol. 3 (Grand Rapids: Academie Books, 1987), 94.

underscore the element of privacy. The בְּ preposition attached to the noun תָּוֶךְ is not just locative but also emphasizes the privateness of Noah's location.[88] The occurrence of the construction elsewhere in conjunction with the term אֹהֶל confirms the nuance of privacy that is resident in this construction. For instance, the text reveals that the chosen location of the ark after its repossession by David in 2 Sam 6 was not in the open, where it would be exposed, but בְּתוֹךְ אָהֳלֹה (v. 17, cf. 1 Chr 16:1). Similarly, when Achan sought to keep the stolen loot out of view, his chosen hiding site was בְּתוֹךְ אָהֳלֹה (Josh 7:21). The vice of the story therefore does not lie with Noah's nakedness. His nakedness was hidden by his location.

Ham's Action and His Siblings'
Reaction (vv. 22–23)

Verse 22 starts out by reiterating Ham's paternity. The link between Ham and Canaan was first made in v. 18 via an identifying clause. Verse 22 marks a repeat of this linkage, only this time through an apposition of relationship. We see a similar kind of reiteration in the story about Hamor in Gen 33:18–34:31. Hamor is referred to as the "father of Shechem" at the beginning of the story (33:19) and then again in 34:6.

*The first of Ham's two-fold action (v. 22a).* Having echoed the linking of Ham to Canaan, the text then offers a description of Ham's two-fold action. The first aspect of Ham's action is captured by the verb רָאָה and the accusative phrase עֶרְוַת אָבִיו ("nakedness[89] of his father"). As to the meaning of the phrase, two opposing views exist.

---

[88] Cf. BDB, 1063. To capture the emphatic nuance that is resident in a בְּ preposition attached to the form תָּוֶךְ ("midst"), we prefer the rendering "in the very midst of."

[89] The terms "naked" and "nakedness" in the English Bible are a translation of a set of Hebrew derivatives that includes the nouns עֶרְוָה, מַעַר and מַעֲרֹם, and the adjectives עֵירֹם, עָרֹם and עָרוֹם. The derivatives themselves can be traced back to the twin verbal roots עָרָה and עוּר (cf. *BDB*, 789), or the

The literal reading considers the action as non-sexual, while the idiomatic reading deems the action as sexual. The former reading, unlike the latter, witnesses further contrasting opinions.

One opinion, represented by BDB, supposes sinfulness by its proposal that Ham looked at the nakedness of his father "by direct volition."[90] The opposite opinion, represented by Goodspeed and Welton, maintains that the seeing was actually accidental and therefore an innocent act.[91] In other words, Ham should not be judged as guilty at this level since he did not enter the tent to view his naked father; rather he saw his father naked when he entered the tent.

*The second of Ham's twofold action.* Syntactically, the aspect of the second of Ham's twofold action constitutes four elements. There is the hiphil verb (נגד); a *lamed* of

---

root ערה (cf. *HALOT*, 2:823, 882). According to BDB (789), the derivatives associated with the verbal root ערה are the nouns עֶרְוָה and מַעַר, while those associated with the verbal root עור are the noun מַעֲרֹם and the adjectives עֵירֹם, עֵרֹם, and עָרֹום. Besides associating or recognizing the association of ערה with the forms עֶרְוָה, עֶרְיָה, מַעַר, עָרֹום, עֵירֹם, *HALOT* (2:823, 882) does not recognize the second root עור.

In our opinion, there are two reasons why BDB should be considered as a less reliable lexicon in this particular case. First, BDB admits via its bracketing of the verbal root עור that the form exists only hypothetically. Secondly, certain derivatives classified under one root function synonymously with certain derivatives classified under the second root. For example, Jerusalem's nakedness עֵרֹם in Ezek 16:7 is reversed a verse later because the Lord ends up covering the nakedness עֶרְוָה. Similarly, for uncovering her nakedness עֶרְוָה in whoredom (v. 36), Jerusalem shall be stripped by her lovers and left bare and naked (עֵירֹם, v. 39).

Outside of Hebrew, the verb ערה and the noun ערוה find attestation in several Semitic languages. Counterparts to the verb are Aramaic ערה (hithpael: "to expose oneself") [*Hebrew and Aramaic Dictionary of the Old Testament*, ed. Georg Fohrer (Berlin: Walter de Gruyter, 1973), 213], Akkadian *eru/aru* ("to be naked;" D: "to expose oneself") [*AHw* 1. 247], Arabic *riya* ("to be naked") [*Wehr*, 712], and Ugaritic *rw* ("to expose, empty, destroy") [Joseph Aistleitner, *Wörterbuch der ugaritischen Sprache*, Berichte über die Verhandlungen der Sächsischen Akademie der Wissenschaften zu Leipzig: Philogisch-Historische Klasse, vol. 106 (Berlin: Akademie-Verlag, 1967), 242 (n. 2097)]. Counterparts to the noun include Aramaic ערוה ("nakedness, exposedness, genital area, sex organ") (*HAD*, 213), Akkadian *uru (m)* ("nakedness, shame") (*AHw* 3:1435), Arabic *ury, urya, ara,* and *uryan* ("nakedness, nudity, naked, nude") (*Wehr*, 712), and Ugaritic *ury* ("naked") (*WUS* 242, n. 2097).

[90] BDB, 907.

[91] Goodspeed and Welton, *The Book of Genesis*, 96.

indirect object; and the locative phrase בַּחוּץ (outside). The fourth constituent is the object

of the verb, which, though not explicitly mentioned, is inferentially the nakedness of

Noah.[92]

 *The Siblings' Reaction.* It is clear that the narrator presents the siblings' reaction

in v. 23, and by extension the siblings themselves, as a literary foil with respect to Ham

and his action.[93]  The contradistinction actually starts in the previous verse with the

locative phrase בַּחוּץ ("outside"). Even though the text does not explicitly place Ham

inside Noah's tent, its placement of him outside through the aforementioned locative

phrase implies that he emerged from inside. In contrast to Ham's implied spatial

positioning inside the tent, his siblings had not been inside the tent prior to v. 23. But

even when they finally entered the tent, the narrator goes to great pains to describe the

series of steps taken by the pair to ensure that not only did they not see the nakedness of

their father, but also, unlike Ham, they covered it.[94] First, they took (וַיִּקַּח)[95] a garment

(הַשִּׂמְלָה).[96] Second, they set it[97] upon שְׁכֶם שְׁנֵיהֶם ("both their shoulders").[98] Third, they

---

 [92] It is not uncommon in the book of Genesis that the verb נגד appears without an explicit mention of the object (Gen 14:13; 21:26; 24:3; and 24:49). This phenomenon of an absent but deducible object is attested in GKC, §117f; cf. Joüon, *A Grammar of Biblical Hebrew*, §154c.

 [93] Even though the commonest type of foil is a character, sometimes an event or an action can serve as a foil. In the case of v. 23 the characters and their actions serve as foil (cf. Leland Ryken, *How to Read the Bible as Literature* [Grand Rapids: Zondervan Publishing House, 1984], 54).

 [94] In utilizing the disjunctive clause וְעֶרְוַת אֲבִיהֶם לֹא רָאוּ at the end of v. 23, the author is emphatic that the siblings did not see the nakedness of their father.

 [95] It is not uncommon that a singular verb would serve more than one subject [cf. GKC, §146f, and Joüon, *A Grammar of Biblical Hebrew*, §154d. A search for this phenomenon yielded 72 occurrences. All these occurrences involved proper nouns as the subjects of the singular verb. A few of those examples include Gen 7:13; 11:29; 17:26; 21:22, 32; 24:50; 25:10; 31:14; 33:7; 34:20; 46:12; Num 26:19; Exod 4:29; 7:6, 10; 8:12; 10:3; 16:6; Lev. 9:23; Num 1:17.

 [96] Even though the English rendering of this noun is anarthrous, the noun is actually articulate in the Hebrew (cf. Davidson, *Introductory Hebrew Grammar*, 26). As to the categorization of the article, it is best viewed as an imaginative article. By it the author expresses an awareness of a particular garment. To

walked backwards. Lastly, they covered the nakedness of their father וּפְנֵיהֶם אֲחֹרַנִּית ("while their faces were turned away").[99]

*Analysis of Noah's Utterances (vv. 24–27)*

Verse 24 is better grouped with the following three verses for two reasons. First, the verse marks a change as far as the subject is concerned. Whereas the subject of vv. 22 and 23 is Ham and his siblings, respectively, Noah is the subject of vv. 24–27.

Secondly, that vv. 24 and 25 are a couplet is evidenced by the absence of an expressed subject in v. 25, since the subject of the verb has already been introduced in the preceding verse. In other words, the fact that the antecedent of the incorporated pronominal element in וַיֹּאמֶר (v. 25) is found in v. 24 shows that the two verses are closely connected.

The two occurrences of וַיֹּאמֶר (v. 25) signify the presence of two separate sets of utterances. Moreover, both occurrences should be regarded as consequential, which means that the utterances of Noah in verses 25–27 are to be viewed as a reaction to the discovery he made, upon waking up from his stupor. Since the utterances also mention

claim, as Brunk does, that the garment belonged to Noah's wife is to introduce a character in the scene that the pericope does not accommodate. More likely the garment belonged to Noah since it is he who is depicted in v. 21 as disrobing himself (Ross, "The Table of Nations in Genesis," 231).

[97] The object has to be supplied since it does not feature in the Hebrew. This type of omission is prevalent among constructions involving both לקח and שִׂים (cf. Gen 21:14; 22:6; 28:11; Exod 17:12; 24:6; 1 Sam 7:12; 8:11; 19:13; 2 Kgs 9:13: 20:7; Zech 6:11). There are instances, however, when the object is included in the form of an object pronoun (e.g. Gen 28:18; Deut 31:26; Josh 8:12) or object suffix (e.g. Gen 31:34; Num 16:18; Ezek 19:5; Hag 2:23).

[98] שְׁנַיִם appears in apposition to the preceding noun and in construct with the following suffixed pronoun. The suffixed pronoun functions as a "genitive of measured." The antecedents of the 3mp pronoun are clearly Shem and Japheth, the subject of the verb וַיָּשִׂימוּ.

[99] פְּנֵיהֶם, which constitutes the noun פָּנִים ("faces") in construct form and the pronominal suffix (genitive of possessor) serves as the subject of the noun clause. According to GKC a noun clause connected by a *waw* copulative to a verbal clause always describes a state contemporaneous with the principal action (GKC, §141e). This element of contemporaneity resident in this clause serves to introduce added emphasis that the siblings did not in fact look at the nakedness of their father.

Ham's siblings, we would have to assume that Noah was also informed about the positive actions of his two sons.

Analysis of the Curse Utterance (v. 25)

Using syntax as a criterion, there are three distinguishable curse (אָרַר) formulas. In one formula, a phrase constituting a noun and a relative clause defines the entity being cursed, and an imperfect is employed to describe the manner in which the curse will manifest itself (Jer 17:5–6; 20:15–16; Josh 6:26). The justification for the curse is implicitly wrapped within the noun and the relative clause. There are instances, though, where no description of the manner in which the curse will manifest itself is offered (Deut 27:15; 1 Sam 14:24; Jer 11:3; 20:14).

In the second formula, a participle phrase marks the entity being cursed (Gen 27:29; Num 24:9; Jer 48:10; Mal 1:14; Judg 21:18; Deut 27:16, 17, 18, 19, 20, 21, 22, 23, 24, 25). The justification for the curse is implicitly wrapped within the participle phrase. No mention is made of the manner on which the curse is to manifest itself. In one instance the item being cursed is presented as an אֲשֶׁר clause (Deut 27:26).

In the third formula, the item being cursed is represented by a noun. The formula explicitly states the justification for the curse and employs the imperfect to describe the manner in which the curse will manifest itself (Gen 3:14; 4:11; 49:7; Josh 9:23).[100]

Of the three curse formulas, the third type best reflects the curse utterance in v. 25. At the head of the curse utterance is the passive participle אָרוּר. The entity being cursed is represented by the proper noun "Canaan." The description of the manner in

---

[100] We could classify 1 Sam 26:19 under this category if we keep in mind that the manner in which the curse is to manifest itself is not explicated.

which the curse is to manifest itself is found in the phrase עֶבֶד עֲבָדִים יִהְיֶה לְאֶחָיו, which

contains the imperfect form יהיה.

As regards the reason for the curse, the answer is quite elusive if the question is:
"Why was Canaan cursed?"[101] The puzzlement arises from the fact that the pericope fails

to yield explicit evidence concerning Canaan's guilt.

The answer is more straightforward if the question is why the curse was uttered in

the first case. The pericope presents the curse utterance as a reaction or consequence of

Noah's discovery of what Ham had done to him. Put differently, Ham's infraction was

the motivational cause of the curse utterance.

We now turn from a general analysis of the curse to a more detailed examination

of its various aspects. These are: (1) the meaning and nature of עֶבֶד עֲבָדִים; (2) the

meaning of אָח in the phrase לְאֶחָי; and (3) the object of the curse.

*The meaning and nature of עבד עבדים*. The fact that the phrase constitutes a noun

adjoined to a pluralized genitival form of the same noun connotes a sense of extremity or

superlativeness (cf. Exod 26:33; Isa 34:10; Eccl 1:2; Song 1:1; Ezek 16:7; Deut 10:17;

1 Kgs 8:27).[102] The point of the *hapax* expression, then, is that the object of the curse will

be subject to extreme servitude.

In determining the nature of servitude, we have to rely on the context and what it

reveals regarding עֶבֶד.[103] Elsewhere in the OT we are able to contextually deduce the

---

[101] See a listing of the different rationale offered for the curse in "suggestions of the justification of Canaan's curse" in the appendix.

[102] Davidson, *Introductory Hebrew Grammar*, 49; cf. GKC, §133i; Joüon, *A Grammar of Biblical Hebrew*, §142l; and *IBHS*, 154, 267.

[103] Even though the focus so far has been on the superlative genitive construction, the exact idea of servitude is repeated in Gen 9:26b and 27b without the superlative adjective.

nature of a particular mention of servitude in terms of the kinds of activities to which the

עֶבֶד in view is subjected. Such activities include: conducting military assaults at the

behest of the master (Gen 14:15; 2 Sam 2:15; 14:30; 1 Kgs 16:9); fetching a wife (Gen

24:2–4); digging a well (26:19); serving as an emissary (32:16; Num 22:18; 1 Sam 18:22;

2 Sam 10:3; 1 Kgs 15:18; 20:6; 2 Kgs 19:5); overseeing the affairs of a house (Gen 39:4);

paying taxes (47:24); laboring manually (Josh 9:23; 1 Sam 8:16; 2 Chr 8:8–9); paying

tribute (2 Sam 8:2, 6; 2 Kgs 17:3); tilling the land (2 Sam 9:10); and accompanying the

master/mistress on a trip (1 Kgs 10:13; 2 Kgs 5:13). [104]

In the case of servitude in Gen 9:25, the limited context spanning vv. 18–29 does

not supply us with any data upon which we can deduce the nature of the servitude. This

does not mean that such data does not exist at all.[105]

*The meaning of* אחים *in the phrase* לאחיו.[106] Rashi and Westermann[107] interpret אָח

strictly as the son of one's mother or father. The implication is that the beneficiaries of

Canaan's curse were his own brothers, viz., Cush, Mizraim and Put. The problem with

this interpretation is twofold. First, the interpretation fails to recognize the wide range of

relationships that legitimately fall under the rubric of "brother." Besides the stricter

---

[104] The persons under which an עֶבֶד are said to be vassalized include a fellow brother (Gen 27:37), the patriarchs (such as Abraham [Gen 12:16], Isaac [26:19], Jacob [30:43]), Judges (such as Eglon [Judg 3:24] and Gideon [6:27]), Kings (such as Chedorlamer [Gen 14:4], Saul [1 Sam 16:15], David [25:40], Solomon [1 Kings 3:15] and Hiram of Tyre [5:15]). The identity of עֶבֶד could be an individual, a group of people or a people group such as Israel (Deut 28:68), the Gibeonites (Josh 9:8), Edomites (1 Kgs 11:17), Moabites (2 Sam 8:2), Arameans (8:6), and the Edomites (8:14).

[105] In our analysis of the object of the curse below, we conclude it to be the Canaanites, not merely Canaan (see ch. 3, pp 92–96). If that be so the treatment of the Canaanites in the Bible comes into play on the question of the nature of servitude in Gen 9:25.

[106] The ל in לְאֶחָיו is best classified as a possessive.

[107] *Genesis: A New English Translation*, 129 and Claus Westermann, *Gen 1–11*, trans. John J. Scullion, vol. 1, Genesis: A Commentary (Minneapolis: Augsburg Publishing House, 1984), 1: 492.

meaning of the son of one's mother or father (cf. Gen 4:2; 9:22; Exod 7:2, etc), other relationships include nephew (Gen 14:14, 16; 24:48; 29:12, 15; Lev 10:4), cousin (2 Sam 20:9), uncle (Gen 13:8), a fellow tribesman (Num 8:26), and a member of a related tribe (Num 20:14).

Second, the interpretation displays a lack of sensitivity to the context. As shall be demonstrated later in our analysis of the blessing utterance,[108] the context within which the blessing utterance is embedded favors the identification of the antecedent of the pronominal suffix מוֹ at the end of vv. 26b, 27b as Shem and Japheth, respectively. Shem, as opposed to Elohim, is the antecedent in v. 26b since the preceding parallel clause (v. 25b) identifies the beneficiaries of Canaan's enslavement not as divine, but human. Japheth, as opposed to Shem, is the antecedent in v. 27b since the verse itself begins with and seems to remain focused on Japheth. If Shem and Japheth are regarded as the antecedents of the pronominal suffix in vv. 26b and 27b, and since these two clauses are parallel to v. 25b, it follows that אֶחָיו should be equated with Shem and Japheth. Since Shem and Japheth were not Canaan's brothers in the stricter sense of the term, we have to assume a loose use of "brothers" in v. 25b. If "brothers" is understood loosely, the strict interpretation of Rashi and Westermann must be dismissed.

*The object of the curse.* The two choices offered by the history of interpretation are Canaan and Ham.[109] One argument of the "Ham" view appeals to the variant textual reading, ἐπικατάρατος Χαμ ("Cursed be Ham" [the father of Ham]), attested by certain Greek Byzantine texts and the Old Latin Text of Ambrose (*et dixit maledictus Cham*).

---

[108] See ch. 3, pp. 96–104.

[109] See a fuller discussion of the "Canaan" and the "Ham" views under "History of Interpretation" (chap. 2, pp. 30–45).

The question, then, becomes whether or not the variant reading is inferior or superior to the MT reading, אָרוּר כְּנָעַן. This determination must not be based on external criteria such as the age or the number of the witnesses.[110] Rather the basis of the determination ought to be primarily internal criteria, viz., the merits of the reading itself as opposed to the manuscripts. Of the various internal criteria cited by McCarter, only two are relevant to the evaluation of the alternative reading in v. 25. One criterion is the principle of *lectio difficilior praeferenda est* ("the more difficult reading is to be preferred"). The other is the criterion of resolution of contradictions. Subjecting the alternative reading to these two criteria, the outcome renders the reading inferior because (a) the reading represents the easier and therefore less preferable option when it comes to the relationship between the punished one and the offender; and (b) it resolves the contradiction posed by placement of the curse on a non-offender so to speak.

Another argument advanced by the "Ham" view considers the mention of David's father in 1 Sam 17 as indirect and therefore illustrative of the mention of Canaan's father in Gen 9:25. Such an assertion is incorrect. The mention of David's father (v. 58) in response to Saul's inquiry about him could not be any more direct. This verse could not therefore serve as a parallel to what might be playing out rhetorically in Gen 9:25.

---

[110] P. Kyle McCarter cautions on the reliability of the factors of age and preponderance in determining the value of a reading. The latter factor is dismissed on the basis of the canon *manuscripta ponderantur, non numerantur* ("manuscripts are to be weighed, not counted"). The former factor is disputed on the strength of the slogan *recentiores non deteriores* ("recent documents are not necessarily worse than older ones") (P. Kyle McCarter, *Textual Criticism: Recovering the Text of the Hebrew Bible*, GBS [Old Testament Guides], ed. Gene M. Tucker [Philadelphia: Fortress, 1986], 71). Other works that make the same point include Ralph W. Klein, *Textual Criticism of the Old Testament: The Septuagint after Qumran*, GBS (OTG), ed. Gene M. Tucker (Philadelphia: Fortress, 1974), 74; F. E. Deist, *Towards the Text of the Old Testament: A Systematic Introduction for Students of Biblical Studies, Theology and Classical Hebrew*, trans. W. K. Winckler (Pretoria: N. G. Kerkboekhandel Transvaal, 1978), 243; and Emanuel Tov, *Textual Criticism of the Hebrew Bible*, 2d rev. ed. (Minneapolis: Fortress Press, 2001), 301–302.

The third argument declares Ham the object of the curse based on the fact that it was he who committed the offense against Noah. True, Ham is guilty as charged. Equally true also is the incontrovertible fact that the object of the curse, according to the text, is Canaan, not Ham. In summary, none of the exegetical appeals for regarding Ham as the object of the curse is convincing. The more accurate and preferable view is that Canaan was the object of the curse.

But even if the "Canaan" view was to be declared the more likely one, as we believe it is, we still need to determine if "Canaan" in 9:25 stands for the individual or the name encompasses his descendants, the Canaanites. To put it more broadly, should Japheth, Shem, and Canaan be understood, as Westermann[111] does, as mere individuals so that the outworking of the Noachian utterances (both the curse and the blessing) occurs within the family of Noah and in the time of the trio? Or should they be understood representatively so that the outworking of Noah's utterances cuts across generations?

In the case of the curse utterance vis-à-vis Canaan, a study at the occurrences of the imperfect form יהיה and its *weqatal* counterpart reveals that, more than anything else, it is the context that determines whether or not the verb carries a transgenerational meaning. For instance, the use of the imperfect form תִּהְיֶה in the declaration of Cain's punishment as a fugitive and wanderer in Gen 4:12 is found to be non-transgenerational on the basis of the surrounding data regarding the placement of a mark on him so that no one would kill him (cf. Gen 44:9; Num 14:33; Jer 36:30). On the other hand, the phrase, בֵּין זַרְעִי וּבֵין זַרְעֲךָ עַד־עוֹלָם ("between my descendants and your descendants forever") renders the imperfect in 1 Sam 20:42 transgeneration (cf. 1 Kgs 2:33; Jer 29:32).

---

[111] Westermann, *Genesis 1–11*, 1: 492.

What does context reveal in the case of Gen 9:25? It is our contention that the context supports a transgeneration meaning. By context, we mean not the most immediate context (i.e., vv. 18–29),[112] but rather the much broader context of the pericope, which we have argued elsewhere spans the *Vatergeschichte* and the rest of the Hexateuch, if not the whole Tanakh. This broader context begins by delineating the composition and territory of the Canaanites in Gen 10:15–19. Genesis 13 shows them as already occupying the territory. Next, it marks them out as targets of marital prohibition (Gen 24:3; 28:1; Deut 7:3) and territorial supplantation (Gen 15:18–21), the latter of which commences with the overrunning of the trans-Jordan region by Israel (Num 21:2–35) and continues with the incomplete conquest of the cis-Jordan region by the same (Josh 5:13–12:24; Judg 1:1–36).

More relevant to the question of the function of the imperfect in Gen 9:25 vis-à-vis the broader context is the depiction of Canaanites as objects of harsh labor. Six times they are portrayed as subjects to an imposition of harsh labor by a tribe of Israel, Israel in general, or one of its kings (Josh 16:10; 17:13; Judg 1:28, 30, 33; 1 Kgs 9:21). Granted, the term for forced labor (מַס) in these six passages is different from the term servant or slave (עֶבֶד) in Gen 9:25. However, if Mendelsohn is correct, the distinction between the two is one of kind.[113] But even if מַס were to be regarded as different from slavery altogether,[114] what cannot be easily dismissed is that both עֶבֶד and מַס share the elements

---

[112] There is nothing within this narrow context that would support a transgeneration meaning.

[113] According to him, מַס represents one of the three types of slavery in ANE. The other two were domestic and temple slavery respectively (I. Mendelsohn, "State Slavery in Ancient Palestine," *BASOR* 85 (1942): 14; cf. I. Mendelsohn, "On Corvée Labor in Ancient Canaan and Israel," *BASOR* 167 (1962): 31–35).

[114] Gerald Klingbeil remarks that the term "does not seem to refer to formal slavery" (*NIDOTTE*, 992).

of subserviency and service. In the case of the former, we already listed the kinds of

services that עֶבֶד would render to a superior.[115] In the case of the latter, the types of

services include participating in building projects (Exod 1:11; 1 Kgs 9:15) and providing

lumber (1 Kgs 5:13). The point, then, is that whether עֶבֶד in Gen. 9:25 is substantially

different from מַס, both the progenitor and his seed were nevertheless subjected to a

condition of subserviency and service.

Setting aside the fact that the subjection of the Canaanites to servitude fell short of

Yahweh's requirement of total annihilation (Deut 7:2), this shared experience of

servitude should lead us to accept the possibility of a futuristic connection, however

remote, between the curse of Canaan and the later subordination of Canaanites. Such a

connection, if admitted, allows for the possibility that the outworking of the Noachian

curse utterance was indeed transgenerational.[116] If so, then "Canaan" in 9:25 ought to be

perceived representatively. In other words, "Canaan" is a figure of speech, which could

be classified as a metonymy of cause,[117] or more preferably, a synecdoche of part for

whole since the latter category is designed for generically related ideas as is the case here.

The "whole," we should point out, does not refer to the rest of Ham's family or the

Hamites in general.[118]

---

[115] See pp. 90, ch. 3.

[116] We prefer to regard the connection between the Gen 9:25 and Canaanite subordination as transgenerational rather than etymological. If etymology is understood as basis or rationale, then the etymology of the Canaanite dispossession and enslavement is clearly the Abrahamic covenant with its promise of the land (cf. Gen 15:16, 18).

[117] Ross, "The Table of Nations in Genesis," 317.

[118] See the discussion of the "Ham" view under "history of interpretation" for the enumeration of the various proponents of the position that the object of the curse was either the rest of Ham's family or the Hamites in general (chap. 2, pp. 34–45).

If "Canaan" is representative, are "Japheth" and "Shem" similarly representative? We hold that they are for the following reasons. First, being the primordial family of the postdiluvian generation, Noah and his sons function representatively in the same way that their primeval counterparts, Adam and Eve, functioned during the antediluvian period. For instance, just as the punishments of Adam and Eve (Gen 3:16–17) are transgenerational, so is the placement of the dread of Noah and his children on creatures (Gen 9:2). Second, Genesis 9:19 and the Table of Nations (Gen 10) depict the sons of Noah as postdiluvian progenitors. Third, the possibility that the accompanying maledictive utterance spans beyond the time of Canaan suggests that the blessing utterances may also constitute a futuristic dimension.

Analysis of the blessing utterance (vv. 26–27)

The blessing utterance consists of five parts, which correspond to the two cola (26a, 26b) of the first line and the three cola (27aα, 27aβ, 27b) of the second line. The first part constitutes a God-oriented blessing.

A survey of the blessing utterances that commence with בָּרוּךְ reveals three basic syntactical patterns. One pattern constitutes a human utterer and man or an inanimate item as the entity being blessed.[119] The second pattern constitutes God as the utterer and a

---

[119] Cf. Gen 27:29, 33; Deut 27:14; 28:3, 4 [object = fruit of the womb etc], 5 [object = basket etc], 6; 33:20; 1 Sam 25:33a (object = sense); 33b; 26:25 Jer 20:14 (object = day; object); Ps 118:26; Prov 5:18 (object = fountain); Ruth 2:19; Deut 33:24; Num 24:9.

There are instances in this category when God is depicted as the agent of blessing via a לְ preposition (cf. Gen 14:19; Exod. 18:10; Judg 17:2; 1 Sam 15:13; 23:21; 2 Sam 2:5; Ps 115:15; Ruth 2:20; 3:10). NRSV erroneously depicts Shem in Gen. 9:26, as the person being blessed and God as the agent of blessing. The pattern where God is the agent and person being blessed is man is marked by a לְ of agent. There exists no לְ in Gen. 9:26.

human being as the entity being blessed.[120] The third pattern constitutes a human utterer and God as the entity that is receives the blessing.

The utterance in Gen 9:26 best matches the third pattern since the utterer there is Noah, a human being, and the entity that receives the blessing is יַהְוֶה.[121] In the majority of the examples under this pattern, the reason God is blessed is either deducible from the context (Ps 41:13; 72:18; 135:21; 144:1; 1 Chr 16:36; 29:10) or is explicitly marked by some causal marker. Such markers include אֲשֶׁר,[122] כִּי (Ps 28:6; 31:22), and ו conjunction (Zech 11:5). In the case of Gen 9:26a, no causal markers exist. The absence of the causal markers, however, does not automatically rule out the presence of a reason for, as evidenced by certain examples above, the reason is at times derivable from the context.

So is there a contextually derivable reason for the blessing utterance of 26a? We suggest that there is based on the genitival term שֵׁם after the construct form אֱלֹהֵי.[123] In and of itself, this genitival construction is best classified as relational and therefore highlights the relationship between Yahweh Elohim and Shem.[124] Over and above the relational

---

[120] Num 22:12; Isa 19:25; Jer 17:7.

[121] Nzash Lumeya ("The Curse on Ham's Descendants: Its Missiological Impact on Zairian Mbala Mennonite Brethren" [Ph.D. diss., Fuller Theological Seminary, 1988], 71) and Westermann (*Genesis 1-11,* 493) are probably right when they characterize the utterance here as a doxology for a doxology, by definition, is "an utterance expressing pleasure in or thanksgiving for some event or occurrence."

[122] Gen 14:20; 24:27; 1 Sam 25:32, 39; 2 Sam 18:28; 22:47 (cf. Ps 18:46; 68:35); 1 Kgs 1:48; 5:21 (cf. 2 Chr 2:11); 8:15 (cf. 2 Chr 6:4), 56; 10:9; Ps 66:20; 68:20; 72:19; 89:53; 106:48; 119:21; 124:6; Ruth 4:14; Ezra 7:27.

[123] To this end we are in agreement with Cassuto who holds the opinion that the reason for the blessing is deducible in the phrase אֱלֹהֵי שֵׁם. The verse, according to him, is to be understood as ascribing thanksgiving and praise to YHWH "who guided Shem in the good and taught him to conduct himself with decency and all other virtues" (Cassuto, *From Noah to Abraham,* 166).

[124] Overall this construction involving הלהים linked to a proper name via a construct relationship appears 259 times. In three-fourth of those instances the genitive is "Israel." Other people groups that are linked to הלהים are the Philistines (Judg 10:6), the Sidonians (1 Kgs 11:5, 33). At times the genitive is a region, e.g. Egypt (Exod 12:12; Jer 43:12, 13), Aram (Judg 10:6), Damascus, Jerusalem, Moab

97

function, the construction certainly looks forward to the inclusion of Shem in the chosen line that began with Noah, continued through Seth, included Noah and now Shem and was followed by Abraham ending with the Messiah (cf. Gen 10:11–32; Matt 1:1–16). At the same time, it may be that within a blessing environment the construction looks back to Shem's noble dealing with his father Noah.

The second part constitutes an utterance that approximates the curse utterance of 25b. The difference is that the verb here is a jussive (יְהִי) as opposed to an imperfect (יִהְיֶה), the predicate nominative עֶבֶד is devoid of a superlative genitive, and the indirect object is a suffixed pronoun (מוֹ) as opposed to a noun (אָחִים). Each of these differences require further analysis if the phrase is to be fully comprehended.

Beginning with the suffixed pronoun, what is its antecedent? Is it the construct אֱלֹהֵי or the genitive שֵׁם? Reliance on syntax alone does not yield an unequivocal response. Because the suffix can be parsed as either singular (e.g. Isa 53:8; 44:15) or plural (e.g. Hab 2:7), either the plural form אֱלֹהֵי or the singular proper name שֵׁם can serve as the antecedent. Additionally there is evidence of both constructs (e.g. 2 Kgs 23:19)[125] and genitives (e.g. Ezek 13:16)[126] serving as antecedents. Contextual considerations, however, introduce the needed clarity. Since Gen 9:26b is an echo or

---

(Judg 10:6; 1 Kgs 11:33), Ekron (2 Kgs 1:2, 3, 6, 16) Sidon (Judg 10:6), Jerusalem (2 Chr 32:19), Hamath (2 Kgs 18:34; Isa 36:19), Sepharvaim (2 Kgs 17:31; 18:34; Isa 36:19), Damascus (2 Chr 28:23), Edom (2 Chr 25:20). As here, the genitive is at times a name of an individual, e.g. Abraham (Gen 26:24; 28:13; 31:42, 53; Exod 3:6, 15, 16; 4:5; 1 Kgs 18:36; Ps 47:9; 1 Chr 29:18; 30:6), Elijah (2 Kgs 2:14), Jacob (Exod 3:6, 15; 4:5; 2 Sam 23:1; Isa 2:3; Mic 4:2; Ps 20:1; 46:7, 11; 75:9; 76:6; 81:1, 4, 8; 94:7), Hezekiah (2 Chr 32:17), Isaac (Gen 28:13; Exod 3:6, 15; 4:5), Nahor (Gen 31:53) and David (2 Kgs 20:5; Isa 38:5; 2 Chr 21:12; 34:3).

[125] The antecedent of the masculine plural suffixed pronoun הֶם is the construct form בָּתֵּי.

[126] The antecedent of the feminine singular suffixed pronoun ה is the genitive form יְרוּשָׁלָ͏ִם.

*ceterum censeo*[127] of v. 25b, where the entities whom Canaan will serve as a slave are clearly not divine or deity, the only conclusion that we can come to is that the form which best serves as the antecedent is not the construct, which is divine, but the genitive.[128] Thus a translation that seeks to identify the antecedent of the suffix would read: "Let Canaan serve as a slave of Shem."

Turning now to the substitution of the jussive (יְהִי) for the imperfect (יִהְיֶה), the switch denotes the utterer's representation of enslavement mentioned in v. 25b as a blessing for Shem. In other words, Shem's blessings come in the form of Canaan serving him. As for the predicate nominative, it may be that superlativeness is not so much the issue as is the fact that Canaan(ites) will be enslaved by the Shem(ites) and Japheth(ites).

The third part commences with the *hapax* verbal form יַפְתְּ about which three aspects have to be determined. First, we must determine its root. Of the three options offered by the history of interpretation, the most unlikely one is Targum Jonathan's יפה ("to beautify") since its third person singular form corresponding to the third person *pluralis majestatis* subject, אֱלֹהִים, lacks the ת that we see in יַפְתְּ.[129] Either of the two remaining options— פתה I ("to be simple minded") and its homonym פתה II ("to be

---

[127] We borrow this term from Delitzsch without accepting his conclusion that the suffix ought to be parsed as a plural based on the parallelism between the suffix and the plural noun towards the end of v. 25 (Delitzsch, *A New Commentary on Genesis*, 295).

[128] The failure by Ibn Ezra to appeal to context and to recognize that the number of the pronominal suffix need not be only plural leads him to the awkward conclusion that the recipients of Canaan's servitude are both Sham and God

[129] The only time ת would appear in (I־II פ ( = non-ת)–III-ה) or in a III ה form in general is in the second or first person perfect singular. But even then the *tau* appears with a contiguous י, which is not the case in יפת.

wide")[130]— would qualify as the root since the form exhibits the required *tau* in its third person singular form.

The second issue is the conjugation of יַפְתְּ. It is most certainly a jussive due to the absence of the *waw* consecutive, apocopation of the final ה, and the retraction of the *mahpak* accent. As to the stem, the /a/ class vowel under the preformative strongly suggests a hiphil.

The third issue is which of the two meanings of the homonymous root apply to Gen 9:27. In other words, should the form יַפְתְּ be traced back to פתה I or פתה II? Two basic conditions have to be met by the root of choice. First, it has to comport with the thrust of vv. 26–26. More precisely, the root has to carry a positive meaning befitting a blessing utterance. Second, the root of choice has to correlate well with v. 27aβ.

Starting with the issue of positivity, there are certain meanings of the root פתה I that could not possibly meet the first condition due to their negative connotation. For instance, the meaning "seduce" in Deut 11:16 (cf. Exod 22:16), "deceive" in 2 Sam 3:25 (cf. Ezek 14:9; Prov 24:28), "coax" in Judg 14:15 (cf. 16:5), "entice" in 1 Kgs 22:20 (cf. 21, 22; Jer 20:7, 10; Job 31:9, 27; Prov 1:10; 16:29), "to be simple minded" in Hos 7:11 (cf. Job 5:2) or "flatter" in Ps 78:36, all carry negative connotations and thus fail to meet the required condition of positivity. However, not all meanings of the root carry a negative connotation. Meanings such as "allure" in Hos 2:16 (Heb) or "persuade" in Prov

---

[130] Lexicons and dictionaries that recognize the homonymity of the root I פ–II ת–III ה include: BDB, 834; *Wilhelm Gesenius' Hebräisches und Aramäisches Handwörterbuch über das Alte Testament*, ed. Frants Buhl, 17th ed. (Berlin: Springer, 1962), 666; R. Mosis, "פתה," in *TDOT*, 164; *HALOT* 3:985; Max Wagner, *Die lexikalischen und grammatikalischen Aramaismen im Altestamentlichen Hebräisch*, BZAW, ed. Georg Fohrer, vol. 96 (Berlin: Alfred Töpelmann, 1966), 97. Luther, on the contrary, did not exhibit awareness of the homonymity. He thought the root of "to enlarge" was פתה.

25:15 do have an element of positivity. Considering this positivity, the root פתה I would

have to be retained as a possible candidate in the determination of the meaning of יַפְתְּ.

Turning to the root פתה II, its Aramaic derivative, פתי, carries a positive meaning

in most of its occurrences. Some of the occurrences are found in *Targum Neophyti*[131] and

include, among others, TN's rendering of Gen 26:22, ואמר ארום כען אפתי ייי לן ("and

said: 'Because now the Lord has made room for us'"),[132] Exod 34:24, ואפתי ית תחומכון ("I

will enlarge your borders "),[133] and Deut 33:20, ואמר בריך מן דאפתי דכומה דגד (" and he

said: 'Blessed be he who has enlarged the territory of Gad'").[134] Another occurrence is

Targum Onkelos' rendering of Gen 9:27, which reads: יפתי . . . ליפת ("may the Lord

enlarge Japheth").[135] Considering the positive meaning of פתה II, we must also retain it as

a possible root of choice. With the possibility that either root meets the qualification, we

now need to establish which of them satisfies the second condition, viz., correlating with

v. 27aβ. To make this determination we must bring to bear the meaning of v. 27aβ.

---

[131] The listing of passages can be found in Michael Sokoloff, *A Dictionary of Jewish Palestinian Aramaic of the Byzantine Period*. 2d ed. (Ramat Gan, Jerusalem: Bar Ilan University Press, 2002), 455.

[132] Alejandro Díez Macho, *Neophyti I: Targum Palestinense Ms de la Bibliotheca Vaticana*, trans. Martin McNamara and Michael Maher, vol. 1 (Génesis), Textos y estudios, ed. Federico Peréz Castro (Madrid: Consejo Superior de Investigaciones Científicas, 1968), 161.

[133] Alejandro Díez Macho, *Neophyti I: Targum Palestinense Ms de la Bibliotheca Vaticana*, trans. Martin McNamara and Michael Maher, vol. 2 (Éxodo), Textos y estudios, ed. Federico Peréz Castro (Madrid: Consejo Superior de Investigaciones Científicas, 1970), 231.

[134] Alejandro Díez Macho, *Neophyti I: Targum Palestinense Ms de la Bibliotheca Vaticana*, trans. Martin McNamara and Michael Maher, vol. 5 (Deuteronomio), Textos y estudios, ed. Federico Peréz Castro (Madrid: Consejo Superior de Investigaciones Científicas, 1978), 291.

[135] *Targum Onkelos to Genesis: A Critical Analysis Together with an English Translation of the Text (Based on A. Sperber's Edition)*, trans. Moses Aberbach and Bernard Grossfield (Denver: KTAV Publishing House, 1982), 69.

We must first determine the subject of the clause. History of interpretation offers two choices: Elohim, the subject of the previous clause, or Japheth, the object of the preposition in the previous clause.[136] A search for all the occurrences of the syntactical pattern *imperfect followed by noun followed by preposition followed by proper noun followed by waw conjunction followed by imperfect* yields a total of 56 usages, a majority of which the subject of the previous clause continue to serve as the subject of the next clause (cf. Gen 12:7,18; 17:1; Exod 5:22; 10:24; Num 22:9; 23:16; Judg 9:20, 50; 1 Sam 15:13; 16:8 etc). Were it not for the existence of instances in which the object of the preposition in the previous clause serves as the subject of the next clause (cf. Gen 30:17; 39:2; Num 23:4; Judg 1:19; 1 Sam 3:4; 12:18; 24:23; 2 Sam 5:23; 17:6; Isa 19:21; Hos 5:13; 1 Chr 21:21), we could confidently conclude, on the basis of syntax alone, that the subject of Gen 9: 27b is Elohim. Clearly the search results are sufficiently mixed as to render syntax an ambiguous means of determining the subject of v. 27aβ. Since syntax cannot be relied on to make this determination, we should look to the meaning of the phrase "dwell in the tents of" for clues.

Besides Gen 9:27aβ, the idea of "dwelling in the tents" is represented a total of five times. In four of those usages, the phrase appears in conjunction with the בְּ preposition (Judg 8:11; Ps 78:55; Job 11:14; 18:15) and in the last instance the preposition עִם is utilized (Ps 120:5). In none of these instances does God appear as the subject of the verb. Now, does the fact that God is never the subject in these instances automatically rule out the possibility that God would be the subject in Gen 9:27aβ? We do not think so. Even though God is not depicted as the subject in these instances, there

---

[136] See "history of interpretation" (chap. 2, pp. 49–51).

are sufficient citations in which God is depicted as the subject of the verb. For example, He is depicted as dwelling on Mt. Sinai (Exod 24:16), in the midst of his people Israel (Exod 25:8; 29:45, 46; Num 5:3; Ezek 43:9 etc), and on Mt. Zion (Isa 8:18; Ps 74:2). If the concept of dwelling in the tent does not, in and of itself, rule out God as subject, what else could we rely on to offer us a definitive answer as to the subject of the verb in Gen 9:27aβ? The answer is context. Context seems to favor Japheth as the subject, since he is the object of blessing in v. 27 in the same way that just Shem is the object of blessing in v. 26.

As regards the meaning of the phrase "dwell in the tents," it can connote displacement in Ps 78:55, where the initial dwellers of the tents, the nations, are dispossessed and Israel is settled in the tents in their stead. It could also refer simply to habitation (cf. Judg 8:11; Job 18:15). Lastly, the phrase carries the connotation of co-habitation in Job 11:14, where the injunction is made that wickedness not be allowed to dwell in one's tent. Of the three options, the least likely meaning of the phrase, in so far as Gen 9: 27aβ is concerned, is that of displacement since the negativity attached to the idea of displacement does not harmonize well with the positive attribute of a blessing utterance. Of the remaining two options, the more preferable meaning would be co-habitation since two parties are involved, viz., Shem and Japheth.

We now turn to the meaning of יַפְתְּ in v. 27aα. The two options are the emotional (or mental) idea of persuading someone or the spatial idea of enlarging or making room. It seems that the option of choice would be the spatial meaning, "to make room for, enlarge," since it better correlates with the spatial connotation behind the phrase "dwelling in the tents."

The last of the five parts constituting the blessing utterance (v. 27b) echoes v. 26b. As was in the case of v. 26b, we are here also faced with the question of the number and antecedent of the pronominal suffix מוֹ. Is the suffixed pronoun singular or plural? Is the antecedent the absolute שֵׁם (Shem) in the preceding clause or the subject יֶפֶת (Japheth) of the preceding clause? Whether the suffixed pronoun is parsed as singular or plural depends on its antecedent. The determination of the antecedent in turn depends not on whether the absolute or the subject of the preceding clause elsewhere serves as the antecedent, but on what the context suggests.[137] Assuming that our conclusion concerning the antecedent of מוֹ in v. 26b being Shem is correct, it makes better sense that the antecedent of מוֹ in v. 27b is Japheth, since v. 27 focuses on Japheth.

In summary, the blessing utterance constitutes five parts. The first part is a blessing with God as the object. The reason for the blessing is not explicitly stated. The association of God's name with Shem both highlights Shem's noble reaction and looks forward to the inclusion of Shem in the messianic line. The second part is a re-representation of the curse utterance of v. 25 in blessing terms. The third part calls for spatial blessings on behalf of Japheth. The fourth part petitions for the co-habitation of Shem and Japheth. The last part parallels the second part in its re-representation of the curse utterance in blessing terms. The individual that is to be the beneficiary of Canaan's enslavement this time is Japheth.

---

[137] Examples of instances when the absolute in the preceding clause serves as the antecedent of a pronominal suffix include Deut 5:1, 29:1, 1 Sam 17:8, and 2 Chr 15:2. Examples of instances when the subject of the preceding clause serves as the antecedent include Gen 21:21, 26:25, and Num 17:21.

## Summary

Our goal in this section was to conduct a contextual exegesis of Gen 9:18–27 with a particular emphasis on the nature of the offense and the meaning of Noah's words. We began by determining both the primary and secondary contexts of our pericope. Our conclusion was: (a) the primary contextual parameters of Gen 9:18–29 constitute the whole of the *Urgeschichte*, which spans the first eleven chapters of the book; and (b) the secondary context of the pericope spans not just the *Vatergeschichte*, but also the rest of the Pentateuch if not the whole Tanakh. In either case, the basis of the conclusions was the existence of thematic or literary linkages. In the case the relationship between our text and the *Urgeschichte*, the connectors include the phrase "went out of the ark," the partial genealogical formula at the end of Gen 9, repeated phrases (e.g. "be fruitful and multiply, and fill the earth," and "image of God").

Second, we discussed the role of vv. 18–19 and its contribution to the overall understanding of the nature of the offense and the meaning of Noah's words. One function of the two verses is to supply the reader with the listings of individuals who will constitute the story that is about to unfold. The fact that no female is mentioned stands in the way of a sexual (incest) understanding of Ham's action. Another function of the two verses is to foreground Canaan so the reader does not need to ask the question, "and who is Canaan," when he or she comes to vv. 25–29.

Third, we analyzed Noah's state prior to the offense committed against him. He starts off as drunk, an aftermath of his engagement in viticulture probably for the first time. This is not to say that he was a pioneering viticulturist. Genesis 9:20 does not offer any clue whatsoever that would allow us to read etiology. Additionally, there is evidence

105

that the practice of winemaking predates Noah. Next, the drunkenness brings rise to self-exposure. The *wayyiqtol* form of גלה preceded by the *wayyiqtol* form of שׁכר clarifies the consequential relationship of the two acts of drunkenness and self-stripping. We should reiterate that as shameful as Noah's condition of drunkenness and nakedness was, the passage is not accusatorial towards him. The drunkenness is attributed to his ignorance of the inebriating effect of wine. The self-exposure occurred in the privacy of his tent.

Fourth, we studied Ham's two-fold action and his siblings' reaction. We chose to reserve any discussion on the validity of the various readings of Ham's actions and his siblings' reaction for the next chapter. Instead we stayed with syntactical analysis.

Lastly, we examined in great detail the words of Noah. The curse utterance follows a formula where the item being cursed is represented by a noun (Canaan), the justification for the curse is explicitly stated, and the imperfect (יִהְיֶה) is employed to describe the manner in which the curse will manifest itself. A search for answers on three aspects of the curse revealed the following. Regarding the question of the meaning and nature of עֶבֶד עֲבָדִים, the meaning is clearly servitude and the nature of it is made manifest in Canaanite servitude to Israel. Concerning the meaning of אָח in the phrase לְאֶחָיו; it is clearly "brothers" in the loose sense of the term. Specifically "brothers," here, refer to the Shemites and the Japhethites, the beneficiaries of Canaan's servitude. As for the object of the curse, it is clearly Canaan; not as an individual, though, but as a people group. The blessing utterance follows the pattern where the utterer is a human and God is the entity that receives the blessing. The utterance calls for spatial blessings on behalf of Japheth and petitions for the co-habitation of Shem and Japheth.

CHAPTER 4

CRITIQUE OF VIEWS RELATED TO GEN 9:18–29

Considering that this book is essentially a critique, it is here that the reader will

find a critique of each of six major views related either to the nature of Ham's offense or

Noah's utterances. Those views are: (1) understandings of Noah's state of nakedness, (2)

various literal understandings of Ham's offense, (3) various sexual understandings of

Ham's offense, (4) understandings of the siblings' reaction, (5) proposed fulfillments of

the curse, and (6) proposed fulfillments of the blessing. Subsumed under these six views

are a total of thity-one subviews.

### Evaluation of the Understanding of Noah's Nakedness
### in Either Literal or Sexual Terms

To make the determination as to whether the scene surrounding the nakedness

incident ought to be understood in either literal or sexual terms requires an exegetical

interaction with two literary elements, viz., the verb גלה and the ה at the end of the

locative term אָהֳלֹה. In other words, the two questions that we have to answer are: (a)

Does the verb imply more than just nakedness? (b) Does the suffixed ה connote that

Noah's wife was present in the tent?

The Verb גלה (v. 21) Carries a Sexual Connotation

Brunk perceives a sexual connotation in this verbal form. If the intention was to

relay the mere idea of removing clothes, he argues, the author could have employed

either the niphal stem or the verb פשט (cf. 1 Sam 18:4). He then concludes by opining

107

that, due to the intimate nature of the subject, the writer of Genesis was communicating

in a subtle way that Noah was removing his clothes in preparation for having sexual

relations with his wife.[1]

Rejecting a non-sexual meaning of גלה is really an argument *ex silentio*. There is

no clear-cut evidence that the hithpael form carries a sexual meaning. Its meaning in Prov

18:2, the only other occurrence, is definitely non-sexual. The Proverbs passage speaks of

the fool exposing his heart or thoughts.

The Suffixed ה (v. 21) Indicates the Presence
of Noah's Wife

The sexual interpretation reads the ה as a third person feminine singular suffix.

One argument against the feminine reading is that it goes against the suggested *Qere*

reading, viz., third person masculine singular suffix.[2] Secondly, if the vowel at the end

were really paragogic, the vocalization of the noun would have remained the same, i.e.,

אֹהֶל. Third, reading the feminine suffix introduces a syntactically unknown referent.

**Evaluation of Literal Understandings
of Ham's Offense**

There are three views on the nature of Ham's offense that fit the label "literal."

They are: (a) perceiving the offense as volitionally looking at Noah's nakedness; (b)

treating Noah irreverently by mocking him, jeering at him, or laughing at him; and (c)

Ham disclosing the nakedness of his father to his brothers rather than covering up the

nakedness.

---

[1] William A. Brunk, "The Action of Ham against Noah: Its Nature and Result (Genesis 9:18–27)" (M.Div. thesis, Western Conservative Baptist Seminary, 1988), 59–60.

[2] As pointed out by the Masora Magna, the Qere-Kethiv phenomenon surrounding the form אָהֳלֹה occurs elsewhere in Gen 12:8; 13:3; 35:21.

## The Offense as Volitionally Looking at
## the Father's Nakedness

As already stated, this is the opinion held by BDB.[3] Indeed, a good portion of the examples cited by BDB alongside Gen 9:22 comprise one or two internal clues that allow us undoubtedly to conclude that the act of seeing was indeed purposeful or intentional. Such clues include a *lamed* of purpose (Gen 42:9, 12; 1 Kgs 9:12), an indirect volitive (Josh 2:1), and the idea of an individual appearing before a priest following a detection of leprosy symptoms (Lev 13:3, 5, 15; 14:36). However, this is not the case with Gen 9:22. Its context does not offer any hint that Ham entered the tent with the intention of viewing his father naked. If anything, it is the siblings who would have been at fault if, having been informed by Ham that their father was naked, they had not taken the necessary precaution to avoid looking at his nakedness. As such, the volitional understanding of ראה is less preferable than the opposite understanding of it as accidental or unintentional.[4]

Disagreeing with BDB means embracing the alternative view, viz., the seeing was actually accidental and therefore an innocent act.[5] Additionally, not regarding Ham's first act as the offense suggests that the offense lay with the second act.

## The Offense as Unfilial Irreverence

Whether the reporting amounted to jeering, laughing or mockery is mere conjecture and speculation. The text does not offer a hint of either the motive or the

---

[3] BDB, 907.

[4] Cf. Barnabe Assohoto and Samuel Ngewa, "Genesis," in *ABC*, ed. Tokunboh Adeyemo (Nairobi, Kenya: WordAlive Publishers, 2006), 25.

[5] Calvin Goodspeed and D. M. Welton, *The Book of Genesis*, An American Commentary on the Old Testament (Philadelphia: American Baptist Publication Society, 1909), 96.

format of the reporting. The text's interest is simply to place the divulgence in negative light.

### The Offense as Disclosure of Rather than Covering Up
### Noah's Nakedness

Whether or not Ham's reporting to his siblings about the nakedness of their father was offensive depends on the siblings' reaction to the reporting since a sure way of evaluating the offensiveness of an action or lack of action is the reaction of the affected individual(s). For instance, David's reaction to the messenger's report of Saul's death clearly conveys his displeasure with the messenger's report (2 Sam 4:10).[6] In order to evaluate Ham's reporting, we must take a close look at the reaction of his siblings.

By this depiction of the siblings' reaction as contrary or a literary foil to Ham's actions, the author suggests how Ham should have responded in lieu. Rather than reporting (וַיַּגֵּד) the nakedness of his father, Ham, like his siblings, should have covered his nakedness instead. Indeed, the overall scriptural discussion of nakedness confirms that Ham's choice to broadcast the news about his father's nudity, rather than cover it, went counter to biblical expectation.[7]

According to OT's depiction of nakedness, were it not that the Fall transpired, nudity would have forever remained outside the realm of human consciousness, eternally disassociated from feelings of shame (cf. Gen 2:25), and constantly perceived as normal. As it is, the Fall brought with it an awareness of being unclothed accompanied by

---

[6] Cf. Gen 12:18; 31:20; 43:6; Lev 5:1; Josh 2:14, 20; 7:19; Judg 14:16; 16:15; 1 Sam 20:9; 22:22; 27:11; 2 Sam 4:10.

[7] Indeed, the expectation within the ANE as reflected in the Ugaritic royal epic "the Aqhat legend" was that the son would protect the drunken father from shame. The epic specifically instructs the son "to take his (father's) hand when he is drunk, to bear him up when he is filled with wine" (CTA 17, 1:30).

feelings of shame that were manifested in the first couple's frail attempt to shroud their nakedness (3:7). Henceforth, to be found unclothed would be rendered an abnormal condition that required hiding.

While nakedness throughout the rest of Scriptures continues to be regarded as abnormal, treatment varies depending on whether the exposure is avoidable or beyond the control of the individual. Avoidable nudity is addressed in non-neutral terms. Thus the Covenant Code prohibits the mounting of steps while approaching the altar to avoid exposure (Exod 20:26) and calls on inclusion of linen undergarments as part of the priestly dressing for the same reason (28:42). Unintentional nakedness, on the hand, is noted with neutrality. Examples of nakedness for which the individual cannot be faulted are the Spirit-induced naked condition of Saul (1 Sam 19:24) and the naked state in which man emerges from the womb and departs from this life (Job 1:21; cf. Eccl 5:15).

The appropriate response by one towards an individual whose state of nakedness is beyond his control is to cover him or her. Yahweh illustrates this kind of response. When He comes across Jerusalem in a state of nakedness, He covers her (Ezek 16:7,8; cf. Hos 2:9). When man responds thus, it is touted as an act of righteousness (Ezek 18:7, 16; cf. Isa 58:7; 2 Chr 28:15; Tobit 1:17; 4:16). Acting to the contrary, as in the case of one stripping the poor of their clothing, is condemned as wicked (Job 22:6).

Different from avoidable nudity and unintentional exposure is nakedness imposed by Yahweh as a measure of judgment against sin. This category is unlike avoidable nakedness since it is not necessarily prohibited. It is unlike unintentional nakedness since its covering is not called for and it has an aura of negativity. Such imposition of nakedness, or more accurately the potentiality of it, as acted out by certain prophets (Isa

20:2; Micah 1:8), is intended to shame (Isa 20:4; 47:3; Nah 3:5), and is directed against Israel (Deut 28:48; Hos 2:3; Amos 2:16; Ezek 16:37, 39), Egypt and Ethiopia (Isa 20:3), Babylon (Isa 47:3), and Assyria (Nah 3:5).

The Qumran community holds similar perspectives on avoidable and divinely imposed nakedness.[8] For example, Qumran's *Rule of the Community* calls for the punishment of needless self-exposure (1 QS 7:13–14), while the *War Scroll* records a prohibition against immodest nakedness (1QM 7:7, 10, cf. 4Q491 1:1–3:8). As regards divinely imposed nakedness, the *pesher* on Hosea interprets the goal of the exposure as that of shaming and disgracing (4Q166: 8–12).

The NT continues the OT perspectives on nakedness. There nakedness is associated with shame, and avoidable nakedness is to be covered. Thus the church of Laodicea is counseled to buy white robes to clothe herself and to keep the shame of her nakedness from being seen (Rev 3:18). Those who stay clothed as opposed to "going about naked and exposed to shame" are blessed (16:15).

As in the OT, unintentional nakedness receives mention. Its inducers include want (Math 25:36; 25:44), arrest (Mark 14:52), an evil spirit (Acts 19:16), and persecution (2 Cor 11:27). In each of these cases, the nakedness is addressed in neutral terms. Responding to unintentional nakedness by covering is lauded and marks out the righteous (Matt 25:36, 38). On the other hand, failing to cover it is judged negatively. Such failure is tantamount to faith without works (James 2:15) and marks out those destined for eternal damnation (Matt 25:43).

---

[8] Niehr, *TDOT*, 349.

When viewed through the lens of the overall scriptural data on nakedness, Ham's failure to cover his father's nakedness seems to have been a violation of the expectation to cover up unintentional nakedness. Noah's nakedness was unintentional in the sense that it was wine-induced. The appropriate response in such a case would have been for the one who came across the naked person to have covered him in the same way that Yahweh covered the nakedness of Jerusalem upon catching sight of it (Ezek 16:7, 8; cf. Hos 2:9).

Thus, to answer the question concerning the appropriateness or inappropriateness of Ham's reporting, the fact that the author pairs the reporting with the covering of nakedness suggests a negative evaluation of the former and the commendation of the latter.

## Evaluation of Sexual Understandings
## of Ham's Offense

It is true that the phrase constituting the verb ראה and the construct form עֶרְוַת appears in Lev. 20:17 laden with sexual connotations. The determination that the phrase carries a sexual meaning is based on the following two contextual indicators: (a) the verb לקח, which usually appears in conjunction with a male and a female, marks the establishment of a marital relationship;[9] and (b) the phrase appearing towards the end of the verse, constituting the piel form of גלה, a human male subject, and the construct עֶרְוַת, euphemistically marks a sexual act.[10] Not all occurrences of the phrase, however, carry the literal sexual meaning. For instance, a literal sexual understanding of the phrase as it

---

[9] Cf. Gen 24:61; Exod 6:20; Lev 21:13, etc.

[10] In the majority of the times, the subject is a male and in all these instances the meaning is certainly sexual (cf. Lev 18: 6–19; 20:18-21, etc.).

appears in Ezek 16:37 (cf. Isa 47:3) is negated by the contextual presentation of God as the subject of the verb "to uncover." God's uncovering could not possibly be thought to connote a literal sexual overture; the uncovering is best understood as an extended metaphor.

Based on the phrase's varied senses, it is clear that the real determinant of meaning is not the phrase *per se*, but the context. In other words, whether or not the phrase carries the same meaning in two contexts depends on the similarity or dissimilarity of the contexts.

## The Offense as Incest

It is exactly on this question of identicalness or difference of context that the "incest" reading by Brunk and Bassett is found wanting. As already indicated, the view that the phrase עֶרְוַת . . . ראה in Gen 9:22 denotes an incestuous act hinges on the assumption that Gen 9:22 and both Lev 20:17 and Lev. 18 (vv. 7, 8, 14, 16) share the same context in as far as parallelism is concerned. In our opinion, if there is any resemblance, it is between Gen 9:22 and Lev 20:17—not between Gen 9:22 and Lev 18. The parallel phrase is ראה . . . עֶרְוַת. The similitude, however, is strictly phraseological, not contextual. No contextual indicators such as those tied to Lev 20:17 and which clue the reader to conclude that incest is in view there—no such contextual indicators are present in Gen 9:22. Unlike Lev 20:17, the characters in Gen 9:22 are all males. We have already argued elsewhere that the ה at the end of the locative phrase בְּתוֹךְ אָהֳלֹה (v. 21) does not denote the presence of Noah's wife in the scene. The concept of גלה . . . עֶרְוַת ("uncovering a person's nakedness"), present in Lev. 20:17 (cf. Ezek 22:10), is absent altogether in Gen. 9:22. True, the preceding verse (v. 21) speaks of uncovering. But the

114

uncovering in view there is not that of an individual uncovering the nakedness of another

individual. The uncovering involves only Noah (v. 21) who engages in self-uncovering.

In view of the absence of any contextual indicators that would clue us to read the phrase

in Gen 9:22 as indicating incest, we have no option but to conclude that the "incest"

reading is erroneous.

## The Offense as Homosexuality

If our dismissal of the "incest" reading is convincing, is the homosexual[11]

understanding in any way whatsoever preferable? In terms of its argumentation, the

homosexual interpretation stands or falls with the incest reading since both appeal to the

same Leviticus passages. The only difference is that whereas the latter zeroes in on those

passages that carry the formula "uncovering the nakedness of X. . . the nakedness of Y"

(e.g. Lev 18:7, 8), the former makes the formula "X . . . uncovering the nakedness of Y"

(e.g. Lev 20:17, 18) the cornerstone of its rationale. Either way the supposed parallelism

between these two sets of passages and Gen 9:22 is erroneous.

Additionally, Robertson's argument that the phrase וַיֵּדַע אֵת אֲשֶׁר־עָשָׂה־לוֹ (v. 24b)

lends itself towards a homosexual understanding is not all that convincing.[12] The fallacy

of this argument rests in its implication that the expression "doing something to

someone" can only refer to a bodily act. There is no doubt that the expression does carry

such a meaning. Examples of such bodily acts include disfigurement (Lev 24:19), being

thrown into a cistern (Jer 38:9), being spat on (Deut 25:9), and rape (Judg 19:24; Gen

---

[11] Proponents include O. Palmer Robertson, "Current Critical Questions Concerning the 'Curse of Ham'," *JETS* 41 [1998], 179; and Anthony Phillips, "Uncovering the Father's Skirt," *VT* 1 (1980): 38–43.

[12] Robertson opines that Noah would not have remembered what had been done to him if all it was was Ham looking at his nakedness (Robertson, "Current Critical Questions Concerning the 'Curse of Ham,'" 179; cf. Brunk, "The Action of Ham against Noah: Its Nature and Result," 49).

19:8). Other times, however, the expression refers to actions that do not involve making physical contact with the object, e.g. concealing a fact (12:18), birthright theft (27:45), deception (29:25), and snubbing (Judg 8:1). Seeing that the expression can refer to both bodily acts and actions that do not involve physical contact, the onus lies with the homosexual reading to prove that the expression cannot refer to a non-contact an act such as being stared at while naked or being left uncovered while naked.

The Offense as Voyeurism

If both the incest and the homosexual reading are wanting, could the voyeuristic[13] understanding prove to be the more accurate reading? A voyeur is defined as "a person who obtains sexual gratification by looking at sexual objects or acts," or "a person who derives exaggerated or unseemly enjoyment from being an observer."[14] Since there is no textual evidence that Ham entered the tent with the intention of viewing his father's nakedness let alone the idea that he derived sexual gratification or enjoyment from looking at the nakedness of the father, it is problematic to describe his actions as voyeuristic. Our overall conclusion on the question of the nature of Ham's infraction is that it should be thought more as literal in nature and therefore non-sexual than idiomatic and therefore sexual.[15]

---

[13] Randall C. Bailey, "They're Nothing but Incestuous Bastards: The Polemical Use of Sex and Sexuality in Hebrew Canon Narratives," in *In Reading from This Place*, ed. Mary Ann Tolbert, Social Location and Biblical Interpretation in the United States, vol. 1 (Minneapolis: Fortress, 1994), 134.

[14] Sol Steinmetz, ed., *Webster's American Family Dictionary* (New York: Random House, 1989), 1045.

[15] Cf. Allen Paul Ross, "The Table of Nations in Genesis" (Ph.D. diss., Dallas Theological Seminary, 1976), 230; Clyde T. Francisco, "The Curse on Canaan," *CT* 8 (1964): 8–9; Umberto Cassuto, *From Noah to Abraham (Genesis vi. 9–xi. 32)*, trans. Israel Abrahams, A Commentary on the Book of Genesis, vol. 2 (Jerusalem: Magnes Press, 1964), 32, 152; Claus Westermann, *Genesis 1–11*, trans. John J. Scullion, Genesis: A Commentary, vol. 1 (Minneapolis: Augsburg Publishing House, 1984), 488.

## Evaluation of the Understanding of the Siblings' Reaction
## as Either Literal or Sexual

Certain proponents of the sexual reading limit their sexual understanding to

Ham's action by either admitting to the difficulty of interpreting the siblings' reaction as

similarly sexual or interpreting their action along the lines of the non-sexual reading.

O. Palmer Robertson, for instance, shows by his interpretation, that the reactions

of the siblings were, for all intents and purposes, non-sexual. According to him, "because

of the great shame associated with the action of their brother, Shem and Japheth *walked*

*backwards* into their father's tent in order to cover his shame. Due to the recentness of

the defiling action of their brother they restrain themselves from even *glancing* in the

direction of their father ... (emphasis mine)."[16]

Bassett, on the other hand, admits to the difficulty of interpreting the phrase

וַיְכַסּוּ אֵת עֶרְוַת אֲבִיהֶם sexually. But rather than change his mind about his idiomatic stance,

he dismisses the phrase as the work of a redactor who "missed the idiomatic meaning of

the tradition that Noah's son saw his father's nakedness and has added the reference to

the brothers' covering their father's nakedness with a garment."[17]

Maintaining an incestuous reading, Brunk offers the following interpretations: (a)

the antecedents of the 3mp suffixed pronoun in the form שְׁנֵיהֶם are Noah and his wife;

meaning that Shem and Japheth placed the garment not upon their own shoulders, but

rather upon the shoulders of Noah and his wife who would both have been left in the tent

in an exposed state when Ham departed; (b) the phrase וַיְכַסּוּ אֵת עֶרְוַת אֲבִיהֶם probably

---

[16] Robertson, 179.

[17] Frederick W. Bassett, "Noah's Nakedness and the Curse on Canaan: A Case of Incest?," *VT* 21 (April, 1971): 233–34.

means that the two sons covered their mother since "the nakedness of their father" is equivalent to "the nakedness of their mother"; (c) the garment belonged to Noah's wife who was the victim of Ham's attack; and (d) the disjunctive clause וְעֶרְוַת אֲבִיהֶם לֹא רָאוּ implies that, unlike Ham, the two brothers did not have sexual relationship with their mother.[18]

Brunk's interpretation that the phrase וְעֶרְוַת אֲבִיהֶם לֹא רָאוּ carries a sexual connotation can only be validated from context. As we demonstrated earlier in our evaluation of the various sexual understandings of Ham's offense, the phrase comprising "see" and "nakedness" carries both sexual and non-sexual connotation depending on the context. As far as we can tell, there is nothing in the description of the siblings' reaction that warrants a sexual reading.

### Evaluation of the Proposed Fulfillments of the Curse

We will offer a listing of the various proposals of fulfillment.[19] Each listing will be coupled with an evaluation.

#### Ham-related Proposals

*Enslavement of the Egyptians by Pharoah*

The first proposal explains the enslavement of the Egyptians by Pharaoh in terms of the curse. No doubt Egypt experienced slavery under Joseph the surrogate to Pharaoh (Gen 47:21). However, the fact still remains that the object of the curse was not Ham or his other sons like Egypt, but his grandson Canaan.

---

[18] Brunk, "The Action of Ham against Noah," 66–68.

[19] We refer the reader back to our discussion of the various proposals of fulfillment (chap. 2, pp. 30–45). There we packaged the discussion into the "Ham" view and the "Canaan" view. The former referred to the suggestions of fulfillment that were rooted on the understanding that Ham was the object of the curse. The latter stood for the suggestions that considered Canaan to have been the object of the curse.

*Triumph of Israel over Egypt*
*During the Exodus*

The second proposal regards the triumph of Israel over Egypt during the Exodus as fulfillment of the aspect of the utterance pertaining to the enslavement of Canaan by Shem. Again this proposal is unlikely because Egypt is not part of Canaanite ancestry. Moreover, the Exodus is the fulfillment of the promise of the emancipation of Israel from the "house of slavery" (Exod 13:3,14; 20:2; Deut 5:6; 6:12; 7:8; 8:14; 13:6, 11; Josh 24:17; Judg 6:8; Jer 34:13; Micah 6:4). Egypt, under Amenhotep II (1450–1425 B.C.), may have been weakened by the Exodus so much so that the king never again conducted a major incursion into the Sinai or Central Palestine.[20] But it was never weakened to the point of enslavement by any other power, let alone Israel.

*Certain Aspects of Ham's*
*Physical Make-up*

The third proposal makes the African people the center of its discussion of the fulfillment of the curse. The proposal constitutes three facets. The first facet imposes on Ham punishment of anatomical consequences with the consequences themselves being his red eyes, twisted lips, singed (curly) hair, extended prepuce, and dark skin. The other aspect of this facet is its appeal to the etymology of the name "Ham" as proof for regarding Ham as black.[21]

---

[20] Eugene H. Merrill, *Deuteronomy*, NAC, ed. E. Ray Clendenen, Kenneth A. Mathews, and David S. Dockery, vol. 4 (Nashville: Broadman & Holman, 1994), 25.

[21] Josiah Priest is one example of commentators who, on the basis of philology, argued that Ham meant "dark," "hot," and "black" (Josiah Priest, *Slavery, as It Relates to the Negro, or African Race, Examined in the Light of Circumstances, History and the Holy Scriptures; with an Account of the Origin of the Black Man's Color, Causes of His State of Servitude and Traces of His Character as Well in Ancient as in Modern Times* [Albany, New York: C. Van Benthuysen, 1843], 15–20, 27–36).

The supposed image of Ham is built out of a perspective of how an African supposedly looks and the assumption that Ham must have been African. Our contention is that no one can definitively claim that Ham resembled the African as much as the former is the stock of the latter. More certain would be the understanding that Ham resembled his parents and brothers. But who knows how the Noachian family looked like? Moreover, why must Ham be pictured as only looking like the Africans? Why would he not have looked like his other descendants such as the Canaanites or the Egyptians? But even if the assumed picture of Ham were to be granted, the mere fact that the Scriptures do not affix on him any form of punishment makes the idea that his appearance resulted from some type of punishment unfeasible.

*The Etymology of the name "Ham"*

Turning to the philological aspect of this facet, we note that there are at least three avenues by which we can arrive at the meaning of a term. One is via explicative data that would sometimes accompany a particular proper name. The proper name שִׁמְעוֹן in Gen 29:33, for instance, is preceded by data that both supply the rationale for and hint at the meaning of the name.[22] Another is by way of etymology or derivatives. The last is through the presence of other synchronically related terms.

In the case of the proper name חָם, the first avenue is unavailable by virtue of the fact that, in all of its fifteen occurrences,[23] the proper name appears unaccompanied by any type of explicative comments or expressions. The second means is available except that one has to contend with the fact there is more than one suggested derivative and

---

[22] See also Gen 25:30.

[23] Gen 5:32; 6:10; 7:13; 9:18, 22; 10:1, 6, 20; Ps 78:51; 105:23, 27; 106:22; 1 Chr 1:4, 8; 4:40.

therefore meaning. These are (a) the epithet for the Old West Semitic Sun-god, *Hammu* ("hot"), which ended up as חָם through "the loss of the case ending *–u* and loss of germination;[24] and (b) the Coptic term *Kheme* (=*Kem* in Egyptian) meaning "the black land."[25]

As much as the Psalmist refers to Egypt as the "land of Ham" (cf. Ps 105:23, 27; 106:22), the Coptic term is a less likely derivative since its development to חָם would follow the less likely path of converting one consonant into another and an "i" class vowel to an "a" class vowel.[26] The preferred choice of the possible derivative is *Hammu*. Advantageous to this choice is the feasibility of the suggested consonantal and vowel changes in the development of "Ham" from *Hammu*. Loss of gemination during the development of a noun is a well-recognized phenomenon. More frequently than not, a vowel would convert into a vowel of the same class.

The third avenue is only unavailable if one hesitates to allow for the possibility that *Hammu* would be a derivative of "Ham." On the other hand, if the possibility is admitted, then one could consider the various terms that carry the basic meaning of "hot" as fitting the rubric of related terms. These terms are חַמָּה,[27] חֹם ("heat"),[28] חָם ("warm"),[29]

---

[24] Julius Lewy, "The Old West Semitic Sun-God Hammu," *HUCA* 18 (1944): 473–76; cf. L. Hicks, "Ham," in *Interpreter's Dictionary of the Bible: An Illustrated Encyclopedia*, ed. George Arthur Buttrick (Nashville: Abingdon Press, 1962), 515; A. H. McNeile, "Ham," in *Dictionary of the Bible*, ed. John Hastings (New York: Charles Scribner's Sons, 1963), 361.

[25] W. E. Crum, *A Coptic Dictionary* (London: Oxford University Press, 1939; reprint, Oxford: Clarendon Press, 1962), 110; cf. D. S. Margoliouth, "Ham," in *A Dictionary of the Bible: Dealing with Its Language, Literature, and Contents Including the Biblical Theology*, ed. James Hasting (Edinburgh, T. & T. Clark, 1898; reprint, New York: Charles Scribner's Sons 1958), 2:288.

[26] T. G. Pinches, "Ham," in *ISBE*, ed. James Orr (Grand Rapids: Eerdmans, 1939), 1324.

[27] The 1898 edition of the Dictionary edited by Hastings relates the Arabic form *hamma* to "Ham" and interprets this Arabic form as meaning "black" [Margoliouth, "Ham," 288]. *NIDOTTE* (2:176), on the other hand, interprets the same Arabic word as "make hot" and relates it to the verb חמם. The verb itself certainly means "to be hot" (e.g., Exod 16:12; 1 Sam 11:9). Other meanings of the verb are "burning

121

and חֻם.[30] Despite being a color term, the last entry still falls under the sphere of the

concept of "being hot or warm" in the sense that "what is heated, especially anything

heated by fire, is darkened in color."[31]

Summarizing our discussion of the philological aspect of the first facet of the

proposal that makes the African people the center of its discussion of the fulfillment of

the curse, only two avenues of determining the meaning of a term are available in the

case of "Ham" (*contra* Goldenberg[32]): etymology and presence of synchronically related

---

with lust" (Isa 57:5), "being inflamed with wine" (Jer 51:39) and "being warm" (e.g. 1 Kgs 1:1; 2 Kgs 4:34).

[28] With the exception of 1 Sam 21: 6, all the other 8 occurrences (Gen 8:22; 18:1; 1 Sam 11:9, 11; 2 Sam 4:5; Isa 18:4; Jer 17:8; Job 24:19) of this form sit in a meteorological environment.

[29] The two occurrences (Josh 9:12; Job 37:17) of this form carry a non-meteorological sense.

[30] All the four occurrences of this form pertain to color of flock (Gen 30:32, 33, 35, 40).

[31] K. M. Beyse, "חמם," in *TDOT*, 475; cf. *HALOT* 1: 297; *NIDOTTE* 2:176.

[32] Basing his conclusions on discussions by Joshua Blau and J. W. Wevers pertaining to LXX transliteration of ח, Goldenberg essentially shuts down these two avenues. According to him neither the suggested etymologies nor the supposed related terms have any relationship with "Ham" since

> "none of these words begins with the letter "ḥ" as does the name Ham (*ham*) The root *ḥmm* 'to be hot' and its derived forms . . . are always written with a *ḥ* (heyth), even in those languages (Old South Arabian, Arabic, Ugaritic) that preserved the *ḥ*. Similarly *Hammu*, derived from *ḥmm*, is spelled with *ḥ* (heyth) . . . We must also reject a derivation from the Hebrew root *ḥwn* 'to be black' or 'dark.' This theory has been particularly attractive to those who see the descendants of Ham as being dark-skinned peoples. However, the discovery that the initial phoneme of the name Ham was *ḥ* forces us to reject this suggestion, for, in those Semitic languages that preserve both phonemes *ḥ* (heyth) and *ḥ*, the word for black is consistently written with *ḥ* (heyth)" (David M. Goldenberg, *The Curse of Ham: Race and Slavery in Early Judaism, Christianity, and Islam*, Jews, Christians, and Muslims from the Ancient to the Modern World, ed. R. Stephen Humphreys, William Chester Jordan, and Peter Schäfer [Princeton: Princeton University Press, 2003], 147–8).

As much as the later phenomenon of non-distinction between a ח and a ח is a given, the two works that Goldenberg bases his conclusions do not necessarily consider it a given that this phenomenon manifests itself in the case of "Ham." Wevers seems to endorse the possible relationship between "Xam" and "Xammu" (J. W. Wevers, "Heth in Classical Hebrew," in *Essays on The Ancient Semitic World*, ed. J. W. Wevers and D. B. Redford [Toronto: University of Toronto Press, 1970], 106). Blau cites "Ham" under the list of names that "exhibit h (heyth) of uncertain etymology transliterated by X" (Joshua Blau, "On Polyphony in Biblical Hebrew," in *PIASH* [Jerusalem: The Israel Academy of Sciences and Humanities, 1983], 168).

terms. If the most probable derivative of "Ham" is *Hammu*, then "Ham" could be

associated with the verb חמם ("to be hot") and its derivatives.

Seeing that "Ham" might carry the meaning "hot/warm" or could possibly be

linked to the color "black," and considering that one of its related terms does connote

color, are we then to conclude that Ham was black or that he was destined to live in hot

regions? Not necessarily. The unavailability of any explicative comments concerning the

significance of the name should caution us to stop at mere determination of the meaning

of the term. Whether the name has any bearing on Ham's experience or makeup cannot

be determined with any degree of certainty—not when the Scriptures themselves are

silent on the implication or significance of the name.

*The African's Dark Skin*

The second facet of the proposal that makes the African people the center of its

discussion resembles the first in its depiction of physical makeup as resulting from

punishment for Ham's actions. The difference here is the personages in view are the

Africans whose connection with Ham is described in terms of shared physical makeup

such as black complexion and curly hair. Ham's makeup is not known with certainty and

should not be assumed to resemble the African's since the Africans are not the only

people group that traces its lineage back to Ham. Second, Gen 9 does not, in any way

whatsoever, relate Ham, the progenitor of the Africans, to the Noachian curse. Even if the

claim were to be made that Ham was a dark skinned individual or turned dark at some

point, the curse would not be the explanation for the dark skin because Ham was arguably

not the target of the curse. Third, makeup or more specifically, dark skin, is never looked

at punitively in the story. As a matter of fact, instances in the Bible where dark skin is linked to as negative a phenomenon as a curse unexceptionally pertain to acquired skin color as opposed to inborn skin color. Inborn skin color, which is what the Africans have, is never portrayed negatively in the Scriptures. We base our assessment on the following three observations.

First, inborn skin and by extension inborn dark skin is attributable to God's act of creation. The Scriptures discuss humanity's creation at two levels. At one level, creation is a one time historical event, which occurred at the dawn of human history resulting in the genesis of the first two human progenitors (Gen 1:26–27), the *Adam* who was formed (יצר) first (Gen 2:7) and the woman who was consequently built (בנה) from the rib of the *Adam*. From the perspective of the pedigree of these progenitors, this creation, which is echoed numerous times in the Scriptures,[33] is representational because it falls outside the scope of their experience.

At another level, the formation of an individual in the mother's womb could be considered an act of divine creation. That God is responsible for this aspect of creation is clear  (Job 10:8–11; Jer 1:5; and Ps 139:13–15). The designation of the formation of an individual in the womb as an act of creation is based on shared vocabulary between the two levels.[34] Creation at the second level (level "b") is no longer representational for

---

[33] Gen 5:1, 2; 6:1, 7; 9:6; Zech 12:1; Isa 45:12.

[34] The three common vocabularies that appear in level "a" are also employed in level "b."

| Shared Vocabulary | Level "a" | Level "b" |
|---|---|---|
| 1.  עשׂה | Gen 1:26; 6:1; 9:6 | Job 10:8, 9; 31:15; Ps 119:73 |
| 2.  ברא | Gen 1:27; 6:7; Isa 45:12 | Isa 54:16; Eccl 12:1 |
| 3.  יצר | Gen 2:7; Zech 12:1 | Jer 1:5 |

124

Adam's pedigree. It is their experience and that is why we term this aspect of creation experiential. Job declares this aspect of creation his experience (10:8) and considers it to be the experience of others (31:15). The Psalmist too considers this aspect of creation his experience (Ps 139:13). Unique to this level and thus relevant to the issue of dark skin as an act of God's creation is the attribution to God of not just the process of a fetus' formation—the weaving and the knitting (Ps 139:13, 15; Job 10:11)—but the very parts of the fetus' body. These include the flesh (בָּשָׂר, Job 10:11), bones (עֶצֶם, Job 10:11), sinews (גִּיד, Job 10:11), kidneys (כִּלְיָה, Ps 139:13), and *skin* (עוֹר, Job 10:11). If God is responsible for clothing us with the skin, it is not at all imaginative to conclude that he also clothes us with skin color—even dark skin color.

Second, the Scriptures, in general, are not pre-occupied with physical appearance as a whole let alone skin color.[35] The Bible certainly makes reference to appearances. However, the number of times that it is silent far surpasses the number of times it makes reference to individual physical aspects. Of the obviously large number of individual and people groups cited in the Bible, mention is made of the appearances of five people groups[36] and approximately thirty individuals,[37] a relatively small number compared to the total number of named characters.[38]

---

[35] Tremper Longman, *Literary Approaches to Biblical Interpretation*, Foundations of Contemporary Interpretation, ed. Moisés Silva, vol. 3 (Grand Rapids: Academie Books, 1987), 89; cf. Leland Ryken, *How to Read the Bible as Literature* (Grand Rapids: Zondervan Publishing House, 1984), 37.

[36] The five people groups are the Anakites (Num 13:32, מִדָּה), Enim (Deut 2:10, גָּדוֹל), Rephaim (2:21, גָּדוֹל), Cushites (Isa 18:2, 7, מְמֻשָּׁךְ וּמוֹרָט), and Sabeans (45:14, מִדָּה).

[37] The thirty or so individuals include: (1) the daughters of men (Gen 6:2, טֹבֹת), (2) Sarah (12:11, יְפַת־מַרְאֶה, cf. v. 14), (3) Rebekkah (24:16, טֹבַת מַרְאֶה מְאֹד; cf. 26:7), (4) Esau (27:11, 23, שָׂעִר), (5) Jacob (vv. 11, 16, חָלָק), (6) Rachel (29:17b, יְפַת־תֹּאַר וִיפַת מַרְאֶה), (7) Leah (v. 17a, רַכּוֹת . . . וְעֵינֵי), (8) Joseph (39:6, יְפֵה־תֹאַר וִיפֵה מַרְאֶה), (9) King Eglon (Judg 3:17, בָּרִיא מְאֹד), (10) Samson's sister-in-law (15:2, טֹבָה), (11) Eli (1 Sam 4:18, כָּבֵד), (12) Saul (9:2, טוֹב), (13) David (16:12; 17:42, יְפֵה עֵינַיִם וְטוֹב רֹאִי

Third, unlike instances where the narrator expresses preference[39] or lack of

preference[40] for a particular appearance, in the one instance where in-born dark skin is

referenced (Jer 13:23: "Can an Ethiopian (כּוּשִׁי) change his skin?"),[41] the text does not

express any prejudice[42] whatsoever. Clearly, the verse is not a commentary on the

---

... (אַדְמוֹנִי), (14) Goliath (v. 4, גָּבְהוֹ שֵׁשׁ אַמּוֹת וָזָרֶת מִנַּת), (15) Abigail (25:3, יְפַת תֹּאַר), (16) Bathsheba (2 Sam 11:2, טוֹבַת מַרְאֶה מְאֹד), (17) Tamar (13:1, יָפָה), (18) Abishag (1 Kgs 1:4, יָפָה עַד־מְאֹד), (19) Adonijah (v. 6, טוֹב־תֹּאַר מְאֹד), (20) Elisha (2 Kgs 2:23, קֵרֵחַ), (21) Queen Vashti (Esth 1:11, טוֹבַת מַרְאֶה), (22) Daniel and 3 his friends (Dan 1:4, כָּל־מְאוּם [מוּם] וְטוֹבֵי מַרְאֶה . . . ¯ אֵין¯), and (26) the Suffering Servant (Isa 52:14, מִשְׁחַת מֵאִישׁ מַרְאֵהוּ וְתֹאֲרוֹ מִבְּנֵי אָדָם).

[38] We have not attempted to do the actual counting individual names and people groups in the OT. But we do have works that have done exactly that and serve as our reference point. One such work is that of O. Odelain and R. Seguineau, which focuses on proper names in the Bible. Their tally of biblical characters in both testaments is between 3000 and 3100. This means that the close to 30 individuals whose looks are referenced represent a mere 1% of the total (O. Oderlain and R. Séguineau, *Lexicon der biblischen Eigennamen*, trans. Franz Joseph Schierse [Düsseldorf: Patmos 1981], xvi).

[39] Examples include: (a) lustful desire by Potiphar's wife for Joseph (Gen 39:6); (b) Amnon's illicit love for Tamar (2 Sam 13:1); (c) marriage between the "sons of God" and the daughters of men (Gen 6:2); (d) David's affair with Bathsheba (2 Sam 11:2); (e) Egyptians' interest in Sarah (Gen 12:1); (f) Samson's father-in-law highlighting the excelling beauty of his unmarried daughter compared to her sister, Samson's wife (Judg 15:2); (g) the Philistines' interest in Rebekah (Gen 24:16); (h) choosing the successor to Queen Vashti (Esth 1:11); and (i) the selection of Daniel and his friends for the king's service (Dan 1:4).

[40] Examples include: (a) the rationale offered by Samson's father-in-law for offering his other daughter as a wife in place of Samson's spouse (Judg 15:2); (b) not staring at the Shulammite woman (Song 1:6); (c) the jeering of Elisha by the children (1 Kgs 2:23).

[41] Even though there is no explicit mention of dark skin, the mention of "Ethiopians" connote it since Ethiopians are thought to have been dark-skinned individuals who resided in Africa. See the following works for either the view that Ethiopians were dark-skinned or resided in Africa: J. A. Thompson, *The Book of Jeremiah*, NICOT, ed. R. K. Harrison (Grand Rapids: Eerdmans, 1980), 374; Jack R. Lundbom, *Jeremiah 1–20*, AB, ed. William Foxwell Albright, vol. 21A (New York: Doubleday, 1999), 687; William L. Holladay, *A Commentary on the Book of the Prophet Jeremiah: Chapters 1–25*, vol. 1, Hermenia— a Critical and Historical Commentary on the Bible, ed. Paul D. Hanson (Philadelphia: Fortress Press, 1986), 415; Robert P. Carroll, *Jeremiah: A Commentary*, OTL (Philadelphia: Westminster Press, 1986), 305; Edwin M. Yamauchi, *Africa and the Bible* (Grand Rapids: Baker Academic, 2004), 41; Roger W. Anderson, "Zephaniah Ben Cushi and Cush of Benjamin: Traces of Cushite Presence in Syria-Palestine," in *The Pitcher Is Broken: Memorial Essays for Gösta W. Ahlström*, ed. Steven W. Holloway and Lowell K. Handy, JSOTsup, vol. 190 (Sheffield: Sheffield Academic Press, 1995), 68; David Tuesday Adamo, *Africa and the Africans in the Old Testament* (San Francisco: Christian University Press, 1998), 109.

[42] We define *prejudice* with Gordon Allport "as an antipathy based upon a faulty and inflexible generalization. It may be felt or expressed. It may be directed toward a group as a whole or toward an individual because he is a member of that group" (Gordon W. Allport, *The Nature of Prejudice* [Cambridge, MA: Addison-Wesley Publishing Company, 1954], 9).

aesthetic quality of dark skin, whether desirable or undesirable, beautiful or ugly, attractive or unattractive.[43] The functional use of the proverbial phrase is to hyperbolically illustrate Israel's unlikelihood of turning away from evil. So on the issue of inborn skin color, the Scriptures are neutral at best.[44]

This is not the case with the three instances involving acquired skin color. That the skin color is acquired in these instances is hardly debatable. Job was certainly not an innately dark-skinned individual (30:30). The fact that the princes in Lamentation 4 were colored one way, according to v. 7, and then turned dark in v. 8 confirms that the coloring was acquired. The female character (Shulammite woman) in Cant 1:5, 6 was probably not innately dark since there is mention therein of the phenomenon that brought about the

---

[43] A common reason why the text references physical aspects of individuals is because the narrative requires it. In the words of Shimon bar-Efrat, "in biblical narrative information about someone's outward aspect serves solely as a means of advancing the plot or explaining its course" [Shimon Bar-Efrat, *Narrative Art in the Bible*, JSOTsup, ed. David J. A. Clines and Philip R. Davies, vol. 70 (Sheffield, England: Sheffield Academic Press, 1989), 48].The mention of Eglon's fatness, for instance, is necessary to explain how it is that Ehud's sword, upon the deadly thrust, remained buried in the king's body. Similarly, the mention of Eli's heaviness is vital in explaining why the fall that he experienced turned lethal. The same could be said of the mention of Goliath's size and the beauty of the king of Tyre. The former's gigantic size explains why the Israelites were so frightened of him. The description of the latter is intended to illustrate the glorious status of the king prior to being cast down.

This type of narrative-driven rationale for citing individual features is also evident in instances where the mention appears as a reported speech and is therefore not attributable to the narrator. An example would be Jacob's reference to his smooth skin and Esau's hairy look. These references are vital to the development of the story. Another example is the mention of the size of the Anakites in the speech of the ten spies. They mention the appearance of these inhabitants of Canaan in the manner that they did to underscore the difficulty of an invasion.

Whether they be descriptions that betray admiration or lack thereof or narrative-driven references, the one thing that is true of all the approximately 35 citations of appearances in the OT is that the references are simply that: descriptions of what the individuals looked like. They do not say anything about the heart or character of the individual or people groups in view. The beauty of Queen Vashti, for instance, is simply that. It does not say anything about her character. The same could be said of the handsomeness of Saul, the beauty of Job's daughters, the handsomeness of David, the beauty of Abigail, the tallness of the Sabeans or the darkness of the Cushites's skin color. For a detailed discussion on function of descriptions in Biblical narrative, see Adele Berlin, *Poetics and Interpretation of Biblical Narrative* (Winona Lake, IN: Eisenbrauns, 1994), 34–37.

[44] See Rodney Steven Sadler, "Can a Cushite Change His Skin? An Examination of Race, Ethnicity, and Othering in the Hebrew Bible" (Ph.D. diss., Duke University, 2001), 214.

dark color.[45] The phenomena that brought about the darkening of skin color in these three instances were disease (heat?), hunger, and the sun, respectively. The first two phenomena are certainly negative. The negativity of the last phenomenon is debatable.

*Enslavement of the African People*

The last facet relates the experience of the enslavement of the African people to the curse in general or to the aspect of the curse regarding the enslavement by Japheth. Enough has been said about the faultiness of this view. Nevertheless the critique is worth repeating. It was Canaan who was cursed. Any fulfillment of this curse must be sought among his descendants. The Africans are not Canaan's descendants.

Canaan-related Proposals

*Invasion of Canaan*

First in the listing is the invasion of Canaan or domination of the Canaanites. We fault this proposal for its generality. The terms "domination" or "invasion" are not precise enough to necessarily include the servitude of the dominated or invaded party.[46] In other words, invasion or domination does not automatically equal servitude in as much as servitude is at times an outgrowth of conquest.

---

[45] Longman's commentary on this verse is worth rehearsing: "The Song neither explicitly or implicitly suggests that white is inherently better or more attractive than black skin. Furthermore, the woman was Semitic and likely had a dark complexion to start with. The darkness about which she complains is not her natural skin color but a tan or a burn" [Tremper Longman III, *Song of Songs*, NICOT, ed. R. K. Harrison and Robert L. Hubbard (Grand Rapids: Eerdmans, 2001), 96].

Other works that support the assertion that the dark skin color in Cant 1:5, 6 was acquired and thus should not be confused with the African's inborn dark skin include: Michael D. Goulder, *The Song of Fourteen Songs*, JSOTsup, ed. David J. A. Clines and Philip R. Davies, vol. 36 (Sheffield: JSOT Press, 1986), 12; Edwin C. Hostetter, "Mistranslation in Cant 1:5," *AUSS* 34 (1996): 35–36; and Meik Gerhards, "Zum emphatischen Gebrauch der Partikel אַל im biblischen Hebräisch," *BN* 102 (2000): 65.

[46] We are assuming that our previous conclusion regarding the nature of the servitude as some type of enslavement on the basis of the broader context of Gen 9:18–29 is valid.

*Enslavement of the Canaanites*

Unlike the first option, the second proposal describes the fulfillment in more specific terms. The view envisions not simply the conquest, but more specifically the enslavement of the Canaanites in the book of Joshua (16:10; 17:13), Judges (1:28, 30, 33), 1 Kings (9:21), and 2 Chronicles (8:8–9) as fulfillment. By all accounts, this is the most credible proposal in terms of accounting for the Noachian utterance regarding the enslavement of Canaan by Shem. Some type of enslavement is definitely in view. The master is Israel, a descendant of Shem through Abraham.[47]

*Subjugation of the Gibeonites by Israel*

The third proposal points to the subjugation of the Gibeonites by Israel. Like the previous listing, this proposal parallels the curse utterance just as well because it includes the element of enslavement that manifests itself in the form of subjection to manual labor (cf. Josh 9:23). However, for it to correlate perfectly with the curse utterance, the Gibeonites must be shown to constitute the Canaanites. Do they?

There are three sets of Scriptures that speak to the issue of the ethnic identity of the Gibeonites. Joshua 9:7 and 11:19 consider them Hivites. In 2 Sam 21:2, they are referred to as Amorites. This double designation is only apparent for this reason: unlike the instances when "Amorite" refers to a specific distinct people group (cf. Exod 3:8, 17; 13:5; 23:23; 33:2; Deut 7:1), "Amorite" here is meant to underscore the fact that the Gibeonites were a non-Israelite people group living in Canaan. Other occurrences of "Amorite" designating pre- or non-Israelite populations in general include Gen 15:16;

---

[47] See our previous discussion (pp. 94–95, chap. 3) on the credible exegetical link between Gen 9:25 and the harsh labor imposed on the Canaanites by the Israelites following the conquest.

Josh 24:15, 18; Judg 6:10; 2 Kgs 21:11 and Amos 2:9,10.[48] The last passage relating to the Gibeonites' ethnicity is Gen 10:17 where the Hivites are considered descendants of Canaan. On the basis of this last passage, we can respond in the affirmative to the question earlier posed regarding whether the Gibeonites could be classified as Canaanites. And since the answer is positive, the view regarding the servitude of the Gibeonites meets the test of possible fulfillment of the curse utterance.

*The Four Kings Serving the King of Elam*

The fourth view calls attention to Gen 14:4 where four kings, whom the proposal considers Canaanites, are depicted as serving (עבד) the King of Elam, who is identified as a Shemite. For this view to be considered acceptable, it has to pass the two-fold test of servitude as the outworking of the curse and Shemite and Canaanite ancestry of the parties involved.

Regarding the ancestry test, we accede to the claim that the test has been met. The cities cited, whether it be that of Chedorlaomer or those of the opposing confederacy, have some connection to either Shem or Canaan. Sodom, Gomorrah, Admah, and Zeboiim all happen to be territorial markers for the land of Canaan (Gen 10:19). Elam, the land of Chedorlaomer, is probably a namesake of Elam the son of Shem (10:22).

Concerning the servitude test, if we limit ourselves to instances where one set of people is subject to a foreign king, the verb עבד appears twenty-five other times.[49] Also relevant for consideration are five other occasions where the verb appears in the context

---

[48] We are indebted to Blenkinsopp for this analysis of the use of "Amorite" (Joseph Blenkinsopp, "Gibeon and Israel: The Role of Gibeon and the Gibeonites in the Political and Religious History of Early Israel," in *SOTSMS*, ed. J. A. Emerton [Cambridge: University Press, 1972], 22).

[49] Judg 3:8, 14; 9:28, 38; 1 Sam 11:1; 17:9; 2 Sam 10:19; 16:19; 22:44; 1 Kgs 4:21; 12:4, 7; Isa 60:12; Jer 17:4; 27:6, 7, 8, 9, 11, 12, 13, 14, 17; 28:14; 40:9.

of a ruler subjected to another at one point and then the subject rebels.[50] In all these occurrences, there is only one instance when עבד possibly signifies enslavement and that because of the presence of the qualifying expression "placing iron on the neck of" (Jer 28:14). Otherwise, in the rest of the passages it is difficult to categorically conclude enslavement is in view. What we find clearly associated with עבד is tribute payment (cf. Judges 3:15). Based on this brief study, the burden of proof lies with the proposal that suggests that עבד in Gen 14:4 implies enslavement especially because there is no qualifying phrase to lead to this conclusion. Seeing then that the proposal passes only one of the two tests, we find it to be deficient as a possible fulfillment of the utterance pertaining to the enslavement of Canaan by Shem.

*The Four Kings Serving King Tidal*

The fifth proposal sees the fulfillment of the utterance concerning the enslavement of Canaan by Japheth in the person of King Tidal in Gen 14. The view is commendable for seeking to account for an aspect of the Noachian utterance that the first three listings ignored or sidestepped, viz., accounting for the statement regarding the enslavement of Canaan by Japheth (Gen 9:27). However, it falls short for the same reason that the fourth proposal does, considering that both positions appeal to the same passage.

*Subjugation of Tyre and Sidon*

Like the fifth proposal, the sixth proposal also seeks to account for the utterance regarding the enslavement of Canaan by Japheth. According to it, the fulfillment occurs in the subjugation of the Canaanite people of Tyre by the Romans following the destruction of Carthage in 146 BC and the Canaanite people of Sidon by the Greeks

---

[50] 2 Kgs 18:7, 20; 24:1, 20; Ezek 17:15.

131

during the reign of Alexander the Great. Indeed, the Greeks and the Romans practiced slavery extensively. In Rome, for instance, the ratio of the enslaved to the free was 1:3. In Attica, there were between 80,000 and 100,000 slaves in a population of a quarter of a million.[51] The slaves themselves were drawn from the population of war captives and were utilized by the elite to till the land.[52] Given that slavery was practiced by the descendants of Japheth and also that the conquered territories of Carthage (Tyre) and Phoenicia (Sidon) were definitely Canaanite, we ought to render this sixth proposal viable.

*Subjugation of the Egyptians*
*and the Babylonians*

The seventh proposal resembles the sixth in as far as envisioning the subjection of Canaanite-related people groups to the Greeks and the Romans as fulfillment of the utterance concerning the enslavement of Canaan by Japheth.[53] As for the occasion for the fulfillment of the aspect of the utterance concerning the enslavement by Shem, the proposal points to the subjection of the Egyptians and the Babylonians by the Persians (descendants of Shem). Both Babylon and Egypt did fall under the subjection of Persia time and time again. Cambyses I (600–559 B.C.) invaded Egypt and made it a satrapy. Babylon became a satrapy under the governorship of Gubaru around 538 B.C. Cambyses II (530–522 B.C.) reorganized Egypt into a satrapy called Mudraya, with Memphis as its capital. Stemming rebellion, Darius Hystapes (522–486 B.C.) brought Babylon under

---

[51] Keith R. Bradley, "Slavery," in *The Oxford Companion to Classical Civilization*, ed. Simon Hornblower and Anthony Spawforth (Oxford: Oxford University Press, 1998), 670.

[52] Tim J. Cornell, "History of Rome," in *The Oxford Companion to Classical Civilization*, ed. Simon Hornblower and Anthony Spawforth (Oxford: Oxford University Press, 1998), 611.

[53] We need not evaluate the aspect of this proposal concerning the Greeks and the Romans since we already did that while responding to the preceding proposal.

control in 520 B.C. Besides the establishment of satrapies, the subjection of Persia over others evidenced itself in the form of enslavement, for Herodotus says the following concerning Xerxes' response to Egyptian rebellion: "Having been over-persuaded to send an expedition against Hellas, Xerxes first marched against the rebels, in the year after Darius' death. These he subdued, and laid Egypt under the much harder slavery [δουλοτερη] than in the time of Darius; and he committed the governance of it to Achaemenes his own brother, Darius' son."[54] As true as the issue of Persian subjection is, the very fact that the subjects (i.e., Egypt and Babylon) are non-Canaanites causes us to dismiss the proposal altogether.

In summary, of the seven proposals, only three can be regarded as valid. Thus, the possible occasions for the fulfillment of the aspect of the utterance concerning the enslavement of Canaan by Shem are Israel's enslavement of the Gibeonites and the Canaanites. In a sense, these two views are one if the enslavement of the Gibeonites is subsumed under the larger umbrella of the Canaanite enslavement. As regards the aspect of the utterance pertaining to the enslavement of Canaan by Japheth, a possible occasion would be the dominance of Rome and Greece over Tyre and Carthage respectively.

## Evaluation of the Proposed Fulfillments
## of the Blessing

Specifically, the proposals pertain to the enlargement of Japheth and the idea of dwelling in the tents of someone else.

---

[54] *Herodotus* 7.7

Proposals Pertaining to the Enlargement of Japheth

*Japhethites Responding to the Gospel*

The first option takes the form of the Japhethites responding to the gospel through

divine persuasion.[55] Our conclusion elsewhere that the preferable meaning of יפת is "to

enlarge" as opposed to "to persuade" rules out this proposal altogether. In other words,

the spatial meaning of the verb does not allow for an emotional or mental understanding

of possible fulfillment.

*Rebuilding of the Temple as Per*
*Cyrus' Decree*

The second option associates the enlargement with the rebuilding of the temple

following the decree by Cyrus.[56] As much as Cyrus was a Japhethite in the sense that, as a

Persian, he was related to the Medes whose ancestry can be traced back to Madai, a son

of Japheth (Gen 10:2), it is difficult to see the connection between spatial enlargement

and the building of the temple.

*Political and Intellectual Domination*

The third option understands the fulfillment in non-geographical terms such as

political dominance, intellectual promotion and conquest, spread of civilization,

colonization of the rest of the world, and intellectual superiority of the Japhethites over

the Hamites, but specifically the Africans.[57]

---

[55] *Lectures on Genesis Chapters 6–14*, 182–84.

[56] *Gen. Rab.* 36.7.1d

[57] *Practical Reflections Upon Every Verse of the Book of Genesis* (London: Longmans, Green, 1892), 52; John Peter Lange, *Genesis, or the First Book of Moses, Together with a General Theological and Homiletical Introduction to the Old Testament*, trans. Tayler Lewis and A. Gosman, 5th ed., vol. 1, A Commentary on the Holy Scriptures: Critical, Doctrinal, and Homiletical, with Special Reference to Ministers and Students, ed. Johann Peter Lange and Philip Schaff (New York: Charles Scribner's Sons,

The inadequacy of this view lies, first of all, in its assumption that the Hamites are somehow in view in the utterance pertaining to Japheth. The people group that is in view in the utterance pertaining to Japheth are the Canaanites who are mentioned at the end of Gen 9:27. So if non-geographical terms mentioned above were to be regarded as the meaning of יפת, the intended target must be the Canaanites, not the Hamites. Thus, it would be the Canaanites who are colonized, politically dominated, civilized, or intellectually surpassed.

The other point at which this aspect can be faulted is the negative attributes of these non-geographical terms. We have already argued that, in regards to יפת, the candidate of choice as far as meaning is concerned has to match the positive environment upon which the blessing utterance of Gen 9:27 sits. None of these non-geographical terms could truly be regarded as positive in nature.

In rating the Japhethites as intellectually superior, the view would find resonance, for instance, with Rushton's work, which contends that, based on the evolutionary theory and genetic variation, the most intelligent race is the Mongoloid population, followed by Caucasian, and then the Negroid.[58] Reacting to Rushton's conclusions, Joseph Graves questions their legitimacy on the grounds that (a) the theoretical models concerning life

---

1884), 337; J. G. Murphy, *A Critical and Exegetical Commentary on the Book of Genesis: With a New Translation* (Boston: W. H. Halliday and Company, 1868), 214.

[58] J. Philippe Rushton, *Race, Evolution, and Behavior: A Life History Perspective* (New Brunswick, NJ: Transaction Publishers, 1997), 5, 113. Kwame Anthony Appiah labels this kind of thinking "extrinsic racism," which he defines as "belief that members of different races differ in respects that warrant the differential treatment, respects— such as honesty, or courage, or intelligence"(Kwame Anthony Appiah, "Racisms," in *Anatomy of Racism*, ed. David Theo Goldberg [Minnesota: University of Minnesota Press, 1990], 5).

history are antiquated and simplistic, and (b) the concept of r-and K-selection, which he relies on, is virtually useless.[59]

*Geographical Expansion*

The fourth view defines the fulfillment along the lines of geographical expansion enhanced by vast population.[60] Of all the proposals of fulfillment, this aspect rates the best in terms of possibility primarily because of its spatial attribute.

Proposals Pertaining to the Idea of Dwelling
in the Tents of Someone Else

*Dispersion of the Jews by the Romans*

The first proposal considers as fulfillment the dispersion of the Jews by the Romans in the second century.[61] We have already ruled out displacement as the possible meaning of "dwelling in the tents of" because the negativity attached to the idea of displacement does not harmonize well with the positive attribute of a blessing utterance.

*Cooperation Between the Hebrews and*
*the Philistines*

The second suggestion points to the cooperation between the Hebrew invaders from the East and the Pelasgic invaders (Philistines) invaders from the West against the settled population of Canaan.[62] It is true that the Philistines were thrust into Canaan after an unsuccessful attack against Rameses III (1304–1236 B.C.). Nevertheless they would

---

[59] Joseph L. Graves, *The Race Myth: Why We Pretend Race Exists in America* (NewYork: Dutton, 2004), 175, 182; cf. Ashley Montagu, *Man's most Dangerous Myth: The Fallacy of Race*, 4th ed. (Cleveland: World Publishing Company, 1968), 100.

[60] Geerhardus Vos, *Biblical Theology: Old and New Testaments* (Grand Rapids: Eerdmans, 1977), 58; Arthur C. Custance, *Noah's Three Sons: Human History in Three Dimensions*, The Doorway Papers, vol. 1 (Grand Rapids: Zondervan Publishing House, 1975), 28.

[61] Justin Martyr, *Dial.* 139.

[62] A. Van Selms, "The Canaanite in the Book of Genesis," in *Studies on the Book of Genesis*, ed. B. Gemster, Oudtestamentische Studiën, vol. 12 [Leiden, E. J. Brill, 1958], 187.

not fit the fulfillment since the table of nation lists them under Ham, not Japheth (cf. Gen 10:14).

*Exclusive Equation of the Gentiles to Only the Japhethites*

The third view sees fulfillment in the conversion of the Gentiles whom the proposal equates with the Japhethites.[63] To envision conversion as fulfillment is to assume a spiritual meaning of the phrase "dwell in the tents of." Such a spiritual understanding amounts to nothing but allegorization. The interdependence between the phrase "dwelling in the tents of" and יפת does not allow for a non-spatial, non-geographical meaning especially because the latter term clearly carries a spatial meaning.

As for the proposal's equation of the Gentiles with the Japhethites alone, a determination of the composition of the Gentiles should be able to reveal whether the equation is parochial or not.

The English expression "Gentile" is a translation of the Latin term *Gentilis*, which, in and of itself, denotes a "member of the same *gens* ("house, family, tribe, clan, nation, people or race") or "foreigner" (or heathen). The Greek equivalent of *Gentilis* is ἔθνος. Liddell-Scott lists a total of five categories of meanings under ἔθνος.[64] Two of the five categories show a close correspondence with the two meanings associated with the Latin equivalent. Latin's "member of the same *gens*" corresponds to Liddell-Scott's

---

[63] *Lectures on Genesis Chapters 6-14*, 184, 186; John Calvin, *Commentaries on the First Book of Moses, Called Genesis*, trans. John King (Grand Rapids: Eerdmans, 1948), 2: 309; Elisha Fish, *Japheth Dwelling in the Tents of Shem or Infant Baptism Vindicated in a Discourse, the Substance of Which Was Delivered at Upton, January 5, 1772. With Objections Answered* [Boston: Thomas and John Fleet, 1773], 10–11; A. B. Simpson, *Genesis and Exodus*, vol. 1, Christ in the Bible, ed. A. B. Simpson (New York: Word, Work and World, 1888), 98; Ernest Shufelt, "Noah's Curse and Blessing, Gen 9:18–27," *CTJ* 17 (1946): 741; Custance, *Noah's Three Sons: Human History in Three Dimensions*, 23.

[64] Henry George Liddell and Robert Scott, *A Greek-English Lexicon* (Oxford: Clarendon Press, 1968), 480.

"part, member" (category 5). Latin's "foreigner or pagan" parallels Liddell-Scott's "foreign, barbarous nations" (category 2). "Foreign," from a Jews' point of view, referred to non-Jews in the same way that Greeks addressed non-Greeks as "foreign."[65] Other entries under "category 2" include "nation, people, province." The remaining three categories are: (a) number of people living together, company, body of men, band of comrades; (b) class of men, caste, tribe; and (c) sex.

The answer to the question of the composition of the Gentiles depends on whether the criterion for making the determination is strictly that aspect of ἔθνος that means "foreign or barbarous nation," and thus lexical, or any and all data that conceptually refer to non-Jews. Limiting oneself to the former data yields an answer consistent with the view that equates "Gentiles" only with the Japhethites. Indeed, all occurrences of "foreign" or "pagan nation" that are either not subject to debate, in so far as the ethnic identity of the foreigners is concerned, or are not too general to reveal the identity of the particular foreigner, invariably point to the Romans who can be traced back to Japheth.[66] The construction of Matt 10:18 allows for the equation of ἔθνος with the Romans and specifically the Roman administrators.[67] Matthew 20:19 (cf. Acts 4:25, 27) also refers to the Romans since crucifixion was a punishment carried out mainly by the Romans. Another clear reference to the Roman army is Lk 21:24. At the very least, Rome is in

---

[65] Aristotle *Pol.* 1324.[b] 10.

[66] References that are either subject to debate as to the exact identity of the foreigners that they might be referring to or are too general in their description of the foreigners as to contribute to our efforts of determining their composition include: Matt 4:15; 10:5; 12:18, 21; 20:25; Lk 2:32; Acts 13:46; Gal 2:8; Rom 2:24; 3:29; 11:11; and Eph 2:11. Other references too general for our use are those that emphasize the paganism or barbarity of the Gentiles (Matt 6:32; 1 Cor 5:1; 12:2; Eph 4:17; 1 Thess 4:5; 1 Pet 4:3).

[67] W. D. Davies and Dale C. Allison, *A Critical and Exegetical Commentary on the Gospel According to Saint Matthew*, vol 2, ICC, ed. J. A. Emerton, C. E. B. Cranfield, and G. N. Stanton (Edinburgh: T & T Clark, 1991), 184.

view alongside other nations that will plunder Jerusalem in the future. If Acts 9:15 looks forward to Paul's defense before kings, then Roman rulers are again in view. Rome features yet again in the person of Cornelius (Acts 10). As a centurion heading one hundred soldiers, Cornelius was most probably of Roman descent.

If the criterion for determining the composition of the Gentiles is altered from the lexical terms "foreigner" or "pagan" to any and all data that conceptually reference non-Jews, an altogether different picture emerges. To this end we wish to scan two sets of data.

The first set of data is references to the term Ἰουδαῖος ("Jew"). We are particularly interested in occurrences of this term that appear juxtaposed to another people group in a manner suggesting mutual exclusivity of the two people groups in which case the people group would qualify as non-Jewish. Of the 195 occurrences, only 24 are relevant. The non-Jewish people groups that these 24 occurrences highlight are Samaritans,[68] Romans,[69] and Greeks[70] respectively.

The second set of data is the Table of Nations (Gen 10). In it, the Jews find nascent representation in the line of Arpachshad, the son of Shem. We gather this from the instances in the NT where Abraham was considered the ancestor of the Hebrews. Paul, who identified himself before a tribune as a Jew (Acts 21:39), referred to himself as a descendant of Abraham (Rom 11:2; 2 Cor 11:22). Peter, a Jew in the sense that he set

---

[68] John 4:9, 22; 8:48. The history of the formation of the Samaritans attests to their non-Jewishness. In place of the northern Kingdom, which had just been led to captivity, the King of Assyria brought in non-Jews (2 Kgs 17:24).

[69] Luke 7:3; John 18:35.

[70] John 7:35; Acts 14:1; 16:1, 3; 18:4; 19:10, 17; 20:21; Rom 1:16; 2:9, 10; 3:9; 10:12; 1 Cor 1:22, 24; 10:32; 12:13; Gal 3:28; Col 3:11.

himself apart from the Gentiles (Acts 15: 8), traced his ancestry and that of his fellows Israelites back to Abraham, Isaac, and Jacob (3:13). The Jews themselves boasted of their Abrahamic ancestry in John 8:33. This ancestral connection between the Hebrews and Abraham, Isaac and Jacob allows us to trace their lineage back to the Shemites and particularly Arpachshad whose line leads directly to Abraham (cf. Gen 11:11–26).

If Arpachshad is the only "Hebrew" in the table of nations, it follows that every other individual or people group in the table is a "non-Hebrew." Discussing the specifics of these non-Jews would therefore go a long way towards adding to the answer we are seeking.

The first set of non-Hebrews that we would like to discuss is the remaining sons of Shem and the Joktanites. The latter stand outside the stemma of Abraham since at the point where the Abrahamic ancestral line forks it follows the other son of Eber, viz., Peleg.[71]

Elam (עֵילָם), which appears some 30 times in the OT,[72] is the Hebrew equivalent of Elamite's (eighteenth century BC) *Hatamti*, Akkadian's *Elamtu*, Sumerian's (third millennium BC) ideogram NIM, and Greek's *Aylam*. In terms of geography, Elam occupied former Eastern Babylon, present-day Iran, and constituted zones such as Susa, Khuzistan, and Anshan. Thus the Elamites were a heterogeneous group of people who

---

[71] The argument could thus be made that the Joktanites are as much Hebraic as the Jews since both people groups have a common ancestor in Eber. However, the Joktanites are not Jewish since the Abrahamic and therefore the Jewish ancestral line excludes them. Going by the same logic, both the Ishmaelites and the Edomites should be considered non-Jewish since the Abrahamic line bypasses them.

[72] Not all instances actually refer to the Shemitic Elam. References to the Shemitic Elam are: Gen 10:22; 1 Chr 1:17; Gen 14:1, 9; Isa 11:11; 21:2; 22:6; Jer 25:26; 49:34–39; Ezek 32:24; Dan 8:2. Non-Shemitic references are Ezra 2:7, 31; 8:7; 10:2, 26; Neh 7:12, 34; 10:14; 12:42 (cf. 1 Chr 8:24; 26:3). Also non-Shemitic would be the single appearance of the term in the NT (Acts 2:9).

inhabited southwestern Iran. Between the second and first millennium B.C, a new population invaded this region and renamed it Iran.[73]

If the *Ashur* under Shem is the same as that under Ham, then it is a reference to Assyria, whose capitals at various times in its history were Nineveh (seventh century B.C.), Dur-Sharrukin (eigth century B.C.) and Calah (modern Nimrud) (ninth century B.C.), had at one point had Ashur (modern Qalaat Sherqat) for a religious center. The Assyrians, who together with Babylonians, were primarily responsible for the banishment of the Jews, were Akkadian in language, culture and religion and appear to have been a mix of old Akkadian, Hurrian, Northwest Semitic, and other strains.

Aram could be considered the progenitor of the Arameans if he is equated with Aram the grandchild of Nahor whose line had two individuals who were regarded as Arameans, viz., Bethuel and his son Laban (Gen 25:20). Aram had Damascus as its headquarters and was a persistent enemy of Israel beginning as early as the period of the Judges (Judg 3:8).

Lud is mentioned three other times in the Old Testament and in each of these instances it is mentioned alongside Put. It is a target of God's judgment in Ezek 30:5. It appears to have had war tendencies according to 27:10 and Isa 66:19.

Of the thirteen names listed under Joktan, only four receive further mention in the Bible. This is not to say that the *hapax* names are totally unknown in so far as the people groups that they represent. As a matter of fact, most, if not all, of the nine once-cited

---

[73] See further Clarisse Herrenschmidt, "Elamite Civilization and Writing," in *Ancestor of the West: Writing, Reasoning, and Religion in Mesopotamia, Elam, and Greece*, trans. Teresa Lavender Fagan (Chicago: University of Chicago Press, 2000), 69–89; Francois Vallat, "Elam," trans. Stephen Rosoff, vol. 2, ABD, ed. David Noel Freedman (New York: Doubleday, 1992): 424–429; Matthew W. Waters, *A Survey of Neo-Elamite History*, SAAS, ed. Robert M. Whiting, vol. 12 (Helsinki: Vammalan Kirjapaino Oy, 2000), 1–3; and D. T. Potts, *The Archaeology of Elam*, Cambridge World Archaeology, ed. Norman Yoffee (Cambridge: Cambridge University Press, 1999), 1–9.

names appear to refer to Arabs.[74] Almodad, Sheleph, and Hazarmeveth refer to South Arabian peoples. Uzal and Obal are associated with Yemen. Of the four names[75] that receive further mention in the Bible, Jobab appears to refer to four different people in its four occurrences,[76] so that the name should be considered as appearing only once in so far as its reference to the Joktanites.

Sheba shares the name with a Cushite (Gen 10:7) and Abraham's grandson through Keturah (25:3). The Cushitic Sheba seems to be in view in Ezek 27:22; 38:3; and Ps 72:10, since he is mentioned alongside a Cushite. In the first verse, he is paired with Raamah. He is cited together with Dedan in the second verse, while in the last verse he is coupled with Seba. If the act of pairing or bundling together in these three verses serves as a clue that it is the Cushitic Sheba that is in view, the association of this Sheba with precious stone and spices in two of these verses (Ezek 27:22; 38:3; Ps 72:15; Jer 6:20; and Isa 60:6) suggests that the same Sheba might be in view in 1 Kgs 10 with its mention of the Queen of Sheba. As for the geographical location of Sheba, John Philby is of the opinion that Old Testament evidence "seems to favor a north Arabian setting down to the time of Solomon and beyond, until the tribe migrated southwards (probably as a result of

---

[74] Allen P. Ross, "Studies in the Book of Genesis Part 3: The Table of Nations in Genesis 10—Its Content," *BSac* 138, no. 549 (1981): 29; Eugene H. Merrill, "The Peoples of the Old Testament According to Genesis 10," *BSac* 154, no. 613 (1997): 19.

[75] These also referred to Arabs (Ibid.).

[76] The name is shared by an Edomite king (Gen 36:33, 34) and a Canaanite king (Josh 11:1).

Assyrian and Babylonian encroachments) at an unascertainable date."[77] Others, however, prefer an African location.[78]

Also sharing a name with a Cushite is Havilah. Geographically Havilah served as a boundary marker for the area occupied by the Ishmaelites (Gen 25:18) and the Amalekites (1 Sam 15:7) and the Pishon River flowed through it (Gen 2:11).

Lastly, Ophir, renowned for its gold (1 Kings 9:27; Isa 13:12; Ps 45:9; Job 22:24; 28:16), is thought to have been located in Western Arabia.[79] In summary the non-Jewish element of the Shemites constitutes the Elamites, Assyrians, Arameans, the Ludites, and the Arabs.

The second set of non-Jews in the Table of Nations would be the Japhethites. Of the fourteen names mentioned under Japheth, three do not receive further mention in the Bible: Riphath, Rodanim and Tiras. This number could be upped to four if the synonymity between the Japhethic Togarmah and Beth-Torgamah (Ezek 27:14; 38:6) is considered questionable.[80]

The repeated mention of the remaining ten names yields the following individual portraits. Gomer, identified with the Cimmerians, were a nomadic people of antiquity dwelling about the Crimea who overran Asia Minor about 635 B.C. and were succeeded

---

[77] Philby bases the suggestion of an earlier northern provenance partly on the pairing of Sheba with Dedan in Gen 10:7 and partly on the failure of current exploration to turn up any substantial traces of earlier gold or silver mining further south than latitude 21 degrees North (Harry St. John Philby, *The Queen of Sheba* [London: Quartet Books Limited, 1981], 34).

[78] Knut Holter prefers to locate Sheba in Africa on the basis of ancient tradition (Knut Holter, *Yahweh in Africa: Essays on Africa and the Old Testament*, Bible and Theology in Africa, ed. Knut Holter, vol. 1 [New York: Peter Lang, 2000], 105).

[79] See further Kenneth A. Kitchen, "Sheba and Arabia," in *The Age of Solomon: Scholarship at the Turn of the Millennium*, ed. Lowell K. Handy, vol. 11, Studies in the History and Culture of the Ancient Near East ed. B. Halpern and M. H. E. Weippert [New York: Brill, 1997], 143–45).

[80] Our opinion is that the two are synonymous in light of the appearance of Beth-Torgamah alongside Gomer in Ezek 38:6.

in southern Russia by the Sarmatians and Scythians, and served as part of Gog's allied forces in Ezek 38:6.

Gog himself resided in Magog (38:2; 39:6) and was identified as the chief prince of Meshech and Tubal. Magog is identified with the mountainous region between Armenia and Cappadocia; the name seems to represent the Scythian hordes southeast of the Black Sea.[81]

The pair Meshech and Tubal was most certainly non-Jewish based on the use of the adjective "uncircumcised" to describe them (32:26). Tubal is equivalent to *Tibare-ni* in Pontus; and Meshech is located in the Moschian mountains near Armenia. Their range was from eastern Asia Minor to the Black Sea.

Ashkenaz, mentioned in the listing of nations that are signaled to engage in a divinely instigated war against Babylon, represented a northern branch of Indo-Germanic tribes.[82] Also stirred to participate in a judgmental war against Babylon was Madai or Medes (Isa 13:17) who are listed from the time of 840 B.C. as a people who dwelled east of Assyria and southwest of the Caspian Sea.[83] Prophesied in the eighth century B.C., the downfall of Babylon in the hands of the Medes took place when Cyrus II entered Babylon in 539 B.C. In actuality, by the time Babylon was falling, the Median Empire, initially formed in the seventh century, had become a vassal of Persia.

Javan, the equivalent of the Ionians (Hellenistic race) who dwelt in western Asia Minor, is depicted as a trader with Tyre (Ezek 27:13, 19) and featured prominently in the prophetic writings of Daniel (ch. 11). Elishah, Tarshish and Kittim stood for coastal

---

[81] Ross, "The Table of Nations in Genesis," 203; cf. Cassuto, *From Noah to Abraham*, 121.

[82] BDB identifies them as a northern people (BDB, 79).

[83] Ross, 203.

regions. Elishah is identified with the place *Alashiyah* on the island of Cyprus. Tarshish has been identified with several places on the southern coasts of Asia Minor as well as Spain and beyond. Kittim stood for Crete, an island in the eastern part of the Mediterranean Sea. The trio's maritime property is evident in the Bible from the mention of their coastlands and the reference to their ships. Mention is made of the coasts of Elishah (Ezek 27:7) and those of Cyprus (Jer 2:10; Ezek 27:6). Solomon's ships were from Tarshish (1 Kgs 10:22; 22:48). The fugitive Jonah boarded a ship to escape to Tarshish. Kittim's ships would attack Assyria according to Num 24:24. This maritime characteristics of the names under Javan might explain the author's summary depiction of the Japhethites as "coastland" people in Gen 10:5. All in all the non-Hebrew people called the Japhethites consist of the Cimmerians, Scythians, Medes, Greeks, Indo-Europeans (Caucasians), Asians, and Cretians (or Cyprians).

The third and last set of non-Hebrews in Gen 10 is the Hamitic people group. Three of the names under Ham were covered during our treatment of Shem as they appear in both places.[84] The remaining names and the people groups that they represent are as follows: Cush within the Table of Nations stands for Arabs, on the basis of sub-names such as Sheba, Dedan and Havilah; Egypt stands for the inhabitants of the Upper and Lower Delta and the Philistines through Caphtor; Canaan stands for a conglomerate of people groups generally referred to as Canaanites; and Put stands for the Libyans.

In summary, the definition of the composition of Gentiles as only constituting the Japhethites ignores the fact that a conceptual understanding of Gentiles yields a listing of

---

[84] Those names are Assyria, Havilah, and Sheba.

145

the composition of Gentiles that extends beyond the Japhethites to include Shemites and

Hamites. Such a limited understanding is parochial at best.

## Summary

What we have strived for in this chapter is to critique the various interpretations

of the nature of the offense and the meaning and fulfillment of the Noah's utterances. The

bases of the critique were the exegetical findings that emerged out of our exegetical work

in chapter three.

The first critique concerned the proper reading of the verb גלה (v. 21) and the

suffixed ה at the end of v. 21. Do they carry any sexual connotations or not? Our

conclusion here was that (a) there is no clear-cut evidence that יִתְגַּל carries a sexual

meaning; and (b) the suffixed ה does not denote that Ham's wife was present in the tent;

instead it should be parsed as third person masculine in line with the *Qere* reading.

Secondly, we evaluated the various understandings of Ham's offense. In

comparing our exegesis of vv. 22–23 and the various interpretations of Ham's action, we

deduced that the best reading is the literal understanding, not the idiomatic and thus

sexual understanding. Just because the phrase ראה . . . עֶרְוַת in Gen 9:22 carries a sexual

meaning in Lev 20:17 does not mean that the phrase carries a similar sense in Genesis.

As a matter of fact, any similitude between Gen 9:22 and Lev 20:17 is strictly

phraseological, not contextual. No contextual indicators such as those tied to Lev 20:17

and which clue the reader to conclude that incest is in view there—no such contextual

indicators are present in Gen 9:22. Unlike Lev 20:17, the characters in Gen 9:22 are all

males. The concept of גלה . . . . עֶרְוַת ("uncovering a person's nakedness"), present in Lev.

20:17, is absent altogether in Gen. 9:22. As for Ham's offense itself, it was not so much that he saw his father naked than the fact that he neglected his responsibility to cover the involuntary nakedness of his father.

Lastly, we critiqued the numerous proposed fulfillments of both the curse and the blessing utterances. Our conclusions were as follows. Any proposals on the outworking of the curse that are tied to Ham any of his descendants are baseless since the text presents Canaan as the object of the curse. To this end the following proposals are to be rejected: the forced corvée service of the Egyptians by Pharaoh; the triumph of Israel over Egypt during the Exodus; the subjection of the Egyptians and Babylonians by the Persians; the enslavement of the Africans; and the African's dark skin color. The sixth view, the service of the four Kings in Gen 14 under Chedorlaomer and the King of Tidal, is disqualified because it is not clear whether the service that their subjects rendered amounted to slavery.

Of the various suggestions of the fulfillment of the curse, the most viable options are the servitude of the Gibeonite; the enslavement of the Canaanites following the conquest; and the dominance of Rome and Greece over Tyre and Carthage, respectively. The first two correspond to the aspect of the curse utterance that pertains to the enslavement of Canaan by Shem. The last suggestion relates to the enslavement of Canaan by Japheth. Each of these three views meets the textually-based threefold test of servitude as the outworking of the curse, Canaanite ancestry as the object of the curse, and Shemite and Japhethite ancestries as the beneficiaries of the servitude. Moreover, they all satisfy the requirement that "Canaan" be understood representatively as a synechdoche of part for whole and, as such, transgenerationally.

As for Noah's blessing, our conclusion is that none of the proposals pertaining to the phrase וְיִשְׁכֹּן בְּאָהֳלֵי־שֵׁם ("let him dwell in the tents of Shem") correlate well with the exegesis of the blessing remarks. Those proposals are: (1) the conversion of the Gentiles who are equated with the Japhethites; (2) dispersion of the Jews by the Romans in the second century; and (3) the cooperation between the Hebrew invaders from the East and the Pelasgic invaders (Philistines) invaders from the West against the settled population of Canaan. The first suggestion fails to correlate with the spatial connotation behind the phrase "dwelling in the tents." The second is unacceptable on the basis of the fact that the negativity attached to the idea of displacement does not harmonize well with the positive attribute of a blessing utterance. The third does not fit the fulfillment since the table of nation lists the Philistines under Ham, not Japheth (cf. Gen 10:14).

As regards proposals related to the enlargement of Japheth we have a viable candidate among the "non-spiritual" group of views but none within the "spiritual" group. The "spiritual" group consist of two suggestions: (1) the response of the Japhethites to the gospel; and (2) rebuilding of the temple in accordance with Cyrus' decree. The view that the blessing pronounced on Japheth manifested itself in the Japhethites positively responding to the gospel lacks merit since the preferable meaning of יפת is "to enlarge," not "to persuade." The requirement that any proposal on the fulfillment of the blessings on Japheth constitute spatial enlargement disqualifies the following view regarding rebuilding of the temple in accordance with Cyrus' decree.

As a whole, the "non-spiritual" views consist of the following aspects: political dominance, intellectual promotion, intellectual conquest, spread of civilization, colonization of the rest of the world, and geographical expansion enhanced by vast population. With the exception of the last aspect, all of the others lack either the attribute of positivity or spatiality—both of which are inherent in the verb יפת and the context in which it sits. Thus the viable candidate among the "non-spiritual" group of views is "geographical expansion."

## CHAPTER 5

## SUMMARY AND CONCLUSION

The introduction aside, our work constituted two major parts. The first part was a brief history of interpretation. The interpretations whose history the study sought to trace were primarily the nature of the infraction against Noah and the meaning and possible fulfillment of the Noachian utterances.

On the issue of the infraction, five views were detected: sexual, sight, disclosure, unfilial irreverence, and castration. The "unfilial irreverence" view can be further broken down to mockery, laughter, and jeering. The subcategories of the sexual interpretation are: homosexuality, incest, and voyeurism.

On the subject of the utterances, we divided the findings on the meaning and fulfillment of the enslavement utterance into the "Canaan" view and the "Ham" view. Suggestions of fulfillment that would fit the "Canaan" view include the Conquest, subjugation of the Gibeonites, continual subjugation of the Canaanites during the reign of Solomon, the servitude of the five kings to Chedorlaomer in Gen 14, and the domination of the Canaanite people of Tyre and Sidon by the Greek and Roman empires. The identification of the beneficiaries of the enslavement has varied depending on the commentator. Rashi considered Canaan's siblings as the beneficiaries. Ibn Ezra argued that the beneficiaries would have been Shem, Japheth, and God. As regards the "Ham" view, its distinct mark is that the object of the curse was Ham or his descendants who include the Africans. This position arises out of an acceptance of the textual emendation of Gen 9:25, appeal to other biblical texts and ancient social customs, and the fact that the text identifies Ham as the offender. Some who associate the Africans with the curse point to the African's physiognomy as evidence of the curse's aftermath.

Concerning the utterance pertaining to Japheth, three meanings of יפת have been proposed: enlarge, beautify, and persuade. The suggestions of fulfillment of the utterance could be categorized as spiritual and non-spiritual. The spiritual label covers the following three views (a) the Japhethites responding positively to the gospel advances; (b) Cyrus' decree to rebuild the temple; and (c) the establishment of the Church. Proposals that appear under the umbrella of non-spiritual consist of political dominance, intellectual conquest, geographical expansion, and spread of civilization by the nations of Europe and America.

Lastly, the aspects of the phrase "dwell in the tents of" that have been staple for heated discussion are the identity of the antecedent, the meaning of the phrase, and possible fulfillment. The antecedent has been identified as either God or man. The phrase has been understood to connote either hostility or peaceful co-existence. Though there are several suggestions of fulfillment, we highlighted one particular one due to its parochial nature, viz. the conversion of the gentiles.

The second part constituted an exegetical critique of the sexual interpretations of the offense and suggestions of fulfillment of the utterances. The critique was conducted within the framework of the overall exegesis of Gen 9:18–29. Rehearsing the findings of our exegesis, firstly, the role of vv. 18–19 is to introduce the two-fold agenda of the progenitorship of Noah's three sons and the foregrounding of Canaan in anticipation of the mention of him later in the narrative via the phrase "Ham was the father of Canaan."

Second, the vice of the story does not lie with the fact that Noah got drunk and then consequently uncovered himself. Noah's engagement in viticulture was most probably a first for him and so he would have been oblivious of the inebriating effects of wine. Moreover, it so happens that he uncovered himself in private, not in the open.

Third, we consider invalid the sexual understanding of Noah's uncovering of self, the suffixed ה (v. 21), the expression "doing something to someone" (v. 24), and Ham's look at his father's nakedness. The parallelism between the phrase ראה... עֶרְוַת in Gen. 9:22 and Lev 17:20 or Lev. 18 (vv. 7, 8, 14, 16) is only apparent, if not altogether false. The ה does not denote the presence of Noah's wife in the scene. It is fallacious to assume that "doing something to someone" can only refer to as contact a physical act as sexual abuse. The preferred reading is that the offense was of a non-sexual nature. Particularly, the offense lies with Ham disclosing to his brothers the fact of their father's nakedness rather than covering him upon discovering his state. When viewed through the lens of the overall scriptural data on nakedness, Ham's failure to cover his father's nakedness was clearly a violation of the expectation to cover up involuntary nakedness.

Fourth, the curse utterance was a reaction to Ham's action and targeted Canaan, who, like Shem and Japheth, represents a people group as opposed to a historical individual. It cannot be emphasized enough that Ham was never the target of the curse. Neither were the non-Canaanites Hamites, let alone the skin color of people of African descent. The beneficiaries of the intended enslavement of the Canaanites are Shem(ites) and Japheth(ites) since they both qualify as Canaan's "brothers" in the loose sense of the word.

Fifth, the blessing utterance, which like the curse utterance is a reaction of the duo's very noble response to Ham's report regarding Noah's nakedness, must be understood to consist of spatial expansion of Japheth(ites), cohabitation of the Japhethites with the Shemites, and the enslavement of the Canaanites by both the Japhethites and the Shemites.

Sixth, the fulfillment of the curse utterance can be legitimately tied to instances in history when the Japhethites and the Shemites enslaved the Canaanites. Enslavement by the Shemites occurred around the period of the Conquest. The Japhethic enslavement featured the Romans and the Greeks, on the one hand, and Tyre (Carthage) and Sidon (Phoenicia), on the other hand. As for Noah's blessing, none of the proposals pertaining to the phrase וְיִשְׁכֹּן בְּאָהֳלֵי־שֵׁם ("let him dwell in the tents of Shem") correlate well with the exegesis of the blessing remarks. Those proposals are: (1) the conversion of the Gentiles who are equated with the Japhethites; (2) dispersion of the Jews by the Romans in the second century; and (3) the cooperation between the Hebrew invaders from the East and the Pelasgic invaders (Philistines) invaders from the West against the settled population of Canaan. As regards proposals related to the enlargement of Japheth we have a viable candidate among the "non-spiritual" group of views but none within the "spiritual" group. That viable candidate is "geographical expansion."

# APPENDIX

## SUGGESTIONS OF THE JUSTIFICATION
## OF CANAAN'S CURSE

Seven proposals have been offered on the question of the justification of Canaan's curse.[1] One proposal points to some curse-resistant phenomenon that is thought to have shielded Ham from the curse. Two phenomena have been proposed: blood relationship and a previously uttered blessing. The former phenomenon can be traced back to Josephus (first century A.D.), who cites "nearness of blood" as the reason Noah would not curse Ham.[2] The latter phenomenon finds expression in at least three works. According to 4Q252Genesis Pesher[a] I ii 5–7, the reason Noah did not curse Ham is because God has blessed the sons of Noah.[3] Justin Martyr (d. ca. A.D. 165) offered the same reason.[4] So did R. Judah (A.D. 400). In response to the rhetorical question, "Should Ham be the one who sinned yet Canaan (his descendants) be cursed?" he responded: "it is because it is said, 'And God blessed Noah and his sons' (Gen 9:1). Now there cannot be a cursing where there has been a blessing. Accordingly, he said, 'Cursed be Canaan,' (He could not curse Ham, so he cursed his descendants)."[5]

---

[1] The question of the justification of Canaan's curse does not arise for works that regard Ham as the object of the curse in v. 25. Such works include LXX's Byzantine text (John William Wevers, *Notes on the Greek Text of Genesis*, vol. 35, Septuagint and Cognate Studies Series, ed. Leonard J. Greenspoon [Atlanta: Scholars Press, 1993], 124).

[2] Josephus, *Ant.* 1.6.3.

[3] Florentino García Martínez, *The Dead Sea Scrolls Translated: The Qumran Texts in English*, trans. Wilfred G. E. Watson, 2d ed. (Leiden: E. J. Brill, 1996), 214.

[4] Justin Martyr (d. ca. 165), in a chapter entitled *the Blessings and also the curse, pronounced by Noah were prophecies of the future*, suggests that the "Spirit of prophecy would not curse the son that had been by God blessed along with (his brother)" (Justin Martyr, *Dial.* 139).

[5] *Gen. Rab.* 36.7.3.

Luther, though properly a subscriber of the view that some existing phenomenon rendered the curse impotent, proposed a reason other than previously uttered blessing for why Ham was not cursed. According to him, after Noah saw that Ham had been called by the voice of God, had been received into the ark, and had also been saved with the others, he wanted to spare him whom God had spared in the flood. Therefore he transferred the curse, which Ham had deserved by his sin, to his son Canaan, whom Ham undoubtedly wanted to remain with him.[6]

Another suggestion points to some sin or vice on the part of Canaan that served as rationale for the curse. According to Philo, the reason God pronounced that his son Canaan should be the servant of Shem and Japheth even though Ham had sinned was, "God pronounced this sentence because both father and son had displayed the same wickedness, being both united together and not separated, and both indulging in the same disposition."[7] By citing Matthew 7:20 in association with Canaan's punishment, Augustine seemed to understand Canaan as equally guilty. Once perceived as an extension of Ham's wickedness, Canaan could thus be regarded as justifiably punished.[8] Lactantius prefaced his rationale by rebutting the thought that Noah, in announcing the curse, would have been driven by some type of vindictiveness. Noah's words, he continues, were uttered under the suggestion or impulse of the Holy Spirit and not "in a spirit of vengeance or impatience on account of the injury received." Finally, he

---

[6] *Lectures on Genesis Chapters 6–14*, trans. George V. Schick, vol. 2, Luther's Works, ed. Jaroslav Pelikan (St. Louis: Concordia Publishing House, 1960), 182.

[7] Philo, *QG* 2.77.

[8] Augustine, *Civ.* 5.16.2.

concludes that the curse on Canaan was not after all the punishment of the innocent: "His

impiety was foreseen."[9]

Lack of wisdom on the part of Canaan served as rationale for the curse of

enslavement according to St. Basil in chapter 20 of *The Book of Saint Basil on the Spirit*.

Placed on a wider context this suggested rationale belongs to Basil's discourse on the

different circumstances under which men are brought under the yoke of slavery. The first

two circumstances are enslavement after conquest and enslavement due to poverty. Of

pertinence to our discussion is the third circumstance: "by a wise and mysterious

dispensation, the worst children are by the orders of the father condemned to serve the

wiser." As condemnatory as this might sound, Basil argued that the condemnation was

merely apparent. In reality, he reasoned, the enslavement by the wise was meant to

benefit the enslaved:

> it is more profitable that the man who, through lack of intelligence, has no natural
> principle of rule within himself, should become the chattel of another, to the end
> that, being guided by the reason of his master, he may be like a chariot with a
> charioteer, or a boat with a steersman seated at the tiller. To this end Jacob's
> lordship over the foolish and unintelligent Esau was designed to benefit the
> latter.[10]

Later proponents of this second answer included the co-authors Goodspeed, Welton and

Ross. The former held the opinion that Canaan's vices were prophetically anticipated and

---

[9] Lactantius, *Inst.* 2.14.

[10] Basil's second illustration of a beneficial enslavement involves Canaan. Canaan is depicted
as uninstructed and thus deserving of enslavement. Canaan's lack of instruction is tied to his own father
Ham whom Basil labels as unwise (St. Basil, *De Spiritu Sancto*, 20.15).

thus the justification for the curse.[11] According to the latter, Noah saw in Canaan the evil

traits.[12]

The third view is akin to the preceding answer in as far as rendering Canaan

culpable. The uniqueness of this view, though, is in its regarding Canaan as either a co-

offender with Ham or the sole offender in the story. Having attributed to Ham the offense

of divulging the nakedness of his father, Ibn Ezra then attaches to Canaan the offense of

doing "something to Noah" on the basis of Gen 9:24. According to Ibn Ezra, the

undefined "something" is attributable to Canaan as opposed to Ham for two reasons.

First, the antecedent of "youngest" in v. 24 could not be Ham since he was not the

youngest of Noah's sons. "Youngest" there must refer to Canaan since he is presented as

Ham's youngest son in Gen 10:6. Second, attributing the offense in v. 24 to Canaan best

accounts for the reason behind the curse on Canaan in v. 25.[13]

This kind of exegetical argumentation to support Canaan's culpability appears

later in some ninetenth century works. The difference though is that in these later works,

Ham is no longer considered the offender. The sole offender is Canaan. One example is

Cornelius Edgar's 1862 work. Besides appealing to name sequence, as did Ibn Ezra,

Edgar also points to the fact that Ham could not be the offender since his name is not

---

[11] Calvin Goodspeed and D. M. Welton, *The Book of Genesis*, An American Commentary on the Old Testament (Philadelphia: American Baptist Publication Society, 1909), 97.

[12] Allen P. Ross, "The Table of Nations in Genesis" (Ph.D. diss., Dallas Theological Seminary, 1976), 357.

[13] Abraham ben Meir Ibn Ezra, *Genesis*, trans. H. Norman Strickman and Arthur M. Silver, vol. 1, Ibn Ezra's Commentary on the Pentateuch (New York: Menorah Publishing Company, 1988), 128. The Midrash's reasoning that the blessing that Ham received in 9:1 served as some type of curse-proof is unacceptable to him.

mentioned in the curse.[14] Lewis sought to depict Ham's action in verse 23 as non-offensive and argued that "son" in v. 24 can mean "grandson" and thus be considered a reference to Canaan. According to him, the verb ראה could not be regarded as evidence of guilt. If the verb were יבט, then a guilty verdict could be justified since the verb implies interest and emotion. There is in the account no intimation of any of that scoffing demeanor that some commentators have so gratuitously charged upon him. Not only was Ham's sighting of his father's nakedness purely accidental, his reporting was conducted with filial piety. Second, Canaan could just as well be regarded a son of Noah in accordance with the well-established Semitic peculiarity by which all the descendants are alike called sons (e.g. Gen 29:5; Ezra 5:1//Zech 1:1).[15]

To avoid the difficulty of proving the sinfulness of Canaan, the fourth view chooses to understand Canaan figuratively, namely, synecdoche of part for the whole. For instance, Cassuto identifies the "whole" as the Canaanites and pinpoints the reason they suffered bondage as their own transgression and not the sins of Ham. Thus the curse was not directed against the man Canaan, the son of Ham, but against the Canaanite *people*, the descendants of Canaan, who were as far removed from their ancestor Canaan as they

---

[14] Cornelius H. Edgar, *The Curse of Canaan Rightly Interpreted and Kindred Topics: Three Lectures Delivered in the Reformed Dutch Church, Easton, Pa* (New York: Baker & Godwin Printers, 1862), 13–14. An 1892 anonymously written work echoes Edgars's first reason in its argumentation of why Canaan ought to be regarded as a co-offender. The reason according to this work is because Canaan "had a principle share in the doom pronounced" (*Practical Reflections Upon Every Verse of the Book of Genesis* [London: Longmans, Green, and Co., 1892], 158).

[15] John Peter Lange, *Genesis, or the First Book of Moses, Together with a General Theological and Homiletical Introduction to the Old Testament*, trans. Tayler Lewis and A. Gosman, 5th ed., vol. 1, A Commentary on the Holy Scriptures: Critical, Doctrinal, and Homiletical, with Special Reference to Ministers and Students, ed. Johann Peter Lange and Philip Schaff (New York: Charles Scribner's Sons, 1884), 338.

were from Ham. This is not the case, therefore, of a son being punished for his father's sins.[16]

The fifth answer points to the principle of *lex talionis* as the rationale for the curse on Canaan. According to *Genesis Rabbah*, R. Huna in the name of R. Joseph said: "You are the one who prevented me from producing a fourth son, therefore I curse your fourth son [corresponding to the fourth son I never had]."[17] In *Sanhedrin*, the Gemara considered the proposal above as more viable since it blended with its assertion that the punishment of Canaan was motivated by the principle of *lex talionis*.[18] Midrash *Tanhuma Buber* supplied more data surrounding the activation of the *lex talionis*:

> Our masters have said: When Noah was in the ark he said: Oh, that my children had slaves so that, while they were seated, those <slaves> would go forth before them. When, however, I go out from the ark, whomever I beget I shall make into slaves for them. He said to him (Ham): You did not allow me to beget a fourth son who would be a slave for his brothers. By your life, I am making your fourth son a slave.[19]

Two more proposals have recently been added to the list of responses. Hamilton envisions within the text the outworking of the principle of children suffering for the sins

---

[16] Umberto Cassuto, *From Noah to Abraham (Genesis vi. 9–xi. 32)*, A Commentary on the Book of Genesis, trans. Israel Abrahams, vol. 2 (Jerusalem: Magnes Press, 1964), 153–54.

[17] *Gen. Rab.* 36.7.4c.

[18] *Sanh.* 70a.

[19] *Midrash Tanhuma Buber* 2.21. Later proponents of the fourth answer include Derek Kidner, *Genesis: An Introduction and Commentary*, TOTC, ed. D. J. Wiseman (Chicago: Inter-varsity Press, 1967), 104; Kenneth A. Mathews, *Genesis 1–11:26*, vol. 1A, NAC, ed. E. Ray Clendenen (Nashville: Broadman & Holman, 1996), 417–18.

of their parents.[20] Bassett claims that Canaan was cursed in order to stop Ham from

passing on the sexually acquired "potency of leadership" to him.[21]

---

[20] Victor P. Hamilton, *The Book of Genesis: Chapters 1–17*, NICOT, ed. R. K. Harrison (Grand Rapids: Eerdmans, 1990), 325.

[21] Frederick W. Bassett, "Noah's Nakedness and the Curse on Canaan: A Case of Incest?" *VT* 21 (1971): 235.

# BIBLIOGRAPHY

## Biblical Texts

*Biblia Hebraica*. Edited by Rudolf Kittel. Stuttgart: Württembergische Bibelanstalt, 1951.

*Biblia Hebraica Stuttgartensia*. Edited by Adrian Schenker. 5th ed., Stuttgart: Deutsche Bibelgesellschaft, 1997.

*Genesis*. Edited by Bonifatius Fischer, vol. 2. Vetus Latina, ed. Petrus Sabatier. Freiburg: Verlag Herder, 1951.

*Genesis*. Edited by John William Wevers, vol. 1. Septuaginta: Vetus Testamentum Graecum Auctoritate Academiae Scientiarum Gottingensis Editum. Göttingen: Vandenhoeck & Ruprecht, 1974.

## Lexicons, Dictionaries, Lexical Essays

Aistleitner, Joseph. *Wörterbuch der ugaritischen Sprache*. Berichte über die Verhandlungen der Sächsischen Akademie der Wissenschaften zu Leipzig: Philogisch-Historische Klasse. Vol. 106. Berlin: Akademie-Verlag, 1967.

*Akkadisches Handwörterbuch: Unter Benutzung des lexikalischen Nachlasses von Bruno Meissner (1868–1947)*. Edited by Wolfram von Soden. Wiesbaden: Otto Harrassowitz, 1965.

Beyse, K. M. "חמם." In *Theological Dictionary of the Old Testament*, ed. G. Johannes Botterweck and Helmer Ringgren, vol. 4, 473–77. Grand Rapids: Eerdmans, 1980.

Crum, W. E. *A Coptic Dictionary*. Oxford: Oxford University Press, 1939. Reprint, Oxford: Clarendon Press, 1962.

*Hebrew and Aramaic Dictionary of the Old Testament*. Edited by Georg Fohrer. Berlin: Walter de Gruyter, 1973.

Klingbeil, Gerald A. "מס." In *New International Dictionary of Old Testament Theology and Exegesis*, ed. Willem A. VanGemeren, vol. 2, 992–995. Grand Rapids: Zondervan Publishing House, 1997.

Koehler, Ludwig, and Walter Baumgartner. *The Hebrew and Aramaic Lexicon of the Old Testament*. Edited by M. E. J. Richardson. Translated by M. E. J. Richardson. Leiden: E. J. Brill, 1995.

_____. *The Hebrew and Aramaic Lexicon of the Old Testament*. Translated by M. E. J. Richardson. Leiden: E. J. Brill, 1996.

Liddell, Henry George, and Robert Scott. *A Greek-English Lexicon*. Oxford: Oxford University Press, 1843. Reprint, Oxford: Clarendon Press, 1968.

Merrill, Eugene H. "Chronology." In *Dictionary of the Old Testament: Pentateuch*, ed. T. Desmond Alexander and David W. Baker, 113–22. Downers Grove, IL: InterVarsity Press, 2003.

Mosis, R. "פתה." In *Theological Dictionary of the Old Testament*, ed. G. Johannes Botterweck, Helmer Ringgren and Heinz-Josef Fabry, vol. 12 (קום–פסח), 162–172. Grand Rapids: Eerdmans, 2003.

Niehr, H. "ערה." In *Theological Dictionary of the Old Testament*, ed. G. Johannes Botterweck, Helmer Ringgren and Heinz-Josef Fabry, vol. 11 (עזז–פנים), 343–49. Grand Rapids: Eerdmans, 2001.

North, R. "שם." In *Theological Dictionary of the Old Testament*, ed. G. Johannes Botterweck, Helmer Ringgren and Heinz-Josef Fabry, vol. 8 (מר–לכד), 427–30. Grand Rapids: Eerdmans, 1997.

Oderlain, O., and R. Séguineau. *Lexicon der biblischen Eigennamen*. Translated by Franz Joseph Schierse. Düsseldorf: Patmos Verlag, 1981.

Pan, Choo-Wee. "פתה." In *New International Dictionary of Old Testament Theology & Exegesis*, ed. Willem A. VanGemeren, vol. 3 (ש–נ), 714–16. Grand Rapids: Zondervan Publishing House, 1997.

Sæbø, M. "פתה." In *Theological Lexicon of the Old Testament*, ed. Ernst Jenni and Claus Westermann, vol. 2 (חסד–ציון), 1037–1039. Peabody, MA: Hendrickson Publishers, 1997.

Sokoloff, Michael. *A Dictionary of Jewish Palestinian Aramaic of the Byzantine Period*. 2d ed., Baltimore: Johns Hopkins University Press, 2002.

Steinmetz, Sol, ed. *Webster's American Family Dictionary*. New York: Random House, 1989.

*The Brown-Driver-Briggs Hebrew and English Lexicon: With an Appendix Containing the Biblical Aramaic*. Edited by Francis Brown, S. R. Driver and Charles A. Briggs. Boston: Houghton Mifflin, 1906. Reprint, Peabody, MA: Hendrickson Publishers, 1996.

*The Dictionary of Classical Hebrew*. Edited by David J. A. Clines. 5 vols. Sheffield: Sheffield Academic Press, 2001.

Wagner, Max. *Die lexikalischen und grammatikalischen Aramaismen im alttestamentlichen Hebräisch*. Beihefte zur Zeitschrift für die alttestamentliche Wissenschaft, ed. Georg Fohrer. Vol. 96. Berlin: Alfred Töpelmann, 1966.

Wehr, Hans. *A Dictionary of Modern Written Arabic*. Edited by J. Milton Cowan. 4th ed. Wiesbaden: Otto Harrassowitz, 1979.

*Wilhelm Gesenius' Hebräisches und Arämaisches Handwörterbuch über das Alte Testament*. Edited by Frants Buhl. 17th ed. Berlin: Springer, 1962.

## Grammars

Davidson, A. B. *Introductory Hebrew Grammar: Hebrew Syntax*. 3d ed. Edinburgh: T. & T. Clark, 1912.

*Gesenius' Hebrew Grammar*. Edited by E. Kautzsch. Translated by A. E. Cowley. Second English ed. Oxford: Clarendon Press, 1910.

Jenni, Ernst. *Lehrbuch der Hebräischen Sprache des Alten Testaments*. 2d ed. Basel: Helbing & Lichtenhahn, 1981.

Joüon, Paul. *A Grammar of Biblical Hebrew: Syntax*. Translated by T. Muraoka. Vol. 2. Subsidia Biblica. Rome: Editrice Pontificio Istituto Biblico, 2006.

Seow, C. L. *A Grammar for Biblical Hebrew*. Revised ed. Nashville: Abingdon Press, 1995.

Waltke, Bruce K., and M. O'Connor. *An Introduction to Biblical Hebrew Syntax*. Winona Lake, IN: Eisenbrauns, 1990.

Weingreen, J. A. *Practical Grammar for Classical Hebrew*. 2d ed. Oxford: Clarendon Press, 1959.

Williams, Ronald J. *Hebrew Syntax: An Outline*. 2d ed. Toronto: University of Toronto Press, 1976.

## Jewish, Arabic and Aramaic Works

Etheridge, J. W. *The Targums of Onkelos and Jonathan Ben Uzziel on the Pentateuch with the Fragments of the Jerusalem Targum from the Chaldee*. New York: Ktav Publishing House, 1968.

Ginzberg, Louis. *Bible Times and Characters from the Creation to Jacob*. Translated by Henrietta Szold. *The Legends of the Jews*. Vol. 1. Philadelphia: The Jewish Publication Society of America, 1937.

_____. *Notes to Volume 1 and 2: From the Creation to the Exodus*. The Legends of the Jews. Vol. 5. Philadelphia: The Jewish Publication Society of America, 1953.

Grossfeld, Bernard. *Targum Neofiti 1: An Exegetical Commentary to Genesis Including Full Rabbinic Parallels*. Edited by Lawrence H. Schiffman. New York: Sepher-Hermon Press, 2000.

Ibn Ezra, Abraham ben Meir. *Genesis*. Translated by H. Norman Strickman and Arthur M. Silver. Ibn Ezra's Commentary on the Pentateuch. Vol. 1. New York: Menorah Publishing Company, 1988.

*Ibn Khaldun: The Muqaddimah, an Introduction to History*. Translated by Franz Rosenthal, vol. 2. Bollingen Series. New York: Bollingen Foundation, 1958.

Macho, Alejandro Díez. *Neophyti I: Targum Palestinense Ms de la Bibliotheca Vaticana*. Translated by Martin McNamara and Michael Maher. Vol. 1 (Génesis). Textos y estudios, ed. Federico Peréz Castro. Barcelona: Consejo Superior de Investigaciones Científicas, 1968.

_____. *Neophyti I: Targum Palestinense Ms de la Bibliotheca Vaticana*. Translated by Martin McNamara and Michael Maher. Vol. 2 (Éxodo). Textos y estudios, ed. Federico Peréz Castro. Barcelona: Consejo Superior de Investigaciones Científicas, 1970.

_____. *Neophyti I: Targum Palestinense Ms de la Bibliotheca Vaticana*. Translated by Martin McNamara and Michael Maher. Vol. 5 (Deuteronomio). Textos y estudios, ed. Federico Peréz Castro. Barcelona: Consejo Superior de Investigaciones Científicas, 1978.

*Midrash Tanhuma (S. Buber Recension): Translated into English with Introduction, Indices, and Brief Notes*. Translated by John T. Townsend. Hoboken, NJ: Ktav Publishing House, 1990.

*Midrash Tanhuma-Yelammedenu: An English Translation of Genesis and Exodus from the Printed Version of Tanhuma-Yelammedenu with an Introduction, Notes and Indexes*. Translated by Samuel A. Berman. Hoboken, New Jersey: Ktav Publishing House, 1996.

Neusner, Jacob. *Genesis Rabbah: The Judaic Commentary to the Book of Genesis, a New American Translation, Parashiyyot Thirty-Four through Sixty-Seven on Genesis 8:15 to 28:9*. Vol. 2. Brown Judaic Studies, ed. Jacob Neusner, Wendell S. Dietrich, Earnest S. Frerichs, Calvin Goldscheider and Alan Zuckerman. Atlanta: Scholars Press, 1985.

*Pirke De Rabbi Eliezer (the Chapters of Rabbi Eliezer the Great): According to the Text of the Manuscript Belonging to Abraham Epstein of Vienna*. Translated by Gerald Friedlander. 4th ed. The Judaic Studies Library. Vol. 6. New York: Sepher-Hermon Press, 1981.

Rosenberg, A. J. *Genesis: A New English Translation*. Translation of Text, Rashi, and Other Commentaries by A. J. Rosenberg. New York: Judaica Press, 1993.

Steinsaltz, Adin. "Tractate Sanhedrin: Part V." In *The Talmud: The Steinsaltz Edition*. New York: Random House, 1999.

*Targum Onkelos to Genesis: A Critical Analysis Together with an English Translation of the Text (Based on A. Sperber's Edition)*. Translated by Moses Aberbach and Bernard Grossfield. Denver: Ktav Publishing House, 1982.

*The History of Al-Tabari*. Edited by Ehsan Yar-Shater. Translated by William M. Brinner, vol. 2 (Prophets and Patriarchs). Suny Series in Near Eastern Studies, ed. Said Amir Arjomand. Albany, NY: State University of New York Press, 1987.

*The New Complete Works of Josephus*. Translated by William Whiston. Revised and expanded ed. Grand Rapids: Kregel Publications, 1999.

*The Tales of the Prophets of Al-Kisai*. Translated by W. M. Thackston, vol. 2. Library of Classical Arabic Literature, ed. Ilse Lichtenstadter. Boston: Twayne, 1978.

*The Works of Philo: Complete and Unabridged in One Volume*. Translated by C. D. Yonge. New updated ed. Peabody, MA: Hendrickson Publishers, 1993. Reprint, Peabody, MA: Hendrickson Publishers 1997.

*The Zohar*. Translated by Harry Sperling and Maurice Simon. London: The Soncino Press, 1984.

**Patristic and Historical literature**

Kronholm, Tryggve. *Motifs from Genesis 1–11 in the Genuine Hymns of Ephrem the Syrian: With Particular Reference to the Influence of Jewish Exegetical Traditions*. Sweden: CWK Gleerup, 1978.

*Fathers of the Second Century: Hermas, Tatian, Athenagoras Theophilus, and Clement of Alexandria (Entire)*. American ed. The Ante-Nicene Fathers: Translations of the Writings of the Fathers Down to A.D. 325, ed. Alexander Roberts and James Donaldson. Vol. 2. New York: Christian Literature Company, 1886. Reprint, Grand Rapids: Eerdmans, 1975.

*Fathers of the Third and Fourth Centuries: Lactantius, Venantius, Asterius, Victorinus, Dionysius, Apostolic Teaching and Constitutions, Homily, and Liturgies*. Edited by A. Cleveland Coxe. Translated by William Fletcher. American ed. The Ante-Nicene Fathers Translations of the Writings of the Fathers Down to A.D. 325, ed. Alexander Roberts and James Donaldson. Vol. 7. New York: Christian Literature Company, 1886. Reprint, Grand Rapids: Eerdmans, 1975.

*Fathers of the Third Century: Gregory Thaumaturgus, Dionysius the Great, Julius Africanus, Anatolius and Minor Writers, Methodius, Arnobius*. Edited by A. Cleveland Coxe. Translated by William R. Clark. American ed. The Ante-Nicene Fathers Translations of the Writings of the Fathers Down to A.D. 325, ed. Alexander Roberts and James Donaldson. Vol. 6. New York: Christian Literature Company, 1886. Reprint, Grand Rapids: Eerdmans, 1975.

*Herodotus*. Translated by A. D. Godley. Vol. 3 (Books V–VIII). The Loeb Classical Library, ed. T. E. Page, E. Capps, W. H. D. Rouse, L. A. Post and E. H. Warmington. Cambridge, MA: Harvard University Press, 1963.

*Origen: Homilies on Genesis and Exodus*. Translated by Ronald E. Heine. The Fathers of the Church: A New Translation, ed. Hermigild Dressler, Robert P. Russell, Robert Sider, Thomas P. Halton and M. Josephine Brennan. Vol. 71. Washington, D.C: The Catholic University of America Press, 1982.

*Pachomian Koinonia: The Lives, Rules, and Other Writings of Saint Pachomius and His Disciples*. Translated by Armand Veilleux, vol. 3. Cistercian Studies Series. Kalamazoo, MI: Cistercian Publication, 1982.

*Saint Augustine's Anti-Pelagian Works*. Translated by Peter Holmes and Robert Ernest Wallis. A Select Library of the Nicene and Post-Nicene Fathers of the Christian Church, ed. Philip Schaff. Vol. 5. New York: Christian Literature Company, 1886. Reprint, Grand Rapids: Eerdmans, 1978.

*St. Augustine's City of God and Christian Doctrine*. Translated by Rev. Professor J. F. Shaw. A Select Library of the Nicene and Post-Nicene Fathers of the Christian Church, ed. Philip Schaff. Vol. 2. New York: Christian Literature Company, 1886. Reprint, New York: Charles Scribner's Sons, 1987.

*Saint Augustine: The City of God against the Pagans*. Translated by Eva Matthews Sanford and William McAllen Green. Vol. V. The Loeb Classical Library, ed. T. E. Page, E. Capps, L. A. Post, W. H. D. Rouse and E. H. Warmington. London: William Heinemann, 1965.

*Saint Irenaeus of Lyons*. Translated by John Behr. Crestwood, New York: St Vladimir's Seminary Press, 1997.

*Saint John Chrysostom: Homilies on Genesis 18–45*. Translated by Robert C. Hill. Vol. 82. The Fathers of the Church: A New Translation, ed. Thomas P. Halton. Washington, D.C.: The Catholic University of America Press, 1990.

*Saint Justin Martyr: Dialogue with Trypho*. Edited by Michael Slusser. Translated by Thomas B. Falls. Selections from the Fathers of the Church. Vol. 3. Washington, D.C.: The Catholic University of America Press, 2003.

*Selections Translated into English from the Hymns and Homilies of Ephraim the Syrian and from the Demonstrations of Aphrahat the Persian Sage*. Edited by John Gwynn. Translated by J. T. Sarsfield Stopford, J. B. Morris and A. Edward Johnstone. A Select Library of Nicene and Post-Nicene Fathers of the Christian Church, ed. Philip Schaff and Henry Wace. Vol. 13. New York: Christian Literature Company, 1886. Reprint, Grand Rapids: Eerdmans, 1969.

*Some of the Principal Works of St. Ambrose*. Translated by H. De Romestin. A Select Library of Nicene and Post-Nicene Fathers of the Christian Church, ed. Philip Schaff and Henry Wace. Vol. 10. New York: Christian Literature Company, 1886. Reprint, Grand Rapids: Eerdmans, 1969.

*The Apostolic Fathers with Justin Martyr and Irenaeus*. American ed. The Ante-Nicene Fathers Translations of the Writings of the Fathers Down to A.D. 325, ed. Alexander Roberts and James Donaldson. Vol. 1. New York: Christian Literature Company, 1886. Reprint, Grand Rapids: Eerdmans, 1973

*The Commonitory of Vincent of Lerins: For the Antiquity and Universality of the Catholic Faith against the Profane Novelties of All Heresies*. Translated by C. A. Heurtley. A Select Library of Nicene and Post-Nicene Fathers of the Christian Church, ed. Philip Schaff and Henry Wace. Vol. 11. New York: Christian Literature Company, 1886. Reprint, Grand Rapids: Eerdmans, 1973.

*The Homilies of St. John Chrysostom, Archbishop of Constantinople on the Gospel of St. Matthew*. Edited by M. B. Riddle. Translated by George Prevost. A Select Library of the Nicene and Post-Nicene Fathers of the Christian Church, ed. Philip Schaff. Vol. 10. New York: Christian Literature Company, 1886. Reprint, Grand Rapids: Eerdmans, 1978.

*The Select Letters of St. Jerome*. Translated by F. A. Wright. Loeb Classical Library, ed. G. P. Goold, T. E Page, W. H. D. Rouse, E. Capps, L. A. Post, and E. H. Warmington. London: William Heinemann, 1933. Reprint, Cambridge, MA: Harvard University Press, 1980.

*The Treatise De Spiritu Sancto: The Nine Homilies of the Hexaemeron and the Letters of Saint Basil the Great, Archbishop of Caesarea*. Translated by Blomfield Jackson. A Select Library of Nicene and Post-Nicene Fathers of the Christian Church, ed. Philip Schaff and Henry Wace. Vol. 8. New York: Christian Literature Company, 1886. Reprint, Grand Rapids: Eerdmans, 1968.

## Commentaries, Books and Monographs

### Eighteenth and Nineteenth Century Works

Baldwin, Samuel Davies. *Dominion; or the Unity and Trinity of the Human Race with the Divine Political Constitution of the World, and the Divine Rights of Shem, Ham, and Japheth*. Nashville: E. Stevenson and F. A. Owen, 1858.

*The Book of Adam and Eve, also Called the Conflict of Adam and Eve with Satan: A Book of the Early Eastern Church, Translated from the Ethiopic, with Notes from the Kufale, Talmud, Midrashim, and Other Eastern Works*. Translated by S. C. Malan. London: Williams and Norgate, 1882.

Wade, George Woosung. *The Book of Genesis*. London: Hodder Brothers, 1896.

Briggs, Charles Augustus. *Messianic Prophecy: The Prediction of the Fulfillment of Redemption Though the Messiah*. Edinburgh: T. & T. Clark, 1886.

Bush, George. *Notes Critical and Practical on the Book of Genesis: Designed as a General Help to Biblical Reading and Instruction*. Twenty-sixth ed. New York: Ivison, Phiney & Company, 1860.

Calvin, John. *Commentaries on the First Book of Moses Called Genesis*. Translated by John King. Grand Rapids: Eerdmans, 1948.

Candlish, Robert S. *The Book of Genesis: Expounded in a Series of Discourses*. Edinburgh: Adam and Charles Black, 1868.

Delitzsch, Franz. *A New Commentary on Genesis*. Translated by Sophia Taylor. Vol. 1. Clark's Foreign Theological Library. Edinburgh: T. & T. Clark, 1899.

Edgar, Cornelius H. *The Curse of Canaan Rightly Interpreted and Kindred Topics: Three Lectures Delivered in the Reformed Dutch Church, Easton, Pa*. New York: Baker & Godwin Printers, 1862.

Fish, Elisha. *Japheth Dwelling in the Tents of Shem or Infant Baptism Vindicated in a Discourse, the Substance of Which Was Delivered at Upton, January 5, 1772. With Objections Answered*. Boston, New England: Thomas and John Fleet, 1773.

Foster, Benjamin. *The Washing of Regeneration, or, the Divine Rite of Immersion, and a Letter to the Reverend Mr. Fish, on "Japheth yet Dwelling in the Tents of Shem."* Boston: Draper and Folsom, 1779.

Kalisch, M. M. *Genesis*. English ed. Historical and Critical Commentary: The Old Testament with a New Translation. London: Longman, Brown, Green, Longman, and Roberts, 1858.

Lange, John Peter. *Genesis, or the First Book of Moses, Together with a General Theological and Homiletical Introduction to the Old Testament*. Tayler Lewis and A. Gosman. 5th ed. A Commentary on the Holy Scriptures: Critical, Doctrinal, and Homiletical, with Special Reference to Ministers and Students, ed. Johann Peter Lange and Philip Schaff. Vol. 1. New York: Charles Scribner's Sons, 1884.

M'Causland, Dominick. *Adam and the Adamite*. 3d ed. London: Richard Bentley and Son, 1872.

Newton, Thomas. *Dissertations on the Prophecies, Which Have Remarkably Been Fulfilled, and at This Time Are Fulfilling in the World*. London: J. F. Dove, 1830.

Priest, Josiah. Slavery, as It Relates to the Negro, or African Race, Examined in the Light of Circumstances, History and the Holy Scriptures; with an Account of the Origin of the Black Man's Color, Causes of His State of Servitude and Traces of His Character as Well in Ancient as in Modern Times, vol. 1. Anti-Movements in America, ed. Gerald N. Grob. Albany, NY: C. Van Benthuysen; 1843. Reprint, New York, Arno Press, 1977.

_____. *Bible Defense of Slavery; or the Origin, History, and Fortunes of the Negro Race*. Glasgow, KY: W. S. Brown, 1853.

Murphy, J. G. *A Critical and Exegetical Commentary on the Book of Genesis: With a New Translation*. Boston: W. H. Halliday and Company, 1868.

Practical Reflections Upon Every Verse of the Book of Genesis. London: Longmans, Green, and Co., 1892.

Ryle, Herbert E. *The Early Narratives of Genesis: A Brief Introduction to the Study of Genesis 1–11*. London: Macmillan and Co., 1892.

_____. *The Book of Genesis in the Revised Version, with Introduction and Notes by Herbert E. Ryle*. Cambridge, England: University Press, 1914.

Schaff, Philip. *Slavery and the Bible: A Tract for the Times*. Chambersburg, PA: M. Kieffer, 1861.

Simpson, A. B. *Genesis and Exodus*. Vol. 1. Christ in the Bible, ed. A. B. Simpson. New York: Word, Work and World, 1888.

Spurrell, G. J. *Notes on the Hebrew Text of the Book of Genesis with Two Appendices*. Oxford: Clarendon Press, 1887.

Voice, A. *The Mystery Finished! The Negro Has a Soul. His Normal Relation Is That of a Servant of Tribute to Shem and Japheth. The Negro Is Only Made a Citizen While the "Two Witnesses Are Dead"— These Are Moses and Christ, Civil Law and Ecclesiastical or Social Law. This Death is for Forty-Two Months, or for Three and Half Years*. Memphis: Public Ledger Book and Job Printing Establishment, 1868.

Wade, G. Woosung, ed. *The Book of Genesis*. London: Longmans, Green, and Co., 1896.

Weidner, Revere Franklin. *Genesis*. Vol. 1. Studies in the Old Testament. Chicago: Fleming H. Revell Company, 1892.


Twentieth and Twenty-first Century Works

Adamo, David Tuesday. *Africa and the Africans in the Old Testament*. San Francisco: Christian University Press, 1998.

Allport, Gordon W. *The Nature of Prejudice*. Cambridge, MA: Addison-Wesley Publishing Company, 1954.

Bailey, Lloyd R. *Noah: The Person and the Story in History and Tradition*. Studies on Personalities of the Old Testament, ed. James L. Crenshaw. Columbia, SC: University of South Carolina, 1989.

Bar-Efrat, Shimon. *Narrative Art in the Bible*. Journal for the Study of the Old Testament Supplement Series, ed. David J. A. Clines and Philip R. Davies. Vol. 70. Sheffield, England: Sheffield Academic Press, 1989.

Bentzen, Aage. *Introduction to the Old Testament*. Copenhagen: G. E. C. Gads, 1948.

Berlin, Adele. *Poetics and Interpretation of Biblical Narrative*. Winona Lake, IN: Eisenbrauns, 1994.

Blaikie, William G. *A Manual of Bible History in Connection with the General History of the World*. New York: Thomas Nelson and Sons, 1920.

Blenkinsopp, Joseph. *Gibeon and Israel: The Role of Gibeon and the Gibeonites in the Political and Religious History of Early Israel*. Vol. 2. Society for Old Testament Study Monograph Series, ed. J. A. Emerton. Cambridge, MA: University Press, 1972.

Brueggemann, Walter. *Genesis*. Interpretation: A Bible Commentary for Teaching and Preaching, ed. James Luther Mays. Atlanta: John Knox Press, 1982.

_____. *The Land: Place as Gift, Promise, and Challenge in Biblical Faith*. 2d ed. Overtures to Biblical Theology, Minneapolis, MN: Fortress Press, 2002.

Carroll, Robert P. *Jeremiah: A Commentary*. Old Testament Library, Philadelphia: Westminster Press, 1986.

Cassuto, Umberto. *From Noah to Abraham (Genesis vi 9–xi 32)*. Translated by Israel Abrahams. A Commentary on the Book of Genesis. Vol. 2. Jerusalem: Magnes Press, 1949.

Childs, Brevard S. *Old Testament Theology in a Canonical Context*. Philadelphia: Fortress Press, 1985.

Cohen, H. H. *The Drunkenness of Noah*. Tuscaloosa, AL: University of Alabama Press, 1974.

Clines, David J. A. *The Theme of the Pentateuch*. Journal for the Study of the Old Testament Supplement Series, ed. David J. A. Clines, Philip R. Davies and David M. Gunn. Vol. 10. Sheffield: University of Sheffield, 1978.

Custance, Arthur C. *Noah's Three Sons: Human History in Three Dimensions*. The Doorway Papers. Vol. 1. Grand Rapids: Zondervan Publishing House, 1975.

Dayagi-Mendels, Michal. *Drink and Be Merry: Wine and Beer in Ancient Times*. Jerusalem: Israel Museum, 1999.

Davies, W. D., and Dale C. Allison. *A Critical and Exegetical Commentary on the Gospel According to Saint Matthew*, vol. 2 (Matthew VIII–XVIII). The International Critical Commentary on the Holy Scriptures of the Old and New Testaments, ed. J. A. Emerton, C. E. B. Cranfield and G. N. Stanton. Edinburgh: T & T Clark, 1991.

Deist, F. E. *Towards the Text of the Old Testament: A Systematic Introduction for Students of Biblical Studies, Theology and Classical Hebrew*. Translated by W. K. Winckler. Pretoria: N. G. Kerkboekhandel Transvaal, 1978.

Dorsey, David A. *The Literary Structure of the Old Testament: A Commentary on Genesis-Malachi*. Grand Rapids: Baker Books, 1999.

Dunnett, Walter M. *The Interpretation of Holy Scripture*. Nashville: Thomas Nelson Publishers, 1984.

Ericson, David F. *The Debate over Slavery: Antislavery and Proslavery Liberalism in Antebellum America*. New York: New York University Press, 2000.

Fee, Gordon D., and Douglas Stuart. *How to Read the Bible for All It's Worth: A Guide to Understanding the Bible*. 2d ed. Grand Rapids: Zondervan Publishing House, 1993.

Gadamer, Hans Georg. *Truth and Method*. Translated by Joel Weinsheimer and Donald G. Marshall. New York: Continuum, 1994.

García, Martínez  Florentino. *The Dead Sea Scrolls Translated: The Qumran Texts in English*. Translated by Wilfred G. E. Watson. 2d ed. Leiden: E. J. Brill, 1996.

Goldenberg, David M. *The Curse of Ham: Race and Slavery in Early Judaism, Christianity, and Islam*. Jews, Christians, and Muslims from the Ancient to the Modern World, ed. R. Stephen Humphreys, William Chester Jordan and Peter Schäfer. Princeton: Princeton University Press, 2003

Goodspeed, Calvin, and D. M. Welton. *The Book of Genesis*. An American Commentary on the Old Testament. Philadelphia: American Baptist Publication Society, 1909.

Gossett, Thomas F. *Race: The History of an Idea in America*. New York: Schocken Books, 1965.

Goulder, Michael D. *The Song of Fourteen Songs*. Journal for the Study of the Old Testament Supplement Series, ed. David J. A. Clines and Philip R. Davies. Vol. 36. Sheffield: JSOT Press, 1986.

Graves, Joseph L. *The Race Myth: Why We Pretend Race Exists in America*. New York: Dutton, 2004.

Gunkel, Hermann. *Genesis*. Translated by Mark E. Biddle. Mercer Library of Biblical Studies, ed. John Blenkinsopp and Walter Brueggemann. Macon, GA: Mercer University Press, 1997.

_____. *Genesis Übersetzt und Erklärt*. Göttinger Handkommentar zum Alten Testament. Göttingen: Vandenhoeck und Ruprecht, 1902.

Hamilton, Victor P. *The Book of Genesis: Chapters 1–17*. ed. R. K. Harrison. The New International Commentary on the Old Testament. Grand Rapids, MI: Eerdmans, 1990.

Hanson, K. C., ed. *From Genesis to Chronicles: Explorations in Old Testament Theology, Gerhard Von Rad*. Minneapolis, MN: Fortress Press, 2005.

Harrison, R. K. *Introduction to the Old Testament: With a Comprehensive Review of Old Testament Studies and a Special Supplement on the Apocrypha*. Grand Rapids, MI: Eerdmans, 1969. Reprint, Peabody, MA: Prince Press, 1999.

Hartley, John E. *Genesis*. New International Biblical Commentary: Old Testament Series, ed. Robert L. Hubbard Jr. and Robert K. Johnson. Peabody, MA: Hendrickson Publishers, 2000.

Hastings, Adrian. *The Church in Africa (1450–1950)*. Oxford: Clarendon Press, 1994.

Haynes, Stephen R. *Noah's Curse: The Biblical Justification of American Slavery*. Religion in America. New York: Oxford University Press, 2002.

Heidegger, Martin. *Being and Time*. Translated by John Macquarrie and Edward Robinson. New York: Harper, 1962.

Heimerdinger, Jean-Marc. *Topic, Focus and Foreground in Ancient Hebrew Narratives*. Journal for the Study of the Old Testament: Supplement Series, ed. David J. A. Clines and Philip R. Davies. Vol. 295. Sheffield: Sheffield Academic Press, 1999.

Hill, Andrew E., and John H. Walton. *A Survey of the Old Testament*. Grand Rapids: Zondervan Publishing House, 1991.

Hirsch, H. *The Drunkenness of Noah*. Birmingham: University of Alabama, 1974.

Holladay, William L. *A Commentary on the Book of the Prophet Jeremiah: Chapters 1–25*. Vol. 1. Hermenia—a Critical and Historical Commentary on the Bible, ed. Paul D. Hanson. PA: Fortress Press, 1986.

Holter, Knut. *Yahweh in Africa: Essays on Africa and the Old Testament*. Bible and Theology in Africa, ed. Knut Holter. Vol. 1. New York: Peter Lang, 2000.

House, Paul R. *Old Testament Theology*. Downers Grove, IL: InterVarsity Press, 1998.

Hughes, Richard T., and C. Leonard Allen. *Illusions of Innocence: Protestant Primitivism in America, 1630–1875*. Chicago: University of Chicago Press, 1988.

Ide, Arthur Frederick. *Noah and the Ark: The Influence of Sex, Homophobia and Heterosexism in the Flood Story and Its Writing*. Las Colinas, TX: Monument, 1992.

Isichei, Elizabeth Allo. *A History of Christianity in Africa: From Antiquity to the Present*. Grand Rapids: Eerdmans, 1995.

Jackson, Alvin A. *Examining the Record: An Exegetical and Homiletical Study of Blacks in the Bible*. Martin Luther King, Jr. Memorial Studies in Religion, Culture and Social Development, ed. Mozella G. Mitchell. Vol. 4. New York: Peter Lang, 1994.

Jacob, B. *The First Book of the Bible: Genesis*. Translated by Ernest I. Jacob and Walter Jacob. New York: Ktav Publishing House, 1974.

Jordan, Winthrop D. *The White Man's Burden: Historical Origins of Racism in the United States*. Oxford: Oxford University Press, 1974.

Kaiser, Walter C. *Toward an Old Testament Theology*. Grand Rapids: Zondervan Publishing House, 1978.

Keil, C. F., and F. Delitzsch. *Pentateuch*. Translated by James Martin. Vol. 1. Biblical Commentary on the Old Testament. Grand Rapids: Eerdmans, 1951.

Kidner, Derek. *Genesis: An Introduction and Commentary*. Tyndale Old Testament Commentaries, ed. D. J. Wiseman. Chicago: Inter-varsity Press, 1967.

Kikawada, Isaac M., and Arthur Quinn. *Before Abraham Was: The Unity of Genesis 1–11*. Nashville, TN: Abingdon Press, 1985

Klein, Ralph W. *Textual Criticism of the Old Testament: The Septuagint after Qumran*. Guides to Biblical Scholarship (Old Testament Guides), ed. Gene M. Tucker, Philadelphia: Fortress Press, 1974

Kunin, Seth Daniel. *The Logic of Incest: A Structuralist Analysis of Hebrew Mythology*. Journal for the Study of the Old Testament: Supplement Series, ed. David J. A. Clines and Philip R. Davies. Vol. 185. Sheffield: Sheffield Academic Press, 1995.

Leach, Edmund. *Genesis as Myth and Other Essays*. Cape Editions, ed. Nathaniel Tarn. Vol. 39. London: Jonathan Cape, 1969.

*Lectures on Genesis Chapters 1–5*. Translated by George V. Schick. Vol. 1. Luther's Works, ed. Jaroslav Pelikan. Saint Louis: Concordia Publishing House, 1958.

*Lectures on Genesis Chapters 6–14*. Translated by George V. Schick. Vol. 2. Luther's Works, ed. Jaroslav Pelikan. Saint Louis: Concordia Publishing House, 1960.

Leupold, H. C. *Exposition on Genesis*. Grand Rapids: Baker Book House, 1965.

Lewis, Bernard. *Race and Slavery in the Middle East: An Historical Enquiry*. New York: Oxford University Press, 1990.

Lewis, Jack P. *A Study of the Interpretation of Noah and the Flood in Jewish and Christian Literature*. Leiden: E. J. Brill, 1968.

Lim, Johnson T. K. *Grace in the Midst of Judgment: Grappling with Genesis 1–11*. Beihefte zur Zeitschrift für die alttestamentliche Wissenschaft. Vol. 314. Berlin: Walter de Gruyter, 2002.

Longman, Tremper. *Making Sense of the Old Testament: Three Crucial Questions*, ed. Grant R. Osborne and Richard J. Jones. Grand Rapids: Baker Books, 1998.

_____. *Literary Approaches to Biblical Interpretation*. Foundations of Contemporary Interpretation, ed. Moisés Silva, vol. 3. Grand Rapids: Academie Books, 1987.

_____. *Song of Songs*. New International Commentary on the Old Testament, ed. R. K. Harrison and Robert L. Hubbard. Grand Rapids: Eerdmans, 2001.

Lundbom, Jack R. *Jeremiah 1–20*. Anchor Bible, ed. William Foxwell Albright. Vol. 21A. New York: Doubleday, 1999.

*Luther's Commentary on Genesis*. Translated by J. Theodore Mueller. Grand Rapids: Zondervan Publishing House, 1958.

Mathews, Kenneth A. *Genesis 1–11:26*. New American Commentary: An Exegetical and Theological Exposition of the Holy Scripture NIV Text, ed. E. Ray Clendenen. Vol 1A. Nashville: Broadman & Holman Publishers, 1996.

McCarter, P. Kyle. *Textual Criticism: Recovering the Text of the Hebrew Bible*. Guides to Biblical Scholarship (Old Testament Guides), ed. Gene M. Tucker. Philadelphia: Fortress Press, 1986.

Merrill, Eugene H. *Deuteronomy*. New American Commentary, ed. E. Ray Clendenen, Kenneth A. Mathews and David S. Dockery. Vol. 4. Nashville: Broadman & Holman Publishers, 1994.

_____. *Kingdom of Priests: A History of Old Testament Israel*. Grand Rapids: Baker Book House, 1987.

Mullins, Eustace. *The Curse of Canaan: A Demonology of History*. Staunton, VA: Revelation Books, 1987.

Muraoka, T. *Emphatic Words and Structures in Biblical Hebrew*. Leiden: E. J. Brill, 1985.

Nash, Peter T. *Reading Race, Reading the Bible*. Facets. Minneapolis, MN: Fortress Press, 2003.

Osborne, Grant R. *The Hermeneutical Spiral: A Comprehensive Introduction to Biblical Interpretation*. 2d ed. Downers Grove, IL: IVP Academics, 2006.

Packard, Jerrold M. *American Nightmare: The History of Jim Crow*. New York: St. Martin's Press, 2002.

Perryman, Wayne. *The 1993 Trial on the Curse of Ham*. Edited by Hattie Greenhouse, Simone Williams, and Peter P. Parker. Bakersfield, CA: Pneuma Life Publishing, 1994.

Petersen, Thomas Virgil. *Ham and Japheth: The Mythic World of Whites in the Antebellum South*. ATLA Monograph Series. Vol 12. Metuchen, NJ: The Scarecrow Press and the American Theological Library Association, 1978.

Philby, Harry St. John. *The Queen of Sheba*. London: Quartet Books, 1981.

Pleins, J. David. *When the Great Abyss Opened: Classic and Contemporary Readings of Noah's Flood*. Oxford: Oxford University Press, 2003.

Pope, Marvin H. *Song of Songs*. Anchor Bible, ed. William Foxwell Albright and David Noel Freedman. Garden City, NY: Doubleday & Company, 1977.

Potts, D.T. *The Archaeology of Elam*. Cambridge World Archaeology, ed. Norman Yoffee. Cambridge, MA: Cambridge University Press, 1999.

Rigby, Peter. *African Images: Racism and the End of Anthropology*. Global Issues, ed. Bruce Kapferer and John Gledhill. Washington, D.C.: Berg, 1996.

Rendsburg, Gary A. *The Redaction of Genesis*. Winona Lake, IN: Eisenbrauns, 1986.

Roop, Eugene F. *Genesis*. Scottdale, PA: Herald Press, 1987.

Rushton, J. Philippe. *Race, Evolution, and Behavior: A Life History Perspective*. New Brunswick, NJ: Transaction Publishers, 1997.

Ryken, Leland. *How to Read the Bible as Literature*. Grand Rapids: Zondervan Publishing House, 1984.

Ryle, Herbert E. *The Book of Genesis: In the Revised Version with Introduction and Notes by Herbert E. Ryle*. Cambridge Bible for Schools and Colleges, ed. A. F. Kirkpatrick. Cambridge, MA: University Press, 1914.

Sadler, Rodney Steven. *Can a Cushite Change His Skin? An Examination of Race, Ethnicity, and Othering in the Hebrew Bible*. Journal for the Study of the Old Testament: Supplement Series, ed. David J. A. Clines and Philip R. Davies. Vol. 425. Sheffield: Sheffield Academic Press, 2005.

Sarna, Nahum M. *Genesis*. JPS Torah Commentary, ed. Nahum M. Sarna. Jerusalem: Jewish Publication Society, 1989.

Shaw, Mark. *The Kingdom of God in Africa: A Short History of African Christianity*. Grand Rapids, MI: Baker Books, 1996.

Schwartz, Regina M. *The Curse of Cain: The Violent Legacy of Monotheism*. Chicago: University of Chicago Press, 1997.

Skinner, John. *A Critical and Exegetical Commentary on Genesis*. 2d ed. International Critical Commentary on the Holy Scripture of the Old and New Testaments, ed. Samuel Rolles Driver, Alfred Plummer, and Charles Augustus Briggs. Edinburgh: T. & T. Clark, 1930.

Smith, Ralph L. *Old Testament Theology: Its History, Method, and Message*. Nashville, TN: Broadman & Holman Publishers, 1993.

Speiser, E. A. *Genesis*. Anchor Bible, ed. William Foxwell Albright and David Noel Freedman. Vol.1. Garden City, New York: Doubleday, 1964.

Steinmetz, David C. *Luther in Context*. Bloomington: Indiana University Press, 1986.

Swan, Talbert W. *No More Cursing: Destroying the Roots of Religious Racism.* Indian Orchard, MA: Trumpet in Zion Publishing, 2003.

Terry, Milton S. *Biblical Hermeneutics: A Treatise on the Interpretation of the Old and New Testaments.* Grand Rapids: Zondervan Publishing House, 1974.

*The Early Syrian Fathers on Genesis: From a Syriac Ms. On the Pentateuch in the Mingana Collection.* Translated by Abraham Levene. London: Taylor's Foreign Press, 1951.

Thomas, W. H. Griffith. *Genesis: A Devotional Commentary.* Grand Rapids: Eerdmans, 1946.

Thompson, J. A. *The Book of Jeremiah.* The New International Commentary on the Old Testament, ed. R. K. Harrison, Grand Rapids: Eerdmans, 1980.

Tov, Emanuel. *Textual Criticism of the Bible.* 2d rev. ed. Minneapolis, MN: Fortress Press, 2001.

Trapp, John. *Genesis to Second Chronicles.* Edited by W. Webster and Hugh Martin, vol. 1. A Commentary on the Old and New Testaments. London: Richard Dickinson; Tanski Publications, 1865–1868. Reprint, Eureka, CA: Tanski Publications, 1997.

Turner, Laurence A. *Genesis.* Readings: A New Biblical Commentary, ed. John Jarick, Sheffield: Sheffield Academic Press, 2000.

Unwin, Tim. *Wine and the Vine.* New York: Routledge, 1996.

Van Seters, John. *Prologue to History: The Yahwist as Historian in Genesis.* Louisville, KY: John Knox Press, 1992.

Vawter, B. *On Genesis: A New Reading.* Garden City, NY: Doubleday, 1977.

Von Rad, Gerhard. *Genesis: A Commentary.* Old Testament Library, ed. James Barr Peter Ackroyd, Bernhard W. Anderson, and James L. Mays. Philadelphia: The Westminster Press, 1972.

Vos, Geerhardus. *Biblical Theology: Old and New Testaments.* Grand Rapids: Eerdmans, 1948. Reprint, Grand Rapids: Eerdmans, 1977.

Walsh, Carey Ellen. *The Fruit of the Vine: Viticulture in Ancient Israel.* Harvard Semitic Monographs, ed. Peter Machinist. Vol. 60. Winona Lake, IN: Eisenbrauns, 2000.

Waltke, Bruce K. *Genesis: A Commentary.* Grand Rapids: Zondervan Publishing House, 2001.

Walton, John H. *Genesis.* The NIV Application Commentaries Series, ed. Terry Muck. Grand Rapids: Zondervan Publishing House, 2001.

Ware, A. Charles. *Prejudice and the People of God: How Revelation and Redemption Leads to Reconciliation*. Grand Rapids: Kregel Publications, 2001.

Warnke, Goergia. *Gadamer: Hermeneutics, Tradition, and Reason*. Stanford, CA: Stanford University Press, 1987.

Waters, Matthew W. *A Survey of Neo-Elamite History*. State Archives of Assyria Studies, ed. Robert M. Whiting. Vol. 12. Helsinki: Vammalan Kirjapaino Oy, 2000.

Wenham, Gordon J. *Genesis 1–15*. Word Biblical Commentary, ed. David A. Hubbard and Glenn W. Barker. Vol 1. Waco, TX: Word Books, 1987.

Westermann, Claus. *Genesis 1–11*. Translated by John J. Scullion, vol. 1. Genesis: A Commentary. Minneapolis, MN: Augsburg Publishing House, 1984.

Wevers, John William. *Notes on the Greek Text of Genesis*. Septuagint and Cognate Studies Series, ed. Leonard J. Greenspoon. Vol. 35. Atlanta: Scholars Press, 1993.

Whitelaw, Thomas. *Genesis*. New ed., vol. 1. The Pulpit Commentary, ed. H. D. M. Spence and Joseph S. Exell. London: Funk & Wagnalls, 1900.

Wold, Donald J. *Out of Order: Homosexuality in the Bible and the Ancient Near East*. Grand Rapids: Baker Books, 1998.

*World Christian Encyclopedia: A Comparative Survey of Churches and Religions in the Modern World*. Edited by David B. Barrett, George T. Kurian and Todd M. Johnson. Vol. 1 (The World by Countries: Religionists, Churches, Ministries). New York: Oxford University Press, 2001.

Yamauchi, Edwin M. *Africa and the Bible*. Grand Rapids, MI: Baker Academic, 2004.

Zimmerman, M. A. *Studies in Genesis*. 2d ed. Menasha, WI: Fellowship of Protestant Lutherans, 1979.

**Essays and Journal Articles**

Aaron, David H. "Early Rabbinic Exegesis on Noah's Son Ham and the So-Called 'Hamitic Myth'." *Journal of the American Academy of Religion* 63, no. 4 (1995): 721–59

Anderson, Bernhard W. "From Analysis to Synthesis: The Interpretation of Genesis 1–11." *Journal of Biblical Literature* 97 (1978): 23–29.

Anderson, Roger W. "Zephaniah Ben Cushi and Cush of Benjamin: Traces of Cushite Presence in Syria-Palestine." In *The Pitcher Is Broken: Memorial Essays for Gösta W. Ahlström*, ed. Steven W. Holloway and Lowell K. Handy, Journal for the Study of the Old Testament: Supplement Series, ed. David J. A. Clines and Philip R. Davies. Vol. 190, 45–70. Sheffield: Sheffield Academic Press, 1995.

Appiah, Kwame Anthony. "Racisms." In *Anatomy of Racism*, ed. David Theo Goldberg, 3–17. Minneapolis, MN: University of Minnesota Press, 1990.

Assohoto, Barnabe, and Samuel Ngewa. "Genesis." In *African Bible Commentary*, ed. Tokunboh Adeyemo, 10–84. Nairobi, Kenya: WordAlive Publishers, 2006.

Bailey, Randall C. "They're Nothing but Incestuous Bastards: The Polemical Use of Sex and Sexuality in Hebrew Canon Narratives." In *In Reading from This Place*, ed. Mary Ann Tolbert, Social Location and Biblical Interpretation in the United States, vol. 1, 121–38. Minneapolis, MN: Fortress, 1994.

Bassett, Frederick W. "Noah's Nakedness and the Curse on Canaan: A Case of Incest?" *Vetus Testamentum* 21 (April, 1971): 232–37.

Baumgart, Nobert Clemens. "Das End der biblischen Urgeschichte in Gen 9, 29." *Biblische Notizen* 82 (1996): 27–58.

Baumgarten, Albert I. "Myth and Midrash: Genesis 9:20-29." In *Christianity, Judaism and Other Greco-Roman Cults: Studies for Morton Smith at Sixty, Part 3 Judaism before 70*, ed. Jacob Neusner, vol. 12, 55–71. Leiden: E. J. Brill, 1975.

Bergsma, John Sietze, and Scott Walker Hahn. "Noah's Nakedness and the Curse of Canaan (Genesis 9:20-27)." *Journal of Biblical Literature* 124, no. 1 (2005): 25-40.

Blau, Joshua. "On Polyphony in Biblical Hebrew." In *Proceedings of the Israel Academy of Sciences and Humanities*, vol. 6, 105–83. Jerusalem: The Israel Academy of Sciences and Humanities, 1983.

Bond, Selena, and Thomas F. Cash. "Black Beauty: Skin Color and Body Images among African-American College Women." *Journal of Applied Social Psychology* 22 (1992): 874–88.

Bonfante, Larissa. "The Naked Greek." *Archaeology* 43 (1990): 28–36.

Bradley, L. Richard. "The Curse of Canaan and the American Negro." *Concordia Theological Monthly* 42 (February, 1971): 100–10.

Brow, Robert. "The Curse of Ham—Capsule of Ancient History." *Christianity Today* 18 (October, 1973): 8–10.

Coard, Stephanie Irby, Alfiee M. Breland, and Patricia Raskin. "Perceptions of and Preferences for Skin Color, Black Racial Identity, and Self-Esteem among African Americans." *Journal of Applied Social Psychology* 31 (2001): 2256–74.

Cohn, Robert L. "Narrative Structure and Canonical Perspective in Genesis." *Journal for the Study of the Old Testament* 25 (1983): 3–16.

Copher, Charles B. "The Black Presence in the Old Testament." In *Stony the Road We Trod: African American Biblical Interpretation*, ed. Cain Hope Felder, 146–64. Minneapolis, MN: Fortress Press, 1991.

Cornell, Tim J. "History of Rome." In *The Oxford Companion to Classical Civilization*, ed. Simon Hornblower and Anthony Spawforth, 605–623. Oxford: Oxford University Press, 1998.

Evans, William Mckee. "From the Land of Canaan to the Land of Guinea : The Strange Odyssey of the Sons of Ham." *The American Historical Review* 85 (1980): 15–43.

Felder, Cain Hope. "Race, Racism, and the Biblical Narratives." In *Stony the Road We Trod: African American Biblical Interpretation*, ed. Cain Hope Felder, 127–45. Minneapolis, MN: Fortress Press, 1991.

Francisco, Clyde T. "The Curse on Canaan." *Christianity Today* 8 (April, 1964): 8–10.

Geisler, Norman. "The Relation of the Purpose and Meaning in Interpreting Scripture." *Grace Theological Journal* 5 (1984): 229–45.

Gerhards, Meik. "Zum emphatischen Gebrauch der Partikel אל im biblischen Hebräisch." *Biblische Notizen* 102 (2000): 54–73.

Goldenberg, David M. "The Curse of Ham: A Case of Rabbinic Racism?" In *Struggles in the Promised Land: Toward a History of Black-Jewish Relations in the United States*, ed. Jack Salzman and Cornel West, 21–51. New York: Oxford University Press, 1997.

Goldingay, John. "The Patriarchs in Scripture and History." In *Essays on the Patriarchal Narratives*, ed. A. R. Millard and D. J. Wiseman, 1–34. Winona Lake, IN: Eisenbrauns, 1983.

Haran, Menahem. "The Gibeonites, the Nethinim and the Sons of Solomon's Servants." *Vetus Testamentum* 11 (1962): 159–69.

Heras, Henry. "The Curse of Noe." *Catholic Biblical Quarterly* 12 (1950): 64–67.

Herrenschmidt, Clarisse. "Elamite Civilization and Writing." In *Ancestor of the West: Writing, Reasoning, and Religion in Mesopotamia, Elam, and Greece*, 69–89. Chicago: University of Chicago Press, 2000.

Hersch, Joni. "Skin Tone Effects among African Americans: Perceptions and Reality." *American Economic Review Papers and Proceedings* 96, no. 2 (2006): 251–55.

Hicks, L. "Ham." In *The Interpreter's Dictionary of the Bible: An Illustrated Encyclopedia*, ed. George Arthur Buttrick, vol. 2., 515. Nashville: Abingdon Press, 1962.

Hoftijzer, J. "Some Remarks to the Tale of Noah's Drunkenness." In *Studies on the Book of Genesis*, ed. B. Gemster, Oudtestamentische Studien, vol. 12, 22–27: Leiden, E. J. Brill, 1958.

Hostetter, Edwin C. "Mistranslation in Cant 1:5." *Andrew University Seminary Studies* 34 (1996): 35–36.

Kalu, Ogbu U. "African Christianity: An Overview." In *African Christianity: An African Story*, ed. Ogbu U. Kalu, Perspective on Christianity Series, vol. 3, ed. O. U. Kalu, J. W. Hofmeyr and P. J. Maritz, vol. 5, 24–43. Pretoria, South Africa: Business Print Centre, 2005.

Kitchen, Kenneth A. "Sheba and Arabia." In *The Age of Solomon: Scholarship at the Turn of the Millennium*, ed. Lowell K. Handy, Studies in the History and Culture of the Ancient Near East, ed. B. Halpern and M. H. E. Weippert, vol. 11, 126–53. Leiden: Brill, 1997.

Koltun-Fromm, Naomi. "Aphrahat and the Rabbis on Noah's Righteousness in Light of the Jewish-Christian Polemic." In *The Book of Genesis in Jewish and Oriental Christian Interpretation: A Collection of Essays*, ed. Judith Frishman and Lucas Van Rompay, Traditio Exegetica Graeca, vol. 5, 57–71. Lovanii: Aedibus Peeters, 1997.

Lewy, Julius. "The Old West Semitic Sun-God Hammu." *Hebrew Union College Annual* 18 (1944): 429–81.

Margoliouth, D. S. "Ham." In *A Dictionary of the Bible: Dealing with Its Language, Literature, and Contents Including the Biblical Theology*, ed. James Hasting, vol. 2, 288–289. Edinburgh: T. & T. Clark, 1898. Reprint, New York: Charles Scribner's Sons, 1958.

McNeile, A. H. "Ham." In *Dictionary of the Bible*, ed. John Hastings, 361. New York: Charles Scribner's Sons, 1963.

Mendelsohn, I. "State Slavery in Ancient Palestine." *Bulletin of the American Schools of Oriental Research* 85 (1942): 14–17.

_____. "On Corvée Labor in Ancient Canaan and Israel." *Bulletin of the American Schools of Oriental Research* 167 (1962): 31–35.

Merrill, Eugene H. "A Theology of the Pentateuch." In *A Biblical Theology of the Old Testament*, ed. Roy B. Zuck, 7–88. Chicago: Moody Press, 1991.

_____. "Chronology." In *Dictionary of the Old Testament: Pentateuch*, ed. T. Desmond Alexander and David W. Baker, 113–122. Downers Grove, Illinois: InterVarsity Press, 2003.

_____. "The Peoples of the Old Testament According to Genesis 10." *Bibliotheca sacra* 154 (1997): 3–22.

Minow, Martha. "Surprising Legacies of *Brown V. Board*." In *Legacies of Brown: Multiracial Equity in American Education*, ed. Dorinda J. Carter, Stella M. Flores and Richard J. Reddick, 9–35. Cambridge, MA: Harvard Educational Review, 2004.

Neiman, David. "Curse of Canaan." In *Encyclopedia Judaica*, ed. Cecil Roth and Geoffrey Wigoder, vol. 5, 97–98. Jerusalem: Keter Publishing House, 1971.

_____. "The Date and Circumstances of the Cursing of Canaan." In *Biblical Motifs*, ed. Alexander Altmann, 113–134. Cambridge, MA: Harvard University Press, 1966.

Oded, B. "The Table of Nations (Genesis 10) —a Socio-Cultural Approach." *Zeitschrift für die alttestamentliche Wissenschaft* 98 (1986): 14–31.

Odhiambo, Nicholas. "The Nature of Ham's Sin." *Bibliotheca Sacra* 170 (April-June 2013): 154-65.

Pinches, T. G. "Ham." In *The International Standard Bible Encyclopedia*, ed. James Orr, vol. 2, 1324. Grand Rapids: Eerdmans, 1939.

Phillips, Anthony. "Uncovering the Father's Skirt." *Vetus Testamentum* 30 (1980): 38–43.

Powell, Marvin A. "Wine and the Vine in Ancient Mesopotamia: The Cuneiform Evidence." In *The Origins and Ancient History of Wine*, ed. Patrick E. McGovern, Stuart J. Fleming and Solomon H. Katz, Food and Nutrition in History and Anthropology, ed. Solomon H. Katz, vol. 11, 97–122. Toronto, Canada: Gordon and Breach Publishers, 1996.

Rainey, A. F. "Compulsory Labour Gangs in Ancient Israel." *Israel Exploration Journal* 20, no. 3/4 (1970): 191–202.

Robertson, O. Palmer. "Current Critical Questions Concerning the 'Curse of Ham'." *Journal of the Evangelical Theological Society* 41, no. 2 (1998): 177–88.

Robinson, T. L., and J. V. Ward. "African American Adolescents and Skin Color." *Journal of Black Psychology* 21 (1995): 256–74.

Rice, Gene. "The Curse That Never Was (Genesis 9:18–27)." *Journal of Religious Thought* 29 (1972): 5–27.

Ross, Allen P. "The Curse of Canaan." *Bibliotheca Sacra* 137 (1980): 223–240.

_____. "Studies in the Book of Genesis Part 3: The Table of Nations in Genesis 10— Its Content." *Bibliotheca sacra* 138 (1981): 22–34.

Sailhamer, John H. "Genesis." In *A Complete Literary Guide to the Bible*, ed. Leland Ryken and Tremper Longman, 108–120. Grand Rapids: Zondervan Publishing House, 1993.

Sasson, Jack M. "The 'Tower of Babel' as a Clue to the Redactional Structuring of the Primeval History [Gen. 1–11:9]." In *The Bible World: Essays in Honor of Cyrus H. Gordon*, ed. Gary Rendsburg, Ruth Adler, Milton Arfa, and Nathan H. Winter, 211–219. New York: Ktav Publishing House, 1980.

Shufelt, J. Ernest. "Noah's Curse and Blessing, Gen 9:18–27." *Concordia Theological Journal* 17 (1946): 737–42.

Sforim, Mendele Mocher. "Shem and Japheth on the Train (1890)." In *Modern Hebrew Literature*, ed. Robert Alter, Library of Jewish Studies, ed. Neal Kozodoy, 13–38. New York: Behrman House, 1975.

Smith, Gary V. "Structure and Purpose in Genesis 1–11." *Journal of the Evangelical Theological Society* 20 (Dec, 1977): 307–19.

Spear, Thomas. "Toward the History of African Christianity." In *East African Expressions of Christianity*, ed. Thomas Spear and Isaria N. Kimambo, East African Studies, 3–24. Athens, OH: Ohio University Press, 1999.

Stander, H. F. "The Church Fathers on (the Cursing of) Ham." *Acta patristica et byzantina* 5 (1994): 113–24.

Tomasino, Anthony J. "History Repeats Itself: The 'Fall' and Noah's Drunkenness." *Vetus Testamentum* 42 (1992): 128–30.

Vallat, Francois. "Elam." *Anchor Bible Dictionary,* ed. David Noel Freedman, vol. 2, 424–29. New York: Doubleday, 1992.

Wevers, J. W. "Heth in Classical Hebrew." In *Essays on The Ancient Semitic World*, ed. J. W. Wevers and D. B. Redford, 101–12. Toronto: University of Toronto Press, 1970.

Wintermute, O. S. "Jubilees: A New Translation and Introduction." In *The Old Testament Pseudepigrapha*, ed. James H. Charlesworth, Anchor Bible Reference Library, vol. 2, 35–142. New York: Doubleday, 1985.

## Unpublished Works

Brunk, William A. "The Action of Ham against Noah: Its Nature and Result (Genesis 9:18–27)." M.Div. thesis, Western Conservative Baptist Seminary, 1988.

Camara, Evando de Morais. "A Flight into Utopia: The Proslavery Argument of the American South in Social-Hermeneutical Perspective." Ph.D. diss., University of Notre Dame, 1986.

Crowther, Edward Riley. "Southern Protestants, Slavery and Secession: A Study in Religious Ideology, 1830–1861." Ph.D. diss., Auburn University, 1986.

Daly, John Patrick. "The Divine Economy: Evangelicalism and the Defense of Slavery, 1830-1865." Ph.D. diss., Rice University, 1993.

Glaze, William R. "The Curse of Canaan and its Relationship to the Black Race." M.A. thesis, Liberty Baptist College, 1984.

Hutchison, G. Whit. "The Bible and Slavery, a Test of Ethical Method: Biblical Interpretation, Social Ethics, and the Hermeneutics of Race in America, 1830–1861." Ph.D. diss., Union Theological Seminary, 1996.

Lumeya, Nzash U. "The Curse on Ham's Descendants: Its Missiological Impact on Zairian Mbala Mennonite Brethren." Ph.D. diss., Fuller Theological Seminary, 1988.

Maughmer, Noel D. "The Background of the Noahic Curse on Canaan (Genesis 9:22)." M.Div. thesis, Grace Theological Seminary, 1978.

Odhiambo, Nicholas Oyugi. "Ham's Sin and Noah's Curse: A Critique of Current Views." Dissertation, Dallas Theological Seminary, 2007.

Ross, Allen Paul. "The Table of Nations in Genesis." Ph.D. diss., Dallas Theological Seminary, 1976.

Thompson, Jay Everett. "Historical Geography of Shem, Ham and Japheth, Noah's Three Sons." M.A. thesis, Western Evangelical Seminary, 1978.